Common
Differences

...Revisited...

*A cultural and comparative study of
Jewish and Christian
practices and representations*

Common Differences

...Revisited...

A cultural and comparative study of Jewish and Christian practices and representations

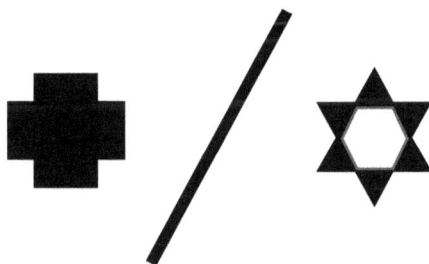

David Prosnitz, Ph.D.

This book is dedicated to my wife Lori for her patience and technical assistance regarding this book and more generally for her love and kindness in all that she does.

Table of Contents

PREFACE

The essays in this book were written over more than a forty-year period. They were not written in the order in which they appear. Ideas change and grow over forty plus years and there are certain inconsistencies and differences in the analysis of varying Christian and Jewish elements in the essays as a result. Blood, for example, in one essay has a flesh aspect when looked at from the viewpoint of spirit, and a spirit aspect when looked at from a flesh standpoint. In another essay, it is interpreted differently. The place of transformation and ideas about *mitzvot* in Judaism change from essay to essay as well. Nonetheless, these essays are a result of a consistent attempt to interpret Jewish and Christian traditions as cultural or semiological systems.

This book is a reworking of an earlier version of <u>Common Differences,</u> which was self-published in 2004. It contains new essays and revisions of old ones.

Most of the material on Pentecostalism comes from my 1978 doctoral thesis entitled: "Spirit in the Flesh: A cultural account of an urban, American Pentecostalism." The essay "Common Differences" was originally delivered as a talk before the LaSalle Street Church of Chicago in 1999.

In these essays, my purpose is not to rewrite, edit or critique the religious ideas studied in this book of essays. Rather, my purpose is to stay true to and understand culturally the terms of the religious language that believers spoke or enacted. I do not entirely succeed in this. I react in these essays to anti-Semitism, to genocidal events in the Bible and to the validity of the kosher laws. While I often give full voice to the Christian materials in this book, I wrestle with Jewish ones. This is a subtheme: the main concern is describing the structure of the religious systems, the Jewish and the Christian, as best I can. I hope my inconsistency here does not undermine my general purpose which is to find the cultural composition of the religious "language" of Judaism and

Pentecostal Christianity. It is important to realize that the analysis of Biblical material is for its cultural meanings, which of course are the very ground of Western culture.

Also, the reader should be prepared for some repetition in the essays that follow. Each essay was originally written to be read independently. Since similar material is often discussed, using the same oppositions, and demonstrating, for example, the same relationship between kinship and religion which appears more than once, the reader is encouraged to skip material he or she already understands. If one essay does not please you, perhaps you might read another.

Finally, I want to thank a few people for their contribution to this book of essays. Firstly, thanks to my wife Lori for her overall support, for her proof-reading and formatting of the manuscript, and for her help with diagrams, particularly the diagram on the System of Common Differences. Thanks to Ruth Grodzins for her editorial help on earlier essays and to Ann Rose Gold for listening many years ago to many of my ideas on Pentecostalism. Thanks to Maurice Said for his more recent editorial work and to Lawrence Bloom for his reading of the manuscript.

David Prosnitz
November 15, 2020

Essay I- Introduction

Common Differences Revisited is a comparative study of Judaism and Christianity written from an unusual viewpoint. It is not about the beliefs and practices of Jewish and Christian religions as they simply differ from one another. Instead, it shows that they derive from the same underlying cultural system. They systematically differ and are similar to one another in terms of the deep distinctions and cultural structure they have in common.

This deep structure is key to the book and to the character of Judaism and Christianity. The deep structure is based on spirit and flesh, something with which the reader is familiar. But new here is that this spirit/flesh distinction acts like the grammar of a sentence. It underlies religious constructs and it can be declined into many different religious ideas. One of them is the distinction between religion and kinship itself; religion and kinship domains are a structured expression of the underlying spirit/flesh distinction. Within the spirit domain of religion, spirit and flesh give us three major religions. One religion is in the spirit, singular like spirit and the other two are flesh religions. It gives us two flesh religions because flesh divides into two and it divides these two religions by spirit and flesh. Christianity here is the spirit religion in the flesh because it is a salvationist religion in the body of Christ. And Judaism is the flesh religion here since it is preoccupied with sanctifying bodily things like eating, behaving, descent, and childbearing. Judaism and Christianity divide by spirit/flesh in the flesh subsystem of the spiritual religious domain.

This spiritual domain as just demonstrated is constructed triadically from a declension of spirit/flesh. There is a one in the spirit

I

over two in the flesh, a triadic relationship, in this case for the three major religions. The godheads of these religions are also structured by a triadic expression of spirit and flesh. This triad is especially clear in the Trinity, whose personages form a three-part structure. This is elaborated in the essays in this book on "Common Differences" and "Godheads". And the content of each of these two religions is further constructed by flesh and spirit, as something like baptism shows. Baptism involves going down in the flesh to come up in the spirit and this is a completely structured baptismal event, deeply composed or structured by spirit/flesh and also up/down. In other essays in the book, the analysis of the flesh/spirit distinction leads to a male and female distinction. This is possible since flesh, which divides in two, has gender which is female and male. Likewise, the spirit is generally but not only singularly declined into male. This forms another triad: male spirit over a male/female distinction; this structure is nearly as important in the system of common differences as spirit and flesh are. This is made clear in the study of the mystical God of Kabbalah, in the Godhead essay. This book extensively explores sex and gender through the structured lens of spirit and flesh. This leads again to an analysis of kinship and religious terms and it gives the reader an unusual idea about how sex and gender work in the western tradition.

Before this is discussed, the philosophic underpinnings of spirit and flesh are explored in an essay called "First Thoughts". Its main point is that spirit and flesh are particular expressions of the basic distinction at the root of all human knowing: identity and differences. Here is what the philosopher Bradley says is most important to know about identity and difference: "if all things were different, there would be no knowledge because nothing could be compared. And if all things were the same, nothing could be distinguished." So identity and difference need one another and are at the root of human sense-making. Spirit is at one with identity, flesh expresses difference so, this essay argues, the system of common difference is a particular expression of a universal relational and knowing construct. And spirit and flesh are linked, just like identity and difference, to form a basic, triadic structure, and this triad structures the Trinity. That is, spirit is one part (identity) and difference in the flesh is two, together they form a triad known in the three-person Trinity.

Hence the second major point of this essay: the Trinity is structured (and its character explained) by something fundamental to all human knowledge. How this forms a unitarian God is the subject of analysis and explanation in the essay "Common Differences" and elsewhere in the book. The broader implications of this explanation of the Trinity are not explored in Common Differences Revisited. Instead, an identical but gendered structure is found in the godhead of Jewish mysticism and in the basic form of the western family. A similar structure is found in the relation of God, Torah and Israel. The book's purpose is a structural explanation of tropes within the kinship-religious system I call the system of common differences. Rather than seeking religious truth, this book of essays looks for the way structure constructs intersubjective, cultural ideas.

In this book of essays, we find the overwhelming presence and importance of (spirit/flesh) structure, not just in God concepts and in kinships forms but also in the cultural literature of our society, namely our Bible. We go from identity to difference, to spirit and flesh, to concepts of God, and then to the religious constructs and practices in the Bible, where structure abounds. Structure is so abundant that Jews even eat it in *kashrut* or the kosher dietary regime, and this is discussed in an essay entitled "Food for Thought". Catholics do the same with the sacraments of the Mass which is analyzed here, and even the storylines of many Biblical tales only make sense if it is structure and not anything else that drives the stories. This is explored here in several essays, including one called "Storied Triads of the Bible".

Here is a sampling of some of the essays in Common Differences Revisited: "Notes on Kinship and Religion: an Intellectual Genesis", "Distinction and Structure in our Religious Culture", "Food for Thought: a Cultural Account of the Jewish Dietary Laws", "Firsts and Seconds in the Bible", "Christianity and Judaism: a Study in Cultural Contrasts", "Priestly Sacrifice", "The Trinity: Its Cultural Definition", "Godheads", "The Eucharist, the Passover and the Word", "Moralizing the West: Pentecostal Revivalism in Western Life"

Islam is hardly discussed in this book. From the standpoint of common differences, its character stands as a future test of the understandings put forward in these essays. Its spiritual character, its encompassing qualities and its shifting of Jewish, Christian and kinship cultural elements in an upward direction deserves future analysis from this point of view. Its relative absence here only results from the author's limited familiarity.

This book was written for serious readers who want to understand the cultural character of religion. It was also written with liberal arts graduates and college students in mind. It is a secular accounting of religious concepts and practices. I hope it might be read by people seriously engaged in the study of religion. It is meant for readers who want to understand the roots of the western tradition. It is for people who want to understand religious language as a human, social product (who could disagree with the perception that our religious traditions come to us in our human languages), but one which sheds a light on who we are and how we know. Hopefully, the reader is open to the possibilities in this. It is also meant to dignify Judaism as a sister religion to Christianity and to strengthen the bonds of tolerance that characterize our society.

Essay 2 - Notes on Kinship and Religion: An Intellectual Genesis

This essay provides a brief historical overview of a key question in the sociology of religion, particularly regarding the Christian religion: "How is religion a natural, human social product?" While many notable thinkers have addressed this question, Ludwig Feuerbach's views are the departure point for the argument of this essay. Others are Karl Marx and Emile Durkheim and the later writings of anthropologists Lloyd Warner and Edmund Leach. These five scholars, all serious students of the same Western-Christian relationship between human kinship and divine paradigms, have very different points of view. Yet their writings show an intellectual progression: from humanistic (Feuerbach), to sociological (Marx, Durkheim, and Warner), to symbolic (Leach). This progression should help the reader understand how I arrive at my symbolic or structuralist interpretations in this study of certain religious practices. Finally, these views are illustrated in conclusion by a structural analysis of the Genesis story, a story that introduces binary opposition and knowledge into Biblical history and a story that also links the themes of kinship and religion which is the key to the argument of these essays. But Feuerbach first.

In 1841, Feuerbach published *The Essence of Christianity* which dialectically took religion from the province of God in heaven and put it squarely in the domain of humans on earth. Feuerbach, a materialist and humanist, asserted that religion is anthropology and the study of Christianity is a study in human self-revelation. In his view, religion is essentially an anthropomorphic projection of human qualities into the divine; the study of religion becomes a study in anthropology. "Theology is anthropology, that is, in the object of religion which we call Theos in *Greek* and Gott in *Genesis,* nothing but the essence of man is expressed."

In Feuerbach's view, all aspects of the Christian God are deifications of man: for example, the human family is reproduced in the Trinity, and God is known as a human person in Jesus. Feuerbach repeatedly argues that human elements compose the divine. The principle premise of Feuerbach's work is that the absolute measure of man, in his language, is man - so human nature is the absolute measure of human religious creation. The Christian religion, like all human projects, is the result and reflection of human character. This premise is the basis for his interpretations of God as a moral being, the mystery and suffering of God, the omnipotence of religious feeling, the mystery of the Trinity and so forth. For example, he writes:

> God as God, that is, as a being not finite, not human, not materially conditioned, phenomenal, is only an object of thought. He is the incorporeal, formless, incomprehensible - the abstract, negative being: he is known, i.e. becomes an object only by abstraction and negation (vid negations). *Why?* Because he is nothing but the objective nature of the thinking power, or in general of the power or activity, name it what you will, whereby man is conscious of reason, of mind, of intelligence. There is no other spirit, that is (for the idea of spirit is simply the idea of thought, of intelligence, of understanding, of every other spirit being a specter of the imagination), no other intelligence which man can believe in or conceive than that intelligence which enlightens him, which is active in him.

Here, Feuerbach does not logically demonstrate that the framing of God as incorporeal and incomprehensible is symbolic of the character of human thought nor does he show how such a symbolic projection could occur. Feuerbach simply points to human abstract thought, discusses a similarly abstract (i.e. infinite and formless) characterization of God. Then connects the two, saying that only the human is real and its projection into the divine only diminishes that which is truly human. He applies these observations to other Christian elements. Feuerbach does not say how Jesus the man is an anthropomorphic presence in the godhead; rather he points to Jesus as a man and posits this manhood as an unwarranted projection of the human into the divine. Feuerbach's argument is an argument by copious example rather than an in-depth analysis of how human elements such as Jesus's manhood are deified.

In making his argument through example, Feuerbach offers a second major premise: the human products which he discovers in religious thought are essentially the objectifications of the sensory, the feeling and the flesh of human life in a symbol-God. These objectifications are at once self-discovery and human alienation. Religion shows us what humans are but religion takes this wonderful character away from people and without warrant, undermines the divine in human nature by attributing it to God. Feuerbach rails against this Christian alienation: "I hate that Idealism which tears man out of nature." Feuerbach only celebrates human nature; this is quintessential Feuerbach, whose idea of truth is rooted in the sensuous and the natural, the things we see in living earthly nature. For him, these are the alpha and omega of Christianity. Feuerbach sees Adam and Eve in nature and understands them only in terms of the living garden where they find themselves, humans only in full human glory.

In emphasizing the sensuous basis of religion, Feuerbach appears to unwittingly use religious notions to break from religious thinking. He asserts that the sensuous in man is primary, rejecting the spiritual language of religion for a strictly natural or carnal view of man which Christianity itself posits. Feuerbach takes the spirit/flesh theological distinction and uses flesh to explain spirit. In his view, the flesh and the sensuous are contrasted with spirit, and flesh is the source and power of Christian divinities. Here, Feuerbach reverses ordinary Christian terms - and in a sense, stays within Christian thought - by revering flesh while abhorring spirit as alienation from the virtues of human fleshly life.

But for all this, Feuerbach does not say how this alienated projection of man into heaven, this tearing of man from his real, sensual being into the spiritualized domain of the deity, occurs. Feuerbach maintains, for example, that the basic principles behind religious tropes is nothing other than the act of human thought in its simplest form made objective. But how is this true? He does not say, though he assumes that human thought ultimately constitutes the character of all its products and that this thought is not historically rooted nor uniquely social in origin, but rather that it is universally human.

7

It is this idea of the universally human that caused Marx to say that Feuerbach's materialism is an abstract, lacking a concrete view of the historical circumstances that produce religious ideas. As Marx wrote in his *Thesis on Feuerbach*:

> and Feuerbach resolves the religious essence into the human essence. But the humane essence is no abstraction inherent in each single individual. In its reality it is the ensemble of social relations. Feuerbach, consequently, does not see that the 'religious sentiment' is itself a *social product* and that the abstract individual whom he analyses belongs in reality to a particular form of society. (Original emphasis)

Feuerbach did not neglect to link Christian religious notions to a particular form of society. He connected the divine family to the human family, which for him was the Western family writ universally large. But he does not say how this connection came to be, was sustained, or is constructed. Nevertheless, Marx's basic sociological observations challenge Feuerbach's theory: Marx wants to view religion as a social product linked to historically-produced social relations. This challenge requires a specific idea of *how* a concrete set of social relations, such as the family in American kinship, forms a deity. In my view, the way social notions form religious ones should have a specific character. This "process" must produce a godhead with qualities in terms of the particular social relations producing it (see the essay on Godheads and other essays on the character of the Deity in this book) and must be free of the notion of man that Feuerbach upholds.

That is, Feuerbach's idea of man is pre-social and merely psychological. He points to personality and feeling in man to say that "religion is feeling" and that Jesus is a projection of human personhood. Feuerbach's ideas universalize something very particular, namely the Western emphasis on feelings in an individualized person. Feuerbach's ideas probably do not adequately interpret the human basis for numinous beliefs in other societies. Any adequate "reduction" of religious elements to their social character requires a theory that accepts the particularity of social and religious life. It seems mistaken to apply universal human psychology to explain diverse religious practices. If they reduce to the same human psyche, why the diversity?

Nonetheless, Feuerbach's reduction of God to man presages other attempts to find the real basis of religious activity in social life. In *The Elementary Forms of the Religious Life,* Durkheim pursued the Feuerbachian challenge and framed it as anthropological by studying the religious lives of Australian aborigines rather than those of Christians. He describes Aranda religious rites in terms of the sociology of the group: ritual conveys the power of society to individualized participants, and this power is conceptualized as God. Further, he holds that deities are societies writ large. God is a symbol of society and His power over all things is a sign of society's power over the individual. Society's force is a natural product of society as a concrete human collectivity, which, when focused on the individual member of society brings to bear a power conceived of as divine.

In this sociological view, ritual provides the setting for manifesting the collective moral power of social life: the group is present and can be tangibly experienced by the individual participant. In the collective rite of the social group, the force of human social life is powerfully, even effervescently real. Here God is created, experienced, established and celebrated. Ritual stamps the moral imprint of group life into the minds of individual celebrants. Here, the ideas and emotions of celebrants are governed by a deified society symbolized in a God who is worshiped and experienced.

Durkheim's views have led to studies of non-Western as well as Western religions. Studies of certain religions have moved in two main directions, both based on the primacy of social organization. First, attempts have been made to show how various subgroups, with common social experiences, gather to share an ecstatic religious life that simultaneously functions as a form of social therapy. Religion then is shaped by social conditions, anomie, for example, or social disorientation. This functional school no longer studies the character of Christianity as a social product but instead views religion as a functional response to other social conditions. In these studies, the character of religion is not examined; instead, they examine the functional consequences of religious activity in the wider lives of believers.

The second trend in the sociological approach to Feuerbach's humanization of religion is truer to Durkheim. Concerned with the nature of shared ideas and values in society, certain sociologists link the character of group life with its ideas. They accept, as objects in themselves worthy of study, the historical social life of the group and its shared beliefs and religious practices. While the nature of social structure is understood differently by the two authors I now consider-Lloyd Warner and Edmund Leach-each one details a view of Christian life that furthers a sociological understanding of Christianity.

Warner, especially, describes actual Christian collective representations. He focuses on the nature of Christian collective representations in relation to family life, which Christianity symbolizes and integrates. Warner believes that the relation between these two levels - family life and religious construction - is a nonrational or structural relationship. He further argues that the expression of conventionalized significances in the Christian realm ultimately (if arbitrarily) relates to the moral imperatives of the familial arena. Warner describes how meanings attached to Christian symbolisms stem from family life and its moral order while also describing how these serve to reinforce the social order they represent. Thus, he posits the centrality of Jesus's birth, life, and death for the sacred realm, because it reinforces family life. Thus, his explanation of Jesus's spirit and flesh character: spirit and flesh is rooted in the character of the family. Warner holds that "Much of the meaning of the 'flesh' in Christian belief has to do with the bodily actions and human emotions and the implications of sexuality for the spiritual order." So sexuality in the family is the social root of the flesh and its meaning in Christian life.

Warner's concern for the concrete nature of Christian symbolism and its relation to the family order is best shown in his detailed discussion of the marriage of the virgins (and the Church) to Jesus. He examines the figures who lead the Mass at the time of the marriage, the vows of the virgins, the relation of this marriage to human marriage and its relation to human passions. He even raises the mechanics issue which Feuerbach did not address: "How is it possible to convert the forms of social life into sacred symbols which express the values and beliefs of human society..." And he answers with a chart (see below) called Man's Sexual Life and Family Structure in the Christian Symbol System.

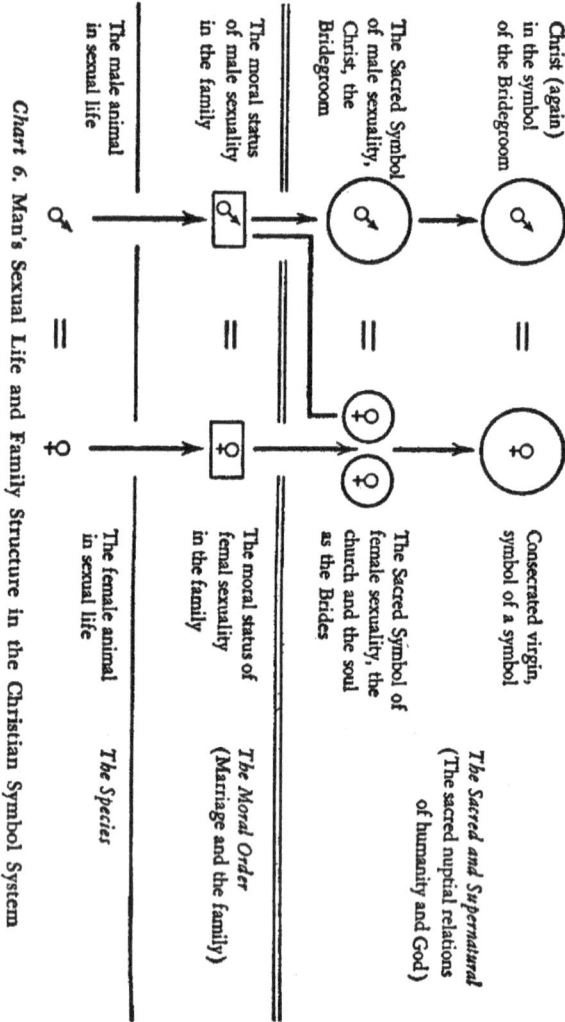

Chart 6. Man's Sexual Life and Family Structure in the Christian Symbol System

Man's Sexual Life and Family Structure in the Christian Symbol System
Source: Warner, L. *The Family of God* Yale University Press, New Haven: 1961 p. 294
ILLUSTRATION I

Warner's chart is more a description than an explanation of how social life shapes religious ideals. Nonetheless, after dissecting the marriage of the virgin, Warner concludes, "the biological family, hard, enduring and central to all life, is the matrix from which the basic beliefs of Christianity emerge." These beliefs are given concrete study in Warner's work. Warner's significant contribution to the sociology of Christianity lies in his attention to the nature of collective representations and their connectedness to the moral, and social level. While Feuerbach and Durkheim echo Warner's words, the family's role as the source of religious ideation remains unclear. Warner's chart only outlines a vague but undetailed connection between biological, moral-social and sacred levels.

Edmund Leach's work advances our understanding of this relationship; particularly his article entitled "Levi-Strauss in the Garden of Eden." (Transactions of the New York Academy of Sciences, 1960, pp. 386-396.) Here, Leach describes the founding of the basic Western family unit in the Bible while detailing a cultural logic that can account for the particulars of religious representation. Leach focuses on the Biblical construction of family relationships as set forth in Genesis. I will use his analysis of these relationships to answer the following question: "How are familial meanings structured into the account of Adam and Eve and what connection does this Biblical account of the family make between kinship and religious thought?".

Leach employs a structural approach that focuses on a cultural logic based on binary elements constructing the character of such collective representations as marriage. Leach looks beneath the surface of the storyline of a myth or a relationship for a deeper linguistic like logic or grammar that can account for similarities between, say, observed religious rite or kinship practice. With Leach, our anthropological understanding of religion and kinship has moved from obvious empiricism in Warner and Durkheim to his deeper logic and meaning. This view remains naturalistic and committed to scientific or intellectual investigation. It regards religious phenomena as a meaningful set of symbols or as quasi-linguistic in character.

Leach's study of Genesis begins with the logical oppositions he isolates from the Biblical text. These include light versus darkness, heaven versus earth, freshwater above versus saltwater below, sea versus dry land, and the creation of the world as a static entity in contrast to the creation of moving, living things. A light/dark opposition is associated with a life/death opposition. In other words, according to Leach and regarding the Genesis story, light is to dark as life is to death. These binary pairs are key to understanding how meaning is developed in the Garden of Eden.

Leach focuses on God's creation of the human couple. This couple is surrounded not only by the unrealized oppositions cited above but also by an unrealized definition of Good and Evil. These nascent oppositions are matched by Adam's "unawareness" of the significance of the tree of knowledge and the tree of life. Adam accepts the presence of these trees though neither aware nor unaware of their implications for ignorance and knowledge, or for death in the face of life. Further, the present but as yet unknown opposition between male and female is exhibited in the couple's sexual ignorance. Leach shows that such binary oppositions have an ordered pattern. His point is that the elements of Genesis are oppositionally organized and are a transformation of the pattern found in the oedipal myth.

This oedipal theme relates to the undervaluing and overvaluing of kinship relations, an opposition that refers to patricide (undervaluing relations) and incest (overvaluing relations) as well as to themes related to the serpent in Genesis. Here is the key part of Leach's analysis.

> Adam and Eve eat the apple and become aware of sexual difference and death becomes inevitable--also of course, pregnancy and life become possible. Significantly, Eve does not become pregnant until after they have been expelled from Paradise. The curse that is imposed on the serpent deserves special note. There is to be enmity between the serpent and the woman and between the "seed of the serpent" and the "seed of the woman"- the latter being specified as male, "he shall bruise thy head and thou shalt bruise his heel" (Leach, 1960 Transactions of the New York Academy of Science, pp. 394-395)

Leach's oedipal theory relates to this passage but needs more detail to be clearly understood. But it sets a new and more structuralist course for the study of religion. His view can be replaced with an alternative structuralist interpretation using the binary oppositions he uncovers. In this view, the Garden of Eden is a story in which the oppositions used both to differentiate and form relations between the spouses are given primacy at the outset of religious thought's development. In short, the Garden of Eden is initially a place of harmony not only between man and beast and between God and man, but also between the distinct (or form) and the indistinct (formlessness). That is, early Eden is characterized by an undifferentiated unity. The river which flows through Eden is not yet forked; Adam and Eve are unaware of sexual differences; and more generally, binary oppositions (such as death/life, male/female, up/down, nature/culture) have not taken hold on the lives of the inhabitants. There is no death, for example, and snakes can talk from tree branches. (Animals speaking is not a nature/culture separation; snakes in trees is not an up/down distinction.) Binary oppositions, however, are nascently present and ready to take center stage in the form of trees of life and death, and knowledge of good and evil. Early Eden reminds one of Rousseau's *Second Discourse*- Adam and Eve are amoral and ignorant. They lack self-consciousness and even their nakedness counts for nothing. What eventually becomes distinct is at this point indistinct. But Eve eats the apple at the serpent's suggestion. The binary distinctions conveyed by the important trees in Eden - - knowledge of good and evil; life and death - - become part of the human condition. Humans are forced to reckon with binary oppositions and moral questions through this new knowledge of life and death, through this new knowledge of distinction.

Garnering distinction or binary opposition brings an end to Eden. With distinction comes knowledge of good and evil and knowledge generally. People suffer the consequences which this knowledge implies. For one, binary distinction implies separation of the terms: God and man now separate, and the separation, newly born of this opposition, is called sin in the Christian tradition. The separation of male and female permits carnal life for Adam and Eve and their descendants. They now know, in the Biblical sense, what nakedness is and with the episodic sex act, humankind knows the difference between acts of carnal relatedness and states of marriage between a husband and wife. Thus, the distinction which God made between static creation of things and the active movement of animate life becomes real for people in history. Again, acts of the flesh produce a spouse-like relationship, which also produces a distinction, if very understated between flesh and spirit. Spouses act together in the flesh but are in a marital, spiritual state. That spouses produce offspring introduces generational relations that are above and below one another. Up and down make their distinctive appearance post-Eden.

This point is emphasized by the character of the serpent. Just as the serpent once stood high in a tree when distinction did not exist, he now lies low, having lost speech and linguistic access to the cultural world of man. He becomes a beast whose head is at the heel of humans. The now inverted serpent is subordinate to Eve, who became subordinate to Adam through her sin (and sexual eagerness). In sum, Eve's sin establishes Adam's dominion, where once they had been undifferentiated equals in Eden. This subordination is a punishment meant to continue down in time. Thus, the story of the snake, the secretive eating of the fruit, the subsequent sin and its sexual consequences, all lead, in part, to a distinction between up and down. Human reproduction and death imply, for example, ascending and descending generations. Again, this implies an up/down distinction coming from the events of Eden.

Thus, the up/down relationship between generations, the active/static opposition in creation, the male/female distinction between persons, even the inside/outside dichotomy established on leaving (or going outside of) Eden - these oppositions become crucial to the relations that Adam and Eve as spouses have with each other. A man dominates or is above the woman in marriage as Adam was to Eve. A man is male and a woman female, an awareness coming from distinction or sin. And to reiterate, couples engage in sexual acts of the flesh that produce states of spiritual relatedness (male/ female, act/state, flesh/spirit).

The more general point is that Adam and Eve, post-Eden, are profoundly associated with and constructed through a series of oppositions that the Bible places at the center of its logic and collective ideas. These distinctions define Adam and Eve as a couple. Hence we begin the Bible with kinship terms and distinctions, distinctions that are used throughout the Bible and in subsequent religious language. This point about religious conceptions is elaborated upon in the following essays.

The argument thus far represents a departure point for the discussion of the relationship between kinship and religious ideation. Oppositions constructing or that frame family relations are also used to construct religious ones. In western culture, kinship is the root of religion just as the family is at the root of the Biblical narrative in Eden. Western religious thinking combines oppositions derived from kinship like up/down, and spirit/flesh to create its numinous concepts in the spirit, which is the domain this system creates as religion. This link is expressed in the first pages of the Bible. It is a married couple that begins the Biblical odyssey.[1] At the level of inner structure or cultural thought, then, the family is enmeshed in, and has a critical relationship to, religious encodings. In other words, the distinctions that form Adam and Eve's relationship are elaborated throughout the Biblical narrative. Hence, kinship structure is the basis of the Bible's stories. This turns out to be true of religious practice generally.

• • •

A brief example of a religious encoding derived from, or better, constructed by the same oppositions that form the Biblical family is seen in baptism by immersion in water. For clarity's sake, remember that structure is like the frame of a house: it gives form or quality to the house it helps to construct. So, the structures or binary distinctions composing baptism give baptism its qualities, again much as a full-frame constructs a house. Now, baptism involves immersing an individual in water: a person must go *down* in the *flesh,* so that he or she may come *up* in the *spirit.* These *actions* lead to a new *state;* where the individual was a *sinner,* he or she becomes *saved.* The relations constructing the term or qualities we find in the term baptism include up/down, spirit/flesh, act/state, sin/salvation and damned/saved. These contrasts give the term baptism most of its representational qualities. Baptism is an initial experience of being saved, of going from low to high etc., all of which is summarized in the term baptism but which is constructed from the structures or distinctions which have just been analyzed. These distinctions undergirding the concept or qualities of baptism. The term baptism becomes the quality that the relations create!

Here, many structures found in kinship such as up down and flesh spirit are used to make baptism a meaningful religious idea just as flesh and spirit construct the native distinction between kinship and religion. In later chapters, many different religious concepts will be amenable to this kind of analysis. The point here is that it is at the level of cultural organization, of binary oppositions constructing family and religious conceptions, that the link between the social and the religious realms is formed.

This relationship points to a working definition of religion which goes beyond religion as a native term. As a native term, religion is a domain in the spirit just as kinship is a domain in the flesh. Religion/kinship is constructed from spirit/flesh. But religion can be given a non-native and more abstract definition that may have use to anthropologists and others. In the West and perhaps elsewhere it is social thought (or specific social distinctions) thinking or organizing themselves together to form numinous ideas and practices. This definition goes beyond religion as a native term and allows for the possibility that similar religious structures exist in other cultures. In this structurally oriented definition, the direction Feuerbach gave to the study of religion is fully expressed. Religion is a human product conveyed in human language and is understandable empirically as something human and it exists within the limits of human understanding (however much it points or doesn't point to the truth). This is Feuerbach's naturalism brought into a symbolic realm; religion is a product and expression of cultural languages. The use of binary cultural logic to discern its character connects it to concrete Western, social relations like husband and wife. Moreover, we now have what was missing – the link between the family and the numinous is not established by Feuerbachian analogy but by structure which is examined in more detail in several of the essays later in this book

Essay 3- Moralizing the West: Pentecostal Revivalism in American Life

The mostly European intellectual history underlying many anthropological studies of religious life may seem very distant from the American frontier. Yet, a culturally significant structuring of religious meanings took place on the frontier, a structuring that can be understood by this European intellectual tradition.

That is, frontier revivals were sociologically significant because their newly obtained Protestantism was cultural in character. In these revivals, we can see structure at work: here a religion of the heart supplants earlier rationalisms to build a society of souls and homes in the American West. In the contrast between the rational and the emotional expression of religion, we see in part the signature of religious culture: a meaningful life is born again into the sinner with his emotional acceptance of religion. This theater of belief becomes an apt field for the European theoretical orientation. A brief history of the early American revivals in addition to a description of the camp meeting I attended in 1975 should help the reader understand how intellectual structure is present, theoretically and concretely, on the revival circuit.

The camp meeting is a traditional form in American Protestantism. Used most widely by Methodists during American's first century, it is essentially an outdoor tent revival where people come great distances to live and worship together for a period of time. The Church of God camp meeting I attended lasted a week and, like others, was marked by continuous preaching, which extended from early in the afternoon to late in the evening. Perhaps a thousand people assembled together, and the preachers ranged from the campground keeper to an international evangelist who specialized in a tongue ministry. The preachers successfully brought a sizeable number of worshippers to religious ecstasy, generally during the evening, at the end of the day's sermons and exhortations. Then hundreds spontaneously did what Pentecostals do when filled with the Holy Spirit: most spoke in tongues; others simply shrieked their praise; still others had the jerks or ran for joy; and numerous people simply lay on the ground, slain by the Lord. These scenes occurred regularly, every evening of the camp meeting. Yet, for all their intensity, they were simply tokens of a type: the camp meeting as a form of worship which became widely popular in the wake of massively ecstatic meetings in Logan County, Kentucky, at the beginning of the nineteenth century.

At the camp meeting I attended, I was accompanied by an informant. During one of our talks - while hundreds of people in the hall were powerfully uplifting the Lord and ecstatically submitting the control of their own flesh - my informant discussed how Pentecostal denominations were going the way of modem Methodism. The Assemblies of God, he said, were further along than the Church of God. They not only were leaving the cities for the suburbs and suburban prosperity; they were also becoming more polished and less enthusiastic in their worship. The shouting Methodists, he said, had once been as enthusiastic as the Church of God is today, but now Methodist churches are quiet and cold. The Methodists changed because they upgraded the educational standards of their ministers. The Church of God and the Assemblies of God were currently upgrading their educational standards, and this dimmed the spontaneity of the spoken spirit and emphasized instead academic discourses on the Bible. In the seminaries and in the practices of better-educated ministries, people were less inclined to preach the Word as the Spirit gave it utterance and were more inclined to develop messages systematically from the study of Scripture. This desire for education and scholarly precision sapped the spirit out of the shouting Methodists, and out of many of today's more educated Pentecostals.

My informant was not as clear as the passages above indicate, but his thought, I believe, was essentially correct. He had located a mechanism and a set of possible uses of the Word upon which the historical changes he described have hinged. His ideas inadvertently emphasize the meaningful organizations or structures within Pentecostalism responsible for movement away from religion of the heart and towards a religion primarily for the head. This shift in emphasis depends on the association of the Word both with Bible study and with direct spiritual intercession. This double association can lead the religious system at issues in at least two directions. Spontaneous mediation of the Word can be judged the more spiritual and desirable religious alternative, while systematic study can be seen as the more scripturally grounded and precise way to religious truth. The choice of one alternative over another has serious consequences for the experiential patterning of the religious language. Systematization of the Word through study, for example, may block the individual's spontaneous mediation of the Holy Spirit - the very core of Pentecostal enthusiasm. This substitution of methodical study for spontaneous mediation may encourage the religious rationalisms characterizing many churches to which Pentecostalism is historically related.

Moreover, within Pentecostalism, this distinction between enthusiasm and scholarship suggests the importance of particular cultural elements in the social and historical development of fundamentalist Christianity in America. In this view, the nature of religious worship is not circumscribed by institutional constraints nor is circumscribed by the experience of social groups, with their backlogs of internal and external interactions. Instead, the nature of religious worship is forged according to the possibilities inherent in the symbolic forms of the religious system itself.

This thesis challenges more traditional church/ sect interpretations of religious change. It suggests that Pentecostal religion, considered as a cultural system, serves a spiritual (and transformational) purpose different from any presumed sociological functions that Pentecostal sects are often alleged to fulfill in a universal and ahistorical manner. In this view, the character of 'sect' worship is not a function of social deprivation, status loss, economic insecurity in a hostile industrial world, or even of the personality types which have been sifted into a variety of anomic social conditions. Here, Pentecostalism is understood as a symbolic form, one that is exercised through and responsive to a social context, but which nonetheless has a distinctive cultural character crucial to its empirical expression. An examination of Pentecostalism's historic relation to Methodism will draw out the binary oppositions which have helped compose differences between these two religions. The importance of oppositions within various religious ideals, like sanctification and tongue- talking, necessarily emerges from the Methodist history which led to Pentecostalism. The old-time itinerant minister, the sinfulness that many of them condemned on the frontier, the development of a seminary system, and the value given to education-all these indicate the various emphases given certain oppositions within the revival tradition. The result is a set of religious convictions that associate spirit as opposed to flesh, with elements like noise as opposed to silence or with enthusiasm as opposed to rationalism. These associations build the character of Pentecostalism, Methodism maintaining a different mix of associations with spirit, as this historical examination will partially confirm.

The general tradition from which Pentecostalism developed is the American revival tradition which has its roots in Methodism. American Methodism fragmented in the late nineteenth century, at first producing an internal holiness movement, which later became independent and which itself produced Pentecostalism. Significantly, the split between the Methodists and the holiness traditions involved not only the issue of sanctification but also the question of educational standards in the ministry and the undisciplined character of wandering revivalists. The historical predecessor to Pentecostalism, the holiness movement, fell away from Methodism principally over educational issues and in doing so sided with the "heart" rather than "head" religion.

Wesleyanism, early on, gave rise to systems that emphasized the more spontaneous holiness mediation of the Spirit, rejecting the elaboration of a more scholarly, Methodist approach to the Word. But even as the splinter groups and the holiness movement stressed emotion rather than intellect, the scholarly road remained an available if latent possibility for them and their heir, the Pentecostal tradition.

21

Common Differences Revisited/Moralizing the West

The holiness tradition, of course, originally existed within Methodism and was true to Wesley's doctrine of perfection and notions of sanctification. The doctrinal issue that divided the Wesleyans was the number of blessings existing in the spiritual life and the nature of spiritual growth once an individual converted. At conversion, everyone agreed, one attained salvation and was justified before God. Nonetheless, a second spiritual blessing was viewed as necessary to removing fully the daily experience of sin in this life. This second blessing was and today is still called sanctification.

Sanctification does not remove one's sinful nature and nor does it free the individual from temptation; this is impossible since humans are in the flesh and are the heirs of Adam and Eve. But sanctification does involve a total purity, a perfecting of one's spiritual life to its earthly extremes. This perfection relates to living a holy and moral life and is intimately connected to codes of conduct. With the second blessing of sanctification comes a moral Christian purity historically related to right living and spiritual holiness. This second blessing is squarely a Wesleyan notion. Historic Methodism never fully denied this doctrine even while the practice of such holiness became the issue that led to the establishment of 'sects' outside of Methodism. That is, the importance and hence the character of this sanctification became a religious issue. Pentecostals added a third blessing to the holiness tradition which they called the spiritual baptism of the Holy Ghost.

These blessings abound in the revivals of the Second Great Awakening. The first took place at Gasper Rivers and the second at Cane Ridge. Tongue talking is the first evidence of this third blessing: like other Pentecostal characteristics, it is intimately linked to a revival tradition. While tongue talking is found throughout Christian history, specific American instances arc noted in the early Methodist revivals of the I8OO's. Students at the University of Georgia spoke in tongues in 1800-01, for example, and more generally people on the frontier camp meetings commonly experience glossolalia.

These early frontier revivals, which began around 1797 and which continued for more than a quarter of a century, were crucial to establishing Arminianism-with its democratic possibility of salvation for all- within almost all-American Protestant denominations. The revivals, moreover, revealed the importance of Christian spirituality in establishing standards for American community life. In fact, the early revivals were commonly viewed not only as necessary to spreading salvation, but also to uplifting morals and establishing codes of conduct for the unchurched and seemingly uncivilized masses who populated American's interior.

The revivals were not the more Calvinistic ones of the eighteenth century but were the explosively popular ones that began on the Western frontier at the outset of the nineteenth century. This Second Great Awakening inaugurated a variety of Christian devices - the camp meeting, the class meeting, the itinerant minister-which aimed at popularizing Christian perfection, and which made its brand of religion crucial to the codes of conduct that tamed a wild and young country.

The Second Great Awakening was an initial popular source for Protestant perfectionism in America and saw itself as the great imposer of moral order on sinners who bordered on the savage. In fact, the itinerants conducting camp meeting revivals frequently began their messages by impressing the perception of self as sinner on the uneducated, unchurched and religiously ignorant people who came to listen. The religious system then suppressed this sinfulness and the evils of the flesh while leading the new believer to the holy life. That this system of categorization defined the nature of immorality as well as the ideal of moral reform is made clear in the biographies of itinerant preachers as well as in the stories of wild Westerners. The historians of the Second Great Awakening also shared the Christian notion of religious dissipation and moral recklessness which they said characterized the frontier. W.W. Sweet, a University of Chicago historian of religion, for example, notes that the great revival began on the Kentucky frontier, following in the wake of vigilante wars, wide-spread drinking, omnipresent violence and frequent and out-of-control crime. He writes:

> That every frontier was in pressing need of moral restraint and guidance there can be no reasonable doubt, and in most instances, the only guardians of the morals of these communities was the little frontier church.

Common Differences Revisited/Moralizing the West

Two great revivals marked the beginning of the Second Great Awakening, both located in Logan County, Kentucky. The Gasper Rivers revival, in July 1800, was an open-air meeting in the Wesleyan tradition. People came from near and far, pitched their tents and got religion in a clearing in the wilderness. Perhaps McGready-the chief revivalist-can give us the best account:

> No person seemed to wish to go home, hunger and sleep seemed to affect nobody-external things were the vast concern. Here awakening and converting work was to be found in every part of the multitude.... Sober professors, who had been communicants for many years, now lying prostrate on the ground, crying out ...

At Gasper Rivers, McGready noted, young men and women, grey-headed people, people of every description, white and black, were to be found in every part of the multitude. Everywhere people were crying out for mercy in the most extreme distress. People fainted; people swooned. They experienced the jerks, the physical sense of religion. People danced together while praying for salvation. At Gasper Rivers, they obtained release and joyfully shouted their deliverance.

A month later, the Cane Ridge gathering took place. This one was also outdoors, and the worshippers were even more numerous. Again, people jerked, rolled, ran, danced, and this time, barked. But unlike Gasper Rivers, the Cane Ridge revival lasted for weeks and drew huge numbers, some estimates ranging as high as twenty-five thousand. It was an almost unceasing affair, the daytime meetings lasting well into the night. There were massive conversions; the scene of Godly beseechers, tearful repentants, God-intoxicated ruffians, the vision questing children dazzled even disbelievers. Never had there been a religious occasion such as this in America. Such manifest ecstasy and such volumes of noise, all these events were astounding for the Kentucky frontier. These revivals were followed by the camp meetings that continued for forty years. This form of Christianity influenced the whole nation, but it spread primarily westward, following the frontier. Two aspects of this movement are noteworthy: first, its theology (or folk beliefs) though Wesleyan was not formally systematic.

Second, the revival's primary concern was that the believer experiences the Holy Spirit and accepts Jesus Christ into his or her life. People sought, as they do today, a felt experience of trust in Christ, and they sought the felt inner purification and cleansing of sin which that faith promised. In a sense, the Methodist and revival notion of the second baptism combines the second and third blessings of Pentecostalism, and perhaps this coalescing of notions is the source of the controversy that sanctification evoked in the late nineteenth century. For early revivalists, sanctification was the result of Christian purification. That is, even after the believer accepted Christ as his personal savior, he remained tainted with sin. This sinfulness could only be removed by an immediate experience of Jesus through God's agent, the Holy Ghost. On having this experience, the individual was perfected and sanctified. The early class meeting formed in the wake of the Kentucky and other revivals furthered the work of sanctification. The converts formed groups where moral standards and practices-"holiness" in later parlance-were strictly enforced. The more Christian conduct was perfected, the holier the believer and the closer, then, to complete and experiential, real sanctification. The churches that followed the revivals and camp meetings linked to this experiential holiness a tradition that emphasized sanctification. This, indeed, was an American Wesleyanism based on the possibility of salvation attainable for all.

The doctrines of salvation, moral reform and Christian perfection were spread throughout American by the chief agent of this revivalism, the itinerant preacher. The life of the frontier itinerant, James Finley, captures the emotional, moral and spiritual experience dramatically realized by converts from Cane Ridge and the camp meeting. His story, moreover, illustrates the character of early Methodism and its itinerants while showing the connection between Christian spirituality and codes of conduct.

Finley, like other itinerants later in their lives, wrote his autobiography so one can see his life in his own terms. Principally, Finley saw himself as a reformed and saved sinner who had once been a near wild man living alone in the wilderness. Finley was a Calvinist's son, brought up in the backwoods of Kentucky where his parents were homesteaders. Life in that early period, as settlers so often noted, was rough and barren. Finley wrote that he, like other backwoods boys, was brought up to "the trade of knock-down and drag-out". While his family had strong religious tendencies, an anomaly for the Appalachian frontier, he himself in his teenage years chose instead to follow the boisterous western life.

In his autobiography, he states that he rejected religion because he had difficulty reconciling God's damnation of the non-elect, who were so by His will, with the idea of God as just and merciful. Having rejected faith, he went full tilt the other way and, as he said, "performed the errant of his destiny." By his own account, he fell into a common frontier pattern: sprees, swearing, fighting and dancing. "Thus I lived thoughtless and wicked, resolving and re-resolving upon amendment, but continuing the same or rather growing worse and worse till I arrived at the twentieth year of age".

During this period, Finley lived in the wilderness as a hunter. While he believed his ways were wicked, he nonetheless was haunted by his family's religiosity. He continued to respect the Sabbath, doing no hunting or labor on this, the day of rest. Earlier in his life he had violated this restriction and as a result, he believed, he subsequently lost his homestead to land speculators: thus, his sojourn in the wilderness. The hunting life, while it had its excitements, also had its melancholy, and it was at this depressed point that friends encouraged him to attend the Kentucky prayer meeting at Cane Ridge. Of it, Finley wrote:

> There would be an unusual outcry, some bustling forth into loud ejaculations of prayer or thanksgiving for the truth...others flying to their careless friends with tears of compassion: beseeching them to turn to the Lord: some struck with terror and hastening through the crowd to make their escape, or pulling away their relations; others fainting and swooning away.

Finley describes seven ministers preaching to thousands with up to five hundred people prostrating themselves at one time:

Common Differences Revisited/Moralizing the West

While witnessing these scenes, a peculiarly strange sensation, such as I had never felt before came over me. My heartbeat tumultuously, my knees trembled, my lips quivered, and I felt as though I must fall to the ground. A strange supernatural power seemed to pervade the entire mass of mind there collected. I became so weak and powerless that I found it necessary to sit down.

Finley eventually went for a walk in the surrounding wood, summoned his courage, and tried to convince himself that this was merely sympathetic excitement. Thinking that this enthusiasm was inspired by the harangues of ministers and not by God, he returned to the scene, but the same awful feeling came over him. He thought he was going to die. So he, like some of the people McGready described, fled to the nearest tavern, which was one half-mile away. Although he thought a drink would calm his nerves, the bar scene made real the very image of sin. It was a place of drunken revelry, of Godless men and uncharitable thoughts.

Finley felt disgust, but he had a drink: "The brandy had no effect in allaying my feelings, but if anything made me worse". In a dazed, religious state, Finley returned and wandered about the campsite. He thought on his sins which were vividly and terrifyingly before him: "Then it was that I saw through the thin veil of Universalism and this refuge of lies was swept away by the Spirit of God." He once was blind, but now, with this realization, he could see. He saw that if he died with his sins, he was a lost man forever. And he dreaded the death of the soul: "Notwithstanding all this, my heart was so proud and hard that I would not have fallen to the ground for the whole state of Kentucky". Falling would have disgraced his manhood and courage, and instead, he left the gathering accompanied by a friend. But miles away, penitence came when he finally turned to his companion and said, "Captain, if you and I don't stop our wickedness, the devil will get us both." Finley began to cry quietly and at first, he kept himself from screaming. But he spent the night weeping aloud and promising God that he would mend his ways. At daybreak, Finley went to the woods to pray. There, crying for salvation and mercy, he fell prostrate. Neighbors, alerted to his cries, brought him inside where a religious man, recently immigrated from Holland, tended him. The man prayed and sang over Finley until nine o'clock in the evening.

> "When suddenly my load was gone, my guilt removed and presently the direct witness from heaven shone full on my soul. Then there flowed such copious streams of love into the hitherto desolate places of my soul, that I thought I should die with excess of joy. I cried, I laughed, I shouted and so strangely did I appear to all but my Dutch brother that they thought me deranged".

The next day, Finley felt he could drink forever from the cup of Jesus. Finley also felt a love for all mankind and reproached himself for living so long in sin and misery when God's mercy was so available to him. Such was the appeal of Cane Ridge. Finley's life is particularly informative since so many of the themes of frontier life converge in him. Like many, in his early adult years, he was a brash, rough man, irreligious and bumptious. His boyhood, in his eyes, had been wicked. His, moreover, had been a lone life, growing up in a backwoods settlement. He had been a hunter, experiencing the loneliness of the woods and knowing its 'lone sickness.' He also was superstitious and a heavy drinker. In many respects, then, he was a man of his time and place, a man of the Wild West. When he finally began to reconcile himself to his calling as a minister and started to attend a denominational church, he discovered that his fellow congregants who knew his past likened him to a devil. In fact, he later became known as the wild hunter preacher. So, Finley had lived the rough and tumble life of the day. His bad conscience, recognition of his sins, and a desire for a decent community contributed to his faith. When he began preaching, he organized class meetings to cleanse the countryside of the very sins he had committed. He tried to bring peace to an area troubled by 'rogues' and with his help, many small towns and churches of the Kentucky frontier developed into peaceful, law-abiding, church-going Christian citadels. Thus, revival Christianity met the perceived needs of frontier life and helped a new society of simple farmers to form communities with common values and moral associations which provided the decency they wished for their lives.

Common Differences Revisited/Moralizing the West

Finley was only one of many itinerant ministers who became the religious mainstay, not only of the frontier but of Methodism through much of the nineteenth century. The itinerant, a wandering minister who was assigned territorial sections, was the principal organizer and preacher to the people in his area. Traveling by horseback, often impoverished, living for God and ordinarily not maintaining a family, the itinerant minister spread the Gospel. Ordinarily without formal training, the early trans-Alleghenian circuit riders were graduates of "Brush College." There:

> The curriculum was constituted of such as 'the philosophy of nature and the mysteries of redemption' while the library consisted of the Word of God, the Discipline and the hymn book, supplemented by trees and brooks and stones, all of which were full of wisdom, and sermons and speeches; and her parchment of literary honors were the horse and the saddlebag."

The itinerants led camp meetings, condemned sin, preached morality, and coordinated the activities of subordinate class leaders, exhorters and local preachers. They were principally concerned with the mediation of the Word to the unsaved, but itinerants also had administrative duties, and in the early Methodist pattern, itinerant preachers reigned supreme.

The enthusiastic but unschooled Methodist circuit riders were eventually replaced by local preachers or ministers with seminary training. This was a decisive point in American Methodist history. The changes induced by the better-educated ministry and the conflicts thus engendered for the preachers and practitioners of old-time Methodism can be dramatically seen in the recollections of Peter Cartwright, one of the most prominent itinerants. His religious fervor and pedagogical power were almost unsurpassed- and there were problems when he encountered the new ministers on his old circuit. His account of the confrontation is revealing enough to quote in full:

> There happened to be at our quarterly meeting a fresh, green, live Yankee from down East. He had regularly graduated and had his diploma, and was regularly called by the Home Missionary Society, to visit the far-off West-

-a perfect moral waste, in his view of the subject-and having been taught to believe that we were almost cannibals and that Methodist preachers were nothing but a poor illiterate set of ignoramuses-he longed for an opportunity to display his superior tact and talent, and throw us poor upstarts of preachers in the West, especially Methodist preachers, into the shades of ever- lasting darkness. He, of course, was very forward and officious. He would, if I had permitted it, have taken the lead of our meeting. At length I thought I would give him a chance to ease himself of his mighty burden, so I put him up one night to read his sermon. The frame building we were worshipping in was not plastered, and the wind blew hard; our candles flared and gave a bad light, and our ministerial hero made a very awkward out in reading his sermon. The congregation paid a heavy penance and became restive; he balked and hemmed and coughed at a disgusting rate. At the end of about thirty minutes the great blessing came: he closed, to the great satisfaction of all the congregation.

I rose and gave an exhortation, and had a bench prepared, to which I invited the mourners. They came in crowds; and there was a solemn power rested on the congregation. My little hot- house reader seemed to recover from his paroxysm of a total failure, as though he had done all right, and uninvited, he turned in to talk to the mourners. He would ask them if they did not love Christ; then he would try to show them that Christ was lovely; then he would tell them it was a very easy thing to become a Christian, that they had only to resolve to be a Christian. I listened a moment and saw this heterodoxy would not do; that it produced jargon and confusion. I stepped up to him and said: 'Brother, you don't know how to talk to mourners. I want you to go out into the congregation, and exhort sinners:

He did not appear the least disconcerted, but at my bidding he left the altar, and out he went into the crowd, and turned in to talking to sinners. There was a very large man, who stood a few steps from the mourners, who weighed about two hundred and thirty pounds; he had been a professor but was backslidden. The power of God arrested him, and he cried out aloud for mercy, standing on his feet. My little preacher turned round and pressed back through the crowd; and coming up to this large man, reached up, and tapped him on the shoulder saying, 'Be composed; be composed.'

Seeing, and indistinctly hearing this, I made my way to him, and cried out at the top of my voice, 'Pray on, brother; pray on, brother; there's no composure in hell or damnation.'

And just as I crowded by way to this convicted man, who was still crying out loud for mercy, the little preacher tapped him again on the shoulder, saying, 'Be composed; be composed, brother.'

I again responded: 'Pray on, brother; pray on, brother; there is no composure in hell.' I said to the throng that crowded the aisle that led to the altar, 'Do, friends, stand back till I get this man to the mourner's bench.'

But they were so completely jammed together that it seemed almost impossible for me to get through with my mourner. I let go of his arm, and stepped forward to open the way to the altar, and just as I had opened the aisle, and turned to go back, and lead him to mourner's bench, the Lord spoke peace to his soul, standing on his feet; and he cried, 'Glory to God', and in the ecstasy of his joy, he reached forward to take me in his arms: but, fortunately for me, two men crowded into the aisle between him and myself and he could not reach me. Missing his arm in catching me, he wheeled around and caught my little preacher in his arms, and lifted him up from the floor; and being a large, strong man, having great physical power, he jumped from bench to bench, knocking the people against one another on the right and left, front and rear, holding in his arms the little preacher. The little fellow stretched out both arms and both feet. expecting every moment to be his last, when he would have his neck broken. Oh, how I desired to be near this preacher at that moment and tap him on the shoulder, and say, 'Be composed; be composed, brother!' But as solemn as the times were, I with many others, could not command my risibilities, and for the moment, it had like to have checked the rapid flow of good feeling with those that beheld the scene: but you may depend on it. as soon as the little hot bed parson could make his escape, he was missing."

Composed Methodism was not itinerant Methodism and the differences Cartwright had with the educated Easterner became a more general problem several decades later. The influence of educated Methodists and rational religious thought became very strong after the Civil War and this situation, especially later in the century, sapped away much enthusiasm. "Traditionalists" began searching for more lively and familiar worship. In fact, *The Autobiography of Peter Cartwright* was published in 1856 when an interest in the holiness Wesleyanism practiced by the early circuit riders was increasing. The book's publication preceded the printing of numerous circuit riders' autobiographies in the 1880's and 1890's. These books popularized old-time virtues and received wide circulation as the question of 'heart religion' in Methodism became increasingly problematic for those who had formed the holiness movement within the church itself.

Common Differences Revisited/Moralizing the West

The holiness movement was nineteenth-century Methodism's internal fundamentalism. It crystallized in opposition to the general direction of Methodist thinking, ultimately opposing the higher Bible criticisms and liberal, socially-minded theology which dominated the divinity schools and intellectual centers of the gilded age. In the seventies, eighties, and nineties, the holiness movement became widespread within the established church. The movement had begun, rather informally, with the idea of returning the church to its sanctified roots. Ostensibly, the issue was doctrinal: the second blessing of sanctification and the possibility of complete perfection provoked much discussion. These intellectual issues, however, were not extremely contentious since John Wesley himself affirmed such ideas. Nonetheless, the renunciation of holiness doctrine in 1894 by the Methodist Episcopal Church reveals the religious nature of the conflict:

> "But there has sprung up among us a party with holiness as a watchword; they have holiness associations, holiness meetings, holiness preachers, holiness evangelists. and holiness property. Religious experience is represented as if it consists of only two steps, the first step out of condemnation into peace and next step into Christian perfection. The effect is to disparage the new birth, and all stages of spiritual growth from the blade to the full corn in the ear, if there be not professed perfect holiness... We do not question the sincerity and zeal of these brethren; we desire the Church to profit by their earnest preaching and Godly example; but we deplore their teaching and methods insofar as they claim a monopoly of the experience, practice, and advocacy of holiness, and separate themselves from the body of ministers and disciples."

It is quite ironic that the Methodist Episcopal Church displayed such hostility to holiness preachers and holiness revivals in its denomination since Methodism began as a holiness movement within Anglicanism, but it is especially revealing that this declaration led to another attack on the holiness revivalists of the decade. Proscriptions against revivalists were written into the Methodist's Discipline by the General Conference of 1894: "No local preacher shall enter into the recognized territory of any of our pastoral charges for the purpose of conducting protracted or revival meetings except upon the invitation of the preacher in charge." This decree represents a rejection of itinerant ministries and a reliance on local ministers who followed the central administration. Not only did this declaration reverse the traditional dominance of the itinerant over the local preacher; it also indicated that the old fashioned and ill-trained heirs to the circuit rider were no longer wanted. This trend is recognized in an official history of Methodism:

"Thus, throughout the twenty years following 1880 Methodist leaders in both North and South witnessed a growing disruption of fellowship in their communions which they seemed powerless to halt. The bishops... were anxious to keep Methodism evangelical and thoroughly Wesleyan... However, wealthy city congregations and their cultivated pastors had rebelled against the class meeting, the revival, and the old standards which an earlier generation had thought to be evidence of holiness."

The cultivated pastors sided with the new Methodism and the older itinerant style, including its revivalism and moral fervor, lost ground. Indeed, educational standards for the ministry during this period were upgraded; seminary training became more common and the older conference courses of study declined. Intellectual and economic advancement increasingly led to a demand for better-equipped ministers.

The established church of this period, moreover, differed from the church of the earlier part of the century. "No longer were Methodists drawn from the lower and humbler economic and social groups," while the church itself was also much richer. This was reflected in the rising scale of ministers' salaries, the building of larger and more costly churches, the introductions of pipe organs and paid choirs, and the frequently voiced complaint that in the local church, the business meeting was replacing the prayer meeting. The church, moreover, was increasingly funding private colleges, which were growing in excellence and endowment as Methodists became wealthier and more addicted to the written word. The church's publishing house also furthered learning and continued to be a financially successful venture.   This increasing prosperity, with its attendant interest in education, was not fully shared in all parts of the country. The South, for example, was impoverished after the Civil War and its educational institutions were in disarray. In the various depressions of the last quarter of the nineteenth century, moreover, the agrarian sector was hardest hit, with Southerners- especially in the depression of 1893 - the heaviest victims. Thus, the South was less wealthy and less enamored of a Methodism increasingly impressed by educational credentials and standards. Southern religion, then, took a different direction from that of the nation. Indeed, the relationship between education and wealth in American Protestantism was reflected in the correspondence, in the South, between low ministerial salaries (compared to those in the nation as a whole) and a general lag in the educational level of the area's religious leadership.

Having retained the less prosperous conditions under which itinerant Methodism thrived, it is therefore not surprising that the holiness movement, while nationwide, was especially strong in this region. The holiness movement was a haven for many of the more traditional ministers and, especially in the South, both revival activity and church membership steadily increased. The revivalists, however, did not easily submit to church authority and their spontaneity clashed with the control local preachers wished to have over religious activities in their territory. They were also disinclined to tolerate the non-perfectionists' view of the church and so many holiness people left the church. The 'sect' building period began in 1894, but earlier 'come-outism' or leaving the parent church was not unknown, especially in the poorer, southern region of the country. In fact, the holiness leaders who wished to remain loyal to Methodism were embarrassed by this tendency and come-outism was one of the many reasons for the Church's hostile declaration of 1894.

The Church of God, or rather the holiness group in North Carolina, which eventually became the Church of God, was one of these early come-outism churches, forming as a Christian Union in 1886. Significantly, it was established by the wandering itinerants, notably Spurling and Tomlinson, and like the itinerants of old, these men made their livings selling religious literature. These were uneducated but faithful men who, true to their alienation from prevailing denominations, believed their new church to be the one and only member of the body of Christ on Earth.

Nonetheless, the Church of God was like many other come-outism churches that had been established in the region. Since the movement toward new congregations was not organized through the essentially loyalist holiness movement within Methodism, there was a kind of denominational splinter effect. Because the conditions were favorable to renewing the region's revivalist tradition the result was a hodge-podge of new names for a myriad of churches which all generally adhered to the same old-fashioned, perfectionist beliefs. In general, these Southern holiness churches became Pentecostal in the twentieth century. While tongue-talking did take place in the early Church of God it was not until 1907 that glossolalia became an explicitly defined third blessing which all Christians were enjoined to seek. Today tongue talking is perhaps the most distinctive feature of Pentecostal faith.

Pentecostalism, then, is holiness perfection with an added blessing. In their terms, Pentecostalism involves strict codes for conduct, but it stresses the *experience* of holiness, often marked by the gift of tongues. Its model is that of Christ's followers on the day of Pentecost in that it emphasizes the direct experience of the Holy Ghost, a tradition harking back to the Second Great Awakening, but one which was underplayed in the moral concerns about sanctification manifest in the National Holiness Association.

The introduction of tongue-talking and a renewed emphasis on religious experience were the hallmarks of the Azusa Street Revival in Los Angeles, which began in 1904. This was, perhaps, the initial Pentecostal event in the twentieth century. Holiness people from throughout the country came to this black revival and soon vast numbers of Southern whites and blacks were following its form and experiencing its spirit. Following on this revival, the Pentecostal-holiness movement groups in the South soon became more systematic in their denominational organization and governance. They have increasingly pursued their evangelical tradition, and the movement has grown phenomenally in this country. In a religious sense, however, little has changed since the Azusa Street Revival and, as far as the religious character of Pentecostalism is concerned, the Second Great Awakening stands as a model for Pentecostal experience.

The Pentecostal movement, then, is the true heir of American revivalism, the class meeting, the itinerant minister, and the holiness movement. It is a Wesleyan religion, like old-time Methodism, and so is a creature of traditional American Protestantism. The Pentecostal movement is not a series of denominational sects but is instead a distinctive cultural idiom built on dichotomies and their associations. It is an idiom or mode of religious expression in which revivalism serves a specifically spiritual purpose. Its history reveals its cultural and systemic character; the enthusiasm it stresses, the naturalism it rejects are clear in the experiential holiness and Holy Ghost enthusiasm and its immediate historical predecessors.

Dichotomies such as spirit/flesh, heart/mind, and enthusiasm/scholarship serve as the generative matrix or basic building blocks of this religious thought. These building blocks are drawn into new configurations in the history of American Methodism and Protestantism. The use of these dichotomies generates the form of religious change, and in this case, explains the form of these Protestant religious movements. Where Methodism takes up the head, Pentecostalism emphasizes the heart as a distinctive feature, though both share the heart/ mind or enthusiasm/ rationalism oppositions. Pentecostal revivalism represents a complex of associated elements which include the Word, the spirit, and the heart. These elements combine, perhaps by chance, to give us the Pentecostal enthusiasm that is so widespread

Essay 4- Concerning Structure: A Little Elaboration

In this book's first essay, the example of baptism was meant to introduce the reader to how religious terms are analyzed in Common Differences Revisited. The term baptism is associated with certain qualities or meanings that are constructed from relations or oppositions such as up/down, spirit/flesh, and act/state that are contained in the term. The distinction up and down, for example, structures or allows baptism to include the idea of being dunked in water. The oppositions constructing or defining the qualities of the term baptism, moreover, have their origin in kinship relations such as husband and wife.

This kind of analysis is meant as an explanation, a cultural explanation of religious language or terms like baptism. And it is explanation that I seek and that this book of essays is about: this essay wants to elaborate how structure allows us to explain the character of religious tropes. In the first essay, I tried to show that the literature viewing religion as a human social product sought a certain kind of explanation. This search began with Feuerbach and his argument by analogy, which explained the numinous by its similarity with family life. The limits of this were uncovered in part by Marx who said a human explanation of religion must relate to particular social relations in a particular historical venue. Feuerbach did however link his explanation to what he viewed as a universal set of social relations. Leach in his Biblical exegesis, found particular and western family constructions and their structures at the root of religion. Using Leach's deep structure approach I would like to further elaborate on how finding the constructing distinctions in a term like baptism explains the term. And using the intellectual histories observations about the family being the root of religious representations, I want to link the structures composing the Western family to those composing Western religious representations.

In my rendition of a clear, objective, and fundamental explanation of religious life, I want to show that the structures organizing kinship relational terms are set against one another to give rise to and to form the qualities of religious terms. This is meant to show how such terms as baptism become imbued with meaning. And this is meant as an explanation of religious tropes. The analysis of baptism in this initial essay was an attempt to do that. It was done by way of deep structures found in kinship terms. Here is what I thought an explanation of baptism consisted of:

> If the basic structures composing baptism could be isolated and if these structures could be shown to construct all the characteristics of baptism, and if these underlying constructions worked according to a determined logic that also and consistently structured all other terms within the religion where baptism occurs, and if these structures were the same structures constructing kinship terms but could be shown to combine in a significant way, then we would have a systematic and objective characterization of baptism and its qualities as a meaningful term.

This would be especially so if all aspects of the system in which baptism exists can be described or explained in the same way. This includes all the ideas of kinship and religious variation between Islamic, Jewish, and Christian constructions but for focus and scope, we will only attempt this analysis on Jewish and Christian ideas in the essays that follow. In any case, if the analysis works consistently, if there are a handful of *common*, deep structures that get *differently* expressed in these religious and kinship domains, then the entire system finds its explanation. This system includes kinship as well as all the different religious expressions found in what some people call the Judeo-Christian tradition but which I call the system of common differences. Here, the term "common differences" conveys the idea that there are distinctions commonly running through the religious/kinship system that construct the differing ideas within Judaism, Christianity, and Islam and their kinship systems. It also conveys the idea that while these religious systems are different from one another, at a deep level, like all human languages, they have much in common.

More on this in the essays that follow but please note that by constructing the various aspects of the system we may do more than clarify the meaning of its terms. We may gain new and unique insights. For example, we might learn in some detail how Judaism, Christianity and Islam relate within a system of common differences with common structural processes. Not only will we see how religious notions and practices are built differently through common structures, but we will also learn that Christian transformation is matched by a process of formation in Judaism and that formation has an oppositional character to transformation. As a future essay will show, one depends on likeness and the other difference. We might learn how the religions relate through a varying use of their most common deep structure or opposition: spirit and flesh. And again, we further could see that common-difference religion is social thought thinking itself; it is underlying, unconscious oppositions from kinship combining in religious terms to produce meaning as the example of baptism here was meant to show. This is an explanation of the how of religious thought.

Again, this goes to finding the oppositions composing a term like baptism and realizing that they also compose family terms like mother, father, sister, and brother. And one might ask if there is a deeper philosophic thought at work in this understanding of how religious/kinship ideation may be explained. There is and the deeper thought about structure and the qualities of terms links to the work of the British philosopher F.H. Bradley in *Appearance and Reality* (Oxford Press London 1969, first published in 1893). The key is Bradley's observation: qualities exist in relation to differences and differences to qualities. If we take Bradley's word "qualities" and imagine it to mean terms like baptism, then the relations or differences composing baptism make for the quality or meaning of the term.

Here is Bradley speaking for himself: "I rest my argument upon this, that if there are no differences, there are no qualities since all must fall into one. But if there is any difference, then that implies a relation"

(1969 pg. 25). So, existent qualities (or identities or things or perhaps religious "objects") imply the existence of relations or differences, and relations require qualities that are discerned, or better constructed through differences. Qualities might be something, sugar for example, or they might be terms, baptism for example. "So far as I can see, relations must depend upon terms, just as much as terms upon relations." (1969 pg.26). A relation without qualities is meaningless and relations and qualities must exist relative to terms.

Take baptism as an example of a term - the term baptism has qualities that define it as an act that initiates spiritual life as a Christian. It is a spiritual rebirth. It involves going down into water (fully in the Pentecostal case) and coming up. The preacher dunks the initiate. Baptism is said to prayers; it involves Christ's words which are spoken by a preacher. All these words, actions and meanings are qualities of the term baptism. There may be more, but for an accounting of baptism's attributes or qualities, this will do.

All these qualities require differences, as Bradley insists. So, baptism's up implies a down. Water must be like something and different from something else (it turns out that blood is the backdrop). Baptism's life of the spirit implies death in the flesh. Its words must be like spirit and unlike something else. These differences can be expressed as binary oppositions: up/down, wet/dry, spirit/flesh, noise/silence, and life/death (oppositions which themselves are qualities in relation). A thoroughly structured system constructs the qualities of its terms through these binary pairs. For baptism to be explained in this manner, all its differences must construct all the qualities associated with the term baptism.

This was what I meant when I wrote earlier that "baptism involves immersing an individual in water: a person must go *down* in the *flesh,* so that he or she may come *up* in the *spirit.* These *actions* lead to a new *state;* where the individual was a *sinner,* he or she becomes *saved.* The relations constructing the term or qualities we find in the term baptism include up/down, spirit/flesh, act/state, sin/salvation and damned/saved. These contrasts give the term baptism most of its representational qualities: baptism is an initial experience of being saved, of going from low to high, etc. all of which is summarized in the term baptism but which is constructed from the structures or distinctions which have just been analyzed. These distinctions undergird the concept or quality of baptism. The term baptism becomes the quality that the relations create!

As the reader will see in more than one essay here, act/state, up/down and spirit/flesh are used to discuss relations between spouses and relations between generations in the terms mother, father, sister and brother. My argument is that these kinship structures are used to construct religious terms as well. They combine in various ways; they operate on one another so to speak, and yield up terms like baptism, the Trinity, and religious practices such as the Jewish dietary laws. My argument is that this is systematic and that there is an underlying logic of religious and kinship terms which is determined by these relations.

Thus, the scope of the book, which examines how structure constructs Pentecostal patterns of culture and Pentecostal transformation as well as various Jewish practices and texts. While this may appear to be an endless mantra of oppositions constructing the qualities of certain religious beliefs and practices, the fact is that this constitutes one kind of explanation. Moreover, the argument will allow us to predict what the qualities of Christian and Jewish thought should be, based on its underlying logic. For example, if spirit/flesh is the key relations in this system, then spirit and flesh ought to define the relationship between different domains such as kinship and religion. Kinship is primarily in the flesh while religion is primarily in the spirit. Kinship should be bifurcated by flesh and spirit, an observation which brothers could make of brothers-in-law. And of course, marriage is in the spirit where generational descent is in the flesh, a thought which is elaborated in an essay that follows. Likewise, this bifurcation should exist in the religious domain and I examine this in the essay entitled "The Eucharist, the Passover, and the Word" and in the essay "Common Differences." And this expected bifurcation of spirit and its domain into spirit and flesh subsets suggests that there are flesh religions and spirit religions in the domain of spirit. This is a prediction, and the essay on

"Judaism/Christianity: a study in cultural contrasts" demonstrates the accuracy of this observation.

Please note, yet again, that religious truths are not the subject of these essays. A religious truth would be something about the character of God and instead, these essays only look at God concepts. These essays examine religious practices and representations, not what these refer to. It is about symbolic and linguistic or cultural understanding, not about an understanding of what is referred to. Faith is not the overriding concern of this book; understanding what religion is, is its focus. And, let me say in passing, that these may be linguistic constructs, but they are also facts in the world and as facts, they need an accounting much as any physical object requires an explanation as real object in the world.

Essay 5- First Thoughts

A professor of mine at Chicago, Professor Stocking, once said that if we could find one true thing, we could build a world up on it. I want to find a simple epistemological truth like the one about identity or quality and difference discussed in the previous essay and see if it figures prominently in our religious culture and then show how a world is built upon it.

What is this truth, a truth I think might be fundamental to both knowing and to our religious - cultural systems? It is this: If everything were the same, then nothing would be knowable because nothing would be distinct. And if everything were different, then nothing would be knowable because nothing would be identifiable or comparable.

To know something, we need both identity and difference. Identity and difference are paired, and both are required to know anything. Differences must occur against something in common to be distinguished (known) and identities must imply differences since in the absence of differences against an identity, nothing is distinguishable, including whatever it is that is the same, which is otherwise unknowable.

Others have also made this fundamental epistemological observation: Heidegger in <u>Identity and Difference</u>, and the British philosopher Bradley in <u>Appearance and Reality</u> come to mind. I have taken this idea from Bradley. Bradley also made a related and important observation: He said that qualities imply relations and relations imply qualities. What he meant was simple and clear: up only exists in contrast to down and their differences are dimensions of a quality, spatial relations. Hot differs from cold according to temperature. Sweet differs from sour in relation to taste. Differs and relates are virtually the same here. Sweet relates to sour, and they relate by a quality of taste, which is a component quality to sweet and sour. Their differences have the quality or identity of taste in common.

Bradley sensibly states in a footnote early in his book that if the reader understood the simple expression, qualities imply relations and relations qualities then there was no need to read on. Still, I want to continue and want to rephrase Bradley's wonderful language into identity and difference. Not only does one imply the other, their relationship is binary. Identity/difference is the binary relationship or difference, and the dimension or quality that they differ along is identity of difference. This is a difficult idea to convey although any intuitive reader should see that identity or unity must imply a unity of differences, otherwise the concept of unity or identity might be meaningless -- what would it be a unity of?

So, identity of differences as a dimension exists. It could be formulated as identity-difference in contrast to identity/difference. The dash is in opposition to the /, which expresses difference. This identity and its symbol - expresses the absence of difference, a quality of unity established by relations of identity-difference, rather than simply as unity. In other words, we have the quality of identity known by a unified binary difference: identity-difference. In any case, we see that relations (binary) need a quality (singularity) to exist and singularity requires relationships, which here are binary. As a result, there are three elements here: the quality, which is singular, and an identity, and then a quality of difference which is a binary contrast. In this view, at the root of all ordinary knowledge, we have a triad, two distinct elements (identity/difference) and one identity made possible by difference. And of course, identity/difference form one pair of binary distinction, so there is a one and a two in this simple opposition but the opposition itself can be declined into or expressed as a more explicitly triadic structure.

Here is a triadic illustration of a version of this identity/difference binary opposition to visualize the points I have been making:

<u>**identity-difference (1)**</u>
identity/difference (2)

44

Identity/difference is a singular but two-part distinction and it can be expressed as the illustration above shows, as a three-part triad. In this triad, a singular unity is above a two-fold difference. This triad is a unity just as the binary distinction it is based on, identity/difference is a unity. Significantly, the triadic version of the opposition, which is just one expression of identity/difference, clearly shows that identity is not just one but is composed of indistinct differences, forming a clear opposition or difference with the difference below.

And significantly, the triadic diagram translates into our religious or cultural terms, and once I show you these, it might become easier to see this triadic structure more clearly. As these essays will show, the basic principle of our culture (I call it the system of common differences) is not identity and difference but spirit and flesh. These are the particular expressions of identity and difference in the western knowledge-relational cultural system. In other words, spirit is readily characterized as an identity and flesh as difference. So, we have a one and a two. To repeat, spirit's main and overriding characteristic or quality is identity; flesh is known in binary difference (two). Together this gives us one, and a two. One is based on identity and the other difference. This is commonly understood as spirit/flesh which are two qualities in one relation. We also have a triad established through one binary opposition. This opposition constructs one triadic singularity -- three elements based on identity or singularity and difference.

Next, let's elaborate on how spirit and flesh form a triad and I want to do this circuitously, by showing various declensions of spirit and flesh. This is consistent with my purpose, which is to introduce the reader to the working of deep structure in cultural representations (for example, in the language of religion) like God (both Jewish and Christian) and the Western family. So first take note of the basic (singular) structure of (binary) spirit and flesh, which can be expressed vertically:

<u>spirit</u>
flesh

Now, as we have said, the top portion is an expression of identity and were this spirit deeply structured, it might consist of spirit-flesh, no

45

distinction but identity (absence of difference) between these differences. The bottom flesh portion might likewise be structured by spirit and flesh, since this is the only distinction at hand to define a flesh built on difference, so we would get:

<u>spirit-flesh</u>
spirit/flesh

Since the top part shows the relationships that compose an identity, (it shows the composition of spirit), this structure can be displayed in the triad most readers will intuitively say they recognize:

<u>spirit</u>
spirit/flesh

Readers may recognize this triad since it principally constructs the Trinity. Let me express the Trinity triadically:

<u>God</u>
flesh/spirit

or rather:

<u>God</u>
Jesus/Holy Ghost

The top portion or God is spirit and one, and the bottom is flesh and two. This gives us a three-person or triadic godhead. But this chart emphasizes the distinctiveness of each divine person and this is not what should occur in a spiritual or religious domain where its godhead emphasizes unity. So, its persons should not be especially distinct, though its flesh aspect should add something of distinction even if its spiritual God character emphasizes unity. This suggests that the bottom portion personages ought to assert their differences somehow through identity even if the contrastive elements of the Trinity ought to be indistinct. So, the original:

<u>spirit</u>
flesh

distinction, though it is a singular unit, is not what rules here. The

spirit-flesh

as an indistinction is the actual declension of spirit and flesh that governs the God person. This is also true for the spirit and flesh

46

distinction that constructs both Jesus and the Holy Ghost and the "distinction" or rather the indistinction between them.

The God person contains spirit-flesh because He is a unity and a unity is of something different, in this case it is a unity of the dominant principle, spirit and flesh. So, God Himself is spirit-flesh. This can present in any order. It is the ordering of spirit and flesh, not their distinctions, that create differences between Jesus and the Holy Ghost who are both composed of spirit and flesh. (The argument for each being composed of spirit and flesh as their dominant distinctions is made in other essays in this book.) Ordered indistinction defines the "difference" between the two bottom flesh persons of the Trinity. That is, spirit-flesh can reverse their order in the two, flesh personages of the godhead (Jesus and the Holy Spirit). Again, this gives us a singular triad composed top (Spirit:), and bottom (Flesh:). Additionally, spirit and flesh manifest themselves on the bottom twice in the two flesh personages and on the top once in God:

Spirit: God as flesh-spirit or spirit-flesh

| |

Flesh: Jesus as flesh—Holy Spirit as spirit

| |

spirit   flesh

ILLUSTRATION 2

Spirit and flesh is present throughout this triad, hence unity or identity, top and bottom and vertically, a unity and identity of common differences. The overall quality of this tripartite structure is a unified God, expressed in triadic difference. The quality of the general and collective term God is constructed though relations that make God's three-person unity possible.

To repeat, God as a singular person is an identity of spirit and flesh while Jesus and the Holy Ghost are also constructed from the same spirit and flesh difference, and they differ as spirit does to flesh. Therefore, the identity of the entire triadic structure, the unity of the Trinity, is constructed through the common use of difference (spirit and flesh) in each person of the Deity. This is the case whether spirit and flesh are expressed as identity above in God, or spirit and flesh are expressed as difference in the character of the two personages below. The personages of the Trinity are unified through their expression of common differences, providing us the overall quality: God or Deity, as a unity of these differences. The line dividing God the person from Jesus and the Holy Ghost is more correctly expressed as an identity, not a difference, demonstrating yet another spirit-flesh dimension of this unified quality or structure.

Additionally, Jesus and the Holy Spirit also introduce gender into this Trinity since Jesus, while in the female flesh, is male and the Holy Spirit, in the spirit, is a male impregnator. Please understand that nothing in what follows diminishes Jesus as a man. As illustrated in other essays in this book, all flesh is fundamentally female and this gendered flesh can also be either male or female, as gendered humans display. Jesus is a man in the female flesh and contrasts to the Holy Spirit. Jesus is, in this relationship, female, especially since the Holy Spirit impregnates spiritually, a very male attribute of this person in the Trinity. Jesus is much like the believer in relation to God, He is His follower, and God is her lead: it is God who has lordship over Him. He (she) submits to His will. Submission in this system, as elaborated in other essays, is a female behavior. Jesus in the flesh, as a man, is female in Trinitarian relations and from a Trinitarian point of view. He is, after all, a person in the flesh.

So, to repeat, this female flesh is both male and female, because people in the female flesh are male and female. Jesus is a male in the female flesh. And this gendering makes it possible for him to emphasize the flesh or female in the Godhead in contrast to the Holy Spirit who as spirit emphasizes male and this point will link to triads, to the Trinity and how its structure works, as the reader will see below.

Now this emphasis on gender in the persons of the Trinity may be a little forced, especially considering a distinction I draw later in this book. Namely, where the Christian religion is a religion in the spirit,

48

Judaism is a religion in the flesh. It follows from this distinction that Judaism emphasizes gender and male/female distinctions far more than Christianity, which emphasizes spirit (in the flesh). But the reason I want to make the point about Jesus representing a female aspect of flesh in the Trinity is to show that spirit and flesh articulate with male and female distinctions used in Judaism and especially in kinship. This becomes important later on. In any case, spirit is male, flesh female and gendered flesh is sub-constructed as male and female. Once Jesus is viewed as male by gender in female flesh, the flesh being paramount, the Trinity's structure may articulate with the structures of kinship. This is the relationship I want to anticipate: the showing of or the profundity of kinship or gendered structures in the Christian divine.

So, male and female through Jesus and the Holy Spirit, make an appearance at the bottom portion of the spirit flesh contrast. That is, we can decline:

$$\frac{\underline{spirit}}{flesh}$$

as:

$$\frac{\underline{spirit}}{female/male}$$

or as:

$$male \mid female\text{-}male$$

or to repeat the argument above diagrammatically using indistinction rather than distinction to characterize the gender expression of the Trinity:

$$male\ God \mid female\ (as\ Jesus) - male\ (or\ Holy\ Spirit)$$

or as:

$$male - female \mid female - male -\!\!- male - female$$

49

or to repeat the argument above somewhat distinctively:

<u>spirit (or God or male)</u>
female (or Jesus) - male (or Holy Spirit)

And to repeat, just to make the gender based Trinitarian Godhead look more like the ones developed later on for the male/female based Kabbala (Jewish) deity, imagine the God personage as male-female (in the image of God He created them - Adam and Eve -, male and female He created them, but God is a unity). And imagine Jesus and the Holy Ghost constructed differently as male/female and female/ male. We then get a declination of the Godhead or Trinity' structure as:

<u>male-female</u>
female/male // male/female

The bottom portion being gendered Flesh, and Jesus and the Holy Ghost each being constructed from male and female, as opposed to spirit and flesh. It is also true that the distinctions on the bottom might best be described as identities like male-female (not male/female), with the reversal in order of gender in the two fleshly personages in the Trinity being more important in establishing their gender. In any case, we are seeing variations of identity and difference, using gender, which describe the unity and differing personages of the Christian Deity.

Thus far, we have argued that identity and difference is the key to knowing, that spirit and flesh express this identity and difference principle and that spirit and flesh likewise structure the Trinity. In addition, flesh can be gendered, and we discover that the Trinity itself can be represented using a male female structure. Where do we go next? Remarkably, having seen gender in the Trinitarian Godhead, we now can take note that the identical structure occurs in marriage and family life.

In the marriage act, God as Spirit joins the couple together, and its structure, to jump ahead, is easily characterized:

<u>God: spirit (which can be characterized as male-female)</u>
the couple: human flesh male-female

This act is in the spirit domain as it involves God (and later a minister who is slotted in the role of God) so it is religious. (The couple when

50

expressed in kinship is in the flesh and so, a distinction at this level between the couple as male/female may rule.) Marriage is a link between the religious domain and the kinship domain, their division following a spirit and flesh distinction. Their division structures the wider love or spiritual or meaning domains of religion and kinship in our society, which is distinct from fleshly work. In any case, marriage as a religious act is singular or unifying, the couple being joined in the spirit.

The entire structure is one in the spirit and it transforms the separateness – pre-marriage – of the spouses. In other words, the couple is uniting in God by having an identical structure to Him: male-female. So, we see unity in the structure: God is male-female as is the couple, much like the Trinity. The couple is transformed from being a separate male person and a separate female person to united bride and groom. This structure is expressed in the spiritual marriage ceremony, where the Minister of God joins the male female couple together. The couple goes from separate male female (male/female) to whole (male-female) and then as a fleshly couple they have children, which is readily expressed structurally as:

the couple (male-female)
the children (male/female)

This structuring of the married couple in the spirit not only repeats the Godhead's gendered structure but also shows that structure – spirit/flesh -- is dynamic, that it declines to create relationships like God and husband and wife. And, of course, the family with children has the structure:

male-female (parents)
male (child) / female (child)

If one imagines God over this last structure, then we have His spirit over the family in the flesh, the family being divided by the spiritually united husband and wife and the children in the flesh. This is of course is spirit over spirit and flesh. This is a replication of the deity's structure, whether the Trinity as discussed above or the Jewish deity as discussed below in the Godhead essay in this book.

So, in addition to the spirit and flesh divvying up of the Trinity and the family, we also have a replication of gender relations between the two entities. The spiritually married and gendered and united couple has distinct male and female children. The Trinity has a male-female God on top and distinctly male and female entities, relatively speaking, on the bottom. The male and female distinction declining to form the Trinity expresses the family's structure as well. Top to bottom, the deep structure of the family and the Trinity, in at least one of its declensions, in this case as expressed as gender, similar. This demonstrates the definition of religion given earlier: kinship which structures a variety of kin personages contains the structures that are set against one another to form the Trinity. And these structures are present endlessly, in the family and in the religious lives of people within this system. The point to underline here is that these observations are deeply Durkheimian. The deep structure of society - family structure in American Kinship (per David Schneider) - is re-presented in the religious constructions of our society, particularly in the concepts of God. This will also be true, as a future essay describes, in the Jewish notions of God, and hence (I suggest) a common kinship structure for Christians and Jews, with traditionally minded Jews perhaps emphasizing descent or children and traditional Christians emphasizing the above, the married couple in family life. But the bigger thought here is also deeply Levi-Straussian. The deep structures of a social system endlessly, in his view, are represented in a society's myth and symbol. The result may well be social solidarity and stronger kinship and more solid family relationships. Perhaps the common presence of the same structures in the Godhead and in kinship make the Levi-Straussian point.

However, this book's key contribution relates to the overwhelming presence and importance of (spirit/flesh) structure, not just in God concepts and in kinships forms but also in the cultural literature of our society, namely our Bible. We go from identity to difference, to spirit and flesh to concepts of God and then to the religious constructs and practices in the Bible, where structure abounds. Structure is so abundant in the religious or spiritual system that Jews even eat properly separated or structured foods in *kashrut* or the kosher dietary regime, and this is discussed in an essay here entitled, Food for Thought.

Catholics do the same with the sacraments of the Mass through the bread and the wine, which express spirit and flesh. This is discussed here in the essay entitled "The Eucharist, the Passover and the Word". And even the story lines of many Biblical tales only make sense if it is structure and not anything else that drive the stories as a later essay entitled Triads in the Bible shows. Structure abounds, structure works logically and consistently and this is the bottom line for much of Western religious representations, including the Bible.

As a modern, secularly oriented (Jewish) person, this is how I manage to routinely read the text, which otherwise hardly makes sense and even appears barbaric in many of the things it says. Let's take a story that has little modern resonance to make the point, the story of Korach.

The story of Korach in Leviticus raises the question, "how did the hierarchy of Priests over Levites become fixed in the Jewish Scriptures?" According to Professor Emerita Berlin, this hierarchy was not present earlier in Torah, a name for Jewish scripture, despite the prior existence of Priests and Levites. While the tribe of Levi had been distinguished from the other tribes of Israel, they only had duties towards the ark and towards the sacrificial altar, but little was said about the authoritative relationship between Priest and Levite. With the Korach rebellion, this changed.

In its description of the rebellion, the Torah records two revolts, one against Moses by the two sons of Eliab and another from Korach and his followers, who were themselves distant relatives of Moses and who were from the tribe of Levi. Moses initially responds to Korach's revolt by saying, "Will you seek the priesthood too". The revolt is against a ranked view of Priest and Levite, which Moses embodied and which in the end, God and Torah sustain. God sustains the position of Moses and the subordinate position of Korach's Levites by killing the rebels. The ground opens and swallows Korach and his followers. More deaths follow the rebellion.

A contemporary reader easily might react in one of two ways. The first reaction is to view the story as dramatic, both visually and in terms of its deadly solution to the rebellion. The other reaction – God simply is a killer, there is no a peace offering or compromise, no truce, no explanation – just killing. God as killer is less than pleasant, and this perception should offend modern sensibilities, perhaps so much so, that this and similar stories fall outside our moral purview. With that question raised, it is important to see what occurs structurally in the story; perhaps something progressive is occurring in the text that also addresses the God as killer morality problem.

The revolt is a revolt in favor of egalitarianism. The question asked of Moses that brought on the rebellion is, "Why do you raise yourself above us?" Why did you assert your authority and force us to wander in the wilderness? The answer is a murderous assertion of structure: the earth opened under a gathering of the rebellious Korach, the sons of Elia and their immediate followers. They descended into the grave alive and the earth closed over them and they vanished. 250 more followers were later killed by fire. Horribly, the next day, God threatens to kill the whole Israelite community. But this is forestalled; God appears distracted from His threat, as He instead makes clear the role of the Priests and Levites. The Priests shall take charge of the altar and partake of all sacred offerings. All offerings shall belong to the Priests, including the best oils and first fruits though they will not have Land. "The sons of Levi shall have the tithe, the uplifted donation as their inheritance for the work they do in the Sanctuary".

So, we get God over Priests and Priests over Levites. We also get Moses over Priests and Levites. The murderous threat is overcome by the victory of structure. Whether it is Moses or Aaron on top, we get a triad which mirrors the Godhead triad, especially since the Priests and Levites, while concrete and in the flesh, are distinguished from one another by the elevation of the tasks they do. The Levites are below the Priests in the nature of the temple service they provide, and their Priestly/Levite up/down articulates with spirit/flesh, as elaborated in later essays. In the story, Aaron also finds himself structured as chief or an equivalent to God, an authority who is above the Levites. The Levites in turn are above the Israelites, who are below, another triad mirroring spirit/flesh:

Aaron the priest
Levite
Israelites

The two down elements are also divided by spirit/flesh, the Levite religious figures (spirit) are over the common Israelite people (flesh). In the Korach story, Moses and God and Aaron occupy the same place in the triad, the above. This makes a strong anti-egalitarian statement in support of Moses and Aaron while showing that the triadic structure is sentence like. Its grammar allows all sorts of subjects on top (God, Moses, Aaron and later, even a woman - Debra) in its senior position. Further, God commands structure rather than murder. In other words, as the text develops, murderous impulses abound but are put aside and there is moral progress coming of a defined Priesthood with Levite assistants: authority takes shape. The potential murder of all the Israelites thankfully gets put behind and a deadly God gets a better people (still alive), with Priests and Levites in triadic harmony with Him. The story is driven by its structure in the sense that the assertion of structure (authority) ended the revolt.

And perhaps parenthetically, the story shows a preliminary and not fully developed God opting for more moral conduct. His evolutionary character is boldly written into the Jewish Scripture when, at the outset of the book of Exodus, God says, "I am what I will be" (a better translation than "I am that I am" according to the footnote at the outset of the Book of Exodus in the Hertz" *Atz Chaim*). In the Korach story, His character at this point is developing against arbitrary killing and hopefully towards a full sanctification (either in this life or the next) of life. That is, He ends his murderous behavior with the death of Korach's followers and establishes proper religious authority. But this observation is parenthetical and is explored in the essay that follows on first and seconds.

In any case, we go from the basic requirements of knowledge, identity and difference, to spirit and flesh, to male and female and family, and then to the texts of our religious tradition. Many of the essays that follow in this book further explore the structure of our religious traditions, especially the essay on "Storied Triads in the Bible". But I would like to speculate a little here on whether the identity and difference theme described thus far also links up to the nature of the world. Perhaps this connection of the conditions of knowing to religious knowledge would be more profound if it were also connected somehow with nature. Is there anything in nature that aligns with how we know?

To make this connection, we need to find something in nature that suggests identity and difference triadically. This requires a natural opposition that can be unified through a quality, as noted earlier. So, what might this be?

Logically at least, it begins with the opposition of a line and a circle. They are, of course, binary in the sense that a circle is enclosed, and a line is not; it extends. And their relationship is well known, it is Pi, the mathematical constant. Now, for us to have a triad we need something in nature something that could be both a line and a circle which would encompass this Pi, and it is a point or dot. To realize this is so, imagine the smallest point possible. It would have radius of 0 and at that radius, it is both a line and a circle. This would represent a singularity consisting of a line and a circle implying one which contained Pi. It would be a triadic unity, a singular point that contained a difference or Pi, which is the value of a binary relationship between a line as radius and a circle.

This structure, a point containing or exhibiting the qualities of a line and a circle, recalls a seminal event in nature, namely the big bang that created the known universe, which began from an infinitesimally small point. A single infinitely small point can be described as a triadic unity of point, circle, and line. Moreover, a point is one and unified, Pi is two and separated, it is circumference divided by diameter. One and two; singularity and multiplicity, the hallmarks of the Pi constructed triad, with unity in the point and the difference in Pi. Amazingly, this initial point displays identity and difference, the requirement of knowing in our knowledge/cultural system. In the beginning, the conditions of knowing were built into existence and later, were built into articulate cognition in the form of our religious cultural, kinship and marriage systems, in almost Hegelian fashion.

This observation is perhaps beyond the scope of this collection of essays since it is not about discovering religious truth. It is about an objective, deep structural analysis of the cultural objects that construct our religious worlds in the system of common differences. This intellectual adventure comes of a desire to know something knowable about religion, which is a knowledge, not a faith undertaking. This knowledge adventure results from something Jewish in me, a struggle or wrestling with the tradition. While this is a traditionally Jewish struggle, the knowledge search is more important than the Jewish one. It is more important to note that struggling is the opposite of submitting and to note that Jews struggle (the meaning of Israel), while in Islam (which means submission) a believer submits. A struggling/submitting contrast displays a binary relationship between the two systems of thought and practice. [2] This is an insight into what religion is, and it is better to first study what religion is before making claims about truth. But it is stunning that in the beginning, identity and difference make possible the beginning of matter, and later also the construction of religious thought in the system of common differences.

Thus, the essays that follow are about the objective structures forming religious and social objects. It is an objective understanding of the deep structure of our social thought that is sought here, not some Hegelian speculation over how it all is true. My hope is that we can celebrate the binary differences composing the system of common differences, and that this book will lead to insight as well as toleration and respect for the cultural traditions that undergird our societies, Christian, Moslem and Jewish.

This collection of essays was written over 40 or so years and my thinking has developed over time. The essays fit together, however much they lack a complete intellectual uniformity, which I tried to write into them as I more recently prepared this book for publication. Triadic thinking came late in my development, but the earlier work is at least consistent with this thinking. So, remember, where there are differences between the earlier and later essays, there are at least thoughts in common, thoughts I'm happy to share and hope you enjoy!

Essay 6- Distinction and Structure in our Religious Culture: A Simple Description of How It Works

This essay provides a general understanding of how Western religious culture works. In that sense, it wants to explain Western religious tropes. The main source of explanation is not very complicated but it is not common sense so this essay also provides tools to facilitate its way of understanding or explaining.

The basic idea is that there exists a deep but very basic, unconscious structure that helps to form most Western religious ideas, customs, stories, and practices. I'll state what that form is, but a tool is needed to see it. That tool is something people learn about in fourth grade: students learn that sentences have a grammar, which consists of a subject a verb and an object. Subjects, verbs and objects can move around or occur in different forms and places, to give us all kinds of sentences. When a person utters a sentence, that sentence is organized by something from below; this is a grammatical structure.

Religious ideas also have something underneath that works like the grammar of a sentence. Here is its basic distinction: spirit/flesh and it lies below most religious ideas we have. Its omnipresence is easily seen – for example, religion is the home of spirit and kinship is the home of the flesh. So, spirit and flesh undergird native concepts like religion and kinship and this suggests rightly that spirit and flesh might further relate to the tropes within these domains. In addition, triadic structures based on spirit and flesh are also omnipresent in the system of common differences and these derive from the character of spirit and flesh themselves.

The first thing to know about spirit and flesh are relatively obvious. Spirit is whole, and spirit does not divide, but flesh divides. It divides in two.

Now, here is the important triadic structure based on the spirit and flesh distinction. Imagine spirit over flesh, the spirit is whole and one, but the flesh level below divides. It divides, of course, into flesh part 1 and flesh part 2. However, the only distinction available here so far is spirit and flesh so let spirit be one of these flesh distinctions and flesh be the second. Imagine a structure in which spirit is on top, and below it, flesh which divides into two: this gives us spirit over spirit/flesh. One spirit is on top and two fleshes are below. This is the structure I referred to and it forms a triad:

<u>spirit</u>
spirit/flesh

If it is not intuitively obvious that this structure acts as a grammar and undergirds religious and kinship tropes, here is a very simple example to help make it concrete: the act of getting married, which uses this triad. But it requires another distinction to make the example work. The bottom portion is flesh, and if we take the flesh as having a gender; this will make the marriage example easier to understand. Again, flesh has sex or gender. And gender is a traditional distinction, male/female. So, imagine someone getting married, the rabbi or priest is above in the spirit, and below are two separate people in the flesh, one is male and the other is female. This is a declension of spirit over flesh, and in marriage, it becomes spirit (God, the preacher, or the rabbi) over male and female, who are at first separated, then united. They become married, male-female. They move from difference to identity, from being separated in the flesh to being united in the spirit. The structure created the act of marriage and the structure declined to make of unmarried people a married couple, which is their new state. Marriage in the language of this essay is a new sentence produced by an underlying cultural grammar based on spirit and flesh which was declined. The cultural sentence is the married couple.

The point here is that underlying the act of getting married is an underlying structure: in this structure, spirit above expresses God or the preacher, flesh below expresses gender which divides into two, a male groom and a female bride. There is a triad here: spirit over spirit and flesh, or spirit over male and female. The male and female distinctions substitute for spirit and flesh in the lower part of the triad. The act of getting married has this structure underlying it, spirit/flesh, in the form of a declined triad,

<u>preacher</u>
bridegroom/bride

or:

<u>spirit</u>
male/female

or:

<u>spirit</u>
spirit/flesh

This is the structure before the service is complete of course and the separate male and female, the bride and groom, become one, so after marriage we get a structure that looks like this:

<u>spirit</u>
male-female

This example shows that the basic structure of spirit and flesh can be expressed in a triad where many different persons or identities may be slotted as the essay here "Storied Triads of the Bible" makes plain. This triad can decline into other triads based in part on gender, which can substitute for flesh. Here is a grammatical, cultural structure that allows for many different sentences.

Now, where does this lead? To most of our religious culture, I believe, and the example underlines the fact that triadic religious ideas reflect social structures. But let's go to the Garden of Eden to make a further point about marriage. God, of course, creates Adam and Eve and they marry but initially they are brother and sister. In this siblingship, it is obvious that a spirit over male/female triad structures the relationship. God is over a distinct male/female — a brother and sister. This is a triad. But I want to go to the creation of Adam and Eve to show spirit and flesh at work yet again. Here is what the Biblical text essentially says: in the image of God did He create them, male and female He created them. So below God, in the flesh, is a distinction of male and female and above, in spiritual God, are male and female, but they are combined. The spirit is a unity, the flesh divides; God is one and in Him so are the two genders which are alike male-female, but below in the flesh they are different and they give us a brother and a sister.

The spirit/flesh distinction governs the story here (and it is a proxy for identity and difference): the marriage of Adam and Eve depends on the structure, the gendered structure of a singular God. God is in the slot of the Rabbi or priest who marries people. That is, His relationship to His two gendered humans is constructed or expressed by an underlying form, He is the Spirit, they are the flesh, He is the one, and they are the two before marriage. He is the male and female together; they are male and female apart. In marriage the couple unite, male-female as one like God male-female. This displays a unity of spirit and flesh, expressed as male-female at the top of the marriage structure and at the bottom. And it is a declension of one binary structure, male over female. The marriage structure becomes one in God since the married couple has the same structure as God though they are in the flesh. Here the flesh is united. The three of them form a unified triad, as unified as the male over female distinction which the story sits on, like a sentence sits on its grammar. It makes the unifying marriage of Adam and Eve possible. The triad is based on a distinction spirit/flesh declined to male/female.

Now, religion in many of its manifestations works by expressing these same structures repeatedly. It is polyphonic perverse, to sound like Levi-Strauss, to a very good purpose. By giving us this distinction and this structure repeatedly, it allows us to have meaningful relationships in the spirit and in the flesh. The repetition gives us a living and mindful structure. Here are some basic triads that we live with.

First, there is Torah or Jewish Scripture, which is clearly in the spirit, and one can even see a triad in its physical form. The Torah itself has two poles, but it forms one Torah scroll. Below it are the Rabbi and the congregation: Torah in the Spirit, the Rabbi a singular and spiritual man in the flesh, who leads his congregation, a flock of the people Israel, a people in the flesh. The triad is apparent here: Torah in the spirit, over both the Rabbi and congregation in the flesh; these two divide into spirit and flesh. Of course, the structuring of the Rabbi has changed here; in the marriage ceremony, he is slotted in the structural position of God, and before his congregation, he is just a Rabbi. Structure or the people taking places within structure move about, they are slotted into spirit and flesh positions, as this example shows. (And while the Rabbi is in the spirit as a man in the flesh, the congregation is spiritually present in the flesh, showing an even further elaboration of structure in these relations)

Here is another triadic example: God with or over the Land of Israel and the People of Israel. And another: Abraham over both Isaac and Ishmael. Now, one could ask, where Sarah is in all this. Interestingly, she is right there, in the same structure we see in the relationship with God and Adam and Eve. God, made of two like genders, is the model for Abraham, who forms a unity with his wife who was also in some sense his sister. So in the sibling relationship between Abraham and Sarah, we have male female apart in one triad with God and we have a second triad, based on their marriage where this couple, in the flesh looks like the gendered-together God united above the couple. Moreover, the triadic relationship of Abraham to Isaac and Ishmael is like that of God to the siblings Adam and Eve. This is not the place to elaborate about Isaac and Ishmael, but the text genders and slots one of these men as female, as that is his place in the triad.

These kinship relations are crafted from the triadic structure deriving from the spirit and flesh distinction. Again, it is easily seen - imagine the relationship of a husband and wife to their children. The couple is married in the spirit, and they have children, descendants in the flesh. The male-female combined couple sits above the distinct male and female siblings. It is the same structure we have for God in the Garden of Eden, over his two sibling offspring, Adam and Eve before they are married (hence God is a Father). In a general sense, the married couple expresses or gives form to spirit; the children express or give form to their flesh. They are the flesh and blood of the parents! The singular married couple is the two that became one, the unity that sits overs the distinctive male and female children that they produce.

Since our family structure is the key to our social system, the importance of the structure is evident: spirit/flesh is what links us to one another. It is how we have mothers and fathers, sisters and brothers, a God of Israel and a people and land of Israel, as religious and kinship concepts. Spirit and flesh link together in the same way as we do, through it, so our Biblical text and our tradition keep the concept alive by repetition. It occurs subtly everywhere throughout the Biblical text and is present even at our household tables.

Turn to Sabbath dinner, for example, and on that Sabbath table sits the candelabra alongside special Sabbath bread and wine. The candelabra stand above the bread and the wine. While it may have two or many lit candles, it forms one light. This is spirit. The bread and the wine are concrete, wine being a spirit or liquor and the bread being flesh. Importantly, the Hebrew word for bread implies flesh, as it does in other languages. In any case, here is a shining example of a triad, sitting at the beginning of the Jewish Sabbath. And, the candlelight is white, and the two flesh items, bread and wine, are both red. Significantly, brown does not appear in Torah, and brown crusted bread, like the wine, would be categorized as red instead. Red is the color of flesh, and white light is the color of spirit, as God's presence in the crossing of the Red Sea proves. He led the people as a white cloud by day and as red fire by night. He was red-white, the color of spirit-flesh. These are the colors of God and the colors of the opposition of spirit and flesh and they appear on the Sabbath table (as parenthetically they appear on the red and white table clothes found in so many restaurants).

Here are more examples of how spirit and flesh come to us, sometimes triadically, sometimes not, just to demonstrate how this system works, focusing on color. As noted, spirit has the color white and flesh the color red. If the theory here is correct, we would expect that twins or paired brothers in the Torah would be distinguished by color, whether they are signified through a triad or if they are distinguished only by spirit and flesh. So, let's find some examples.

The first is Jacob and Esau. Esau was a hairy man with a ruddy complexion. Jacob was smoothed skin. To readers of yore, it is obvious that the Biblical text views Jacob as white and Esau red. Torah makes this clear: Esau was the father of the Edomites and of course, the Hebrew word "*edom*" is a word for red in Torah.

So, that example was obvious, at least to very traditional Bible readers. How about the rest, beginning with Cane and Abel and going to Moses and Aaron, perhaps? Perhaps it is a stretch but the blood of Abel cries from the ground. Now the word blood and ground share a common root for red in *"edom"*. So, the relationship between Cain and Abel is distinguished by the color red. How was Cain white? Some rabbis say he became a leper which is as white as a person can get. God of course was angry at Cain and put a mark on him. When God did something similar to Miriam later in the Bible, she became leprotic. So, perhaps the rabbis were right: Cain became white. As for Moses and Aaron, the color that stands out is the color of Moses' tongue which was burned with red coal. But there is no apparent spirit and flesh distinction between Moses and Aaron (perhaps there is an indistinction). What I see is the exodus, led by a white cloud by day and a column of red fire by night. And I see the former slaves crossing a parted red sea, robed in white, baked cloth, a monument to separation making a people whole, a full and colorful expression of spirit and flesh. They go to the land of milk and honey, honey which likely is red in that part of the world, milk is white. And then there is the repeated use of the red or crimson ribbons put on twins, as when Tamar's twins are distinguished by a crimson thread. Ishmael, Isaac's brother had a red complexion. Brothers seem to be distinguished by red, ruddy or crimson. Or the emphasis in Song of Songs on the mouth of the beloved, those white teeth and red lips.

To reiterate the main point: we are endlessly presented with spirit/flesh in our tradition even if it comes to us colorfully and it often forms a triad that is key to our most important relationships, from God to Israel and from parent to child. Underlining the point, if spirit and flesh have a color, it should run wild in our culture. So, this essay will end with Santa Claus and the American flag.

Santa's red and white colors are spirit and flesh displayed promiscuously and pleasantly in our society's holiday season. For Christians, who are as much in a family and religious system dominated by spirit and flesh as Jews are, this playful man gladly and colorfully brings the most important distinction of our culture to children, with good cheer and happiness in tow.

And then there is the American flag, where the stars seem to be a Biblical reference to the promise given to Abraham, that his descendants would be as numerous as the stars. The blue background is commonly thought of as a reference to the Exodus where a people formed. The flag says that this newly formed American people will be as numerous as the stars, fecund and prosperous. Blue, by the way, is a (spiritualized) expression of red according to Jewish commentators who find this meaning somewhere in Genesis. So, the stars with the blue background are a unity, the light of the stars shines together in the spirit against a spiritualized blue background. And then there are the red and white stripes which in contrast to this unity are distinct. The very distinct alternating red and white stripes. Red and white, flesh and spirit, elevated, proud, and there to affirm that the society this nation leads has its traditional building blocks in place. The stars form one light (from many one) and the distinct stripes are the colors of spirit and flesh, giving us a triad of (singular) stars and (twofold) stripes at the very deepest symbol of American political authority. Here structure, as in the Korach story, gives us authority, triadically displayed in a symbol of authority, the American flag.

It is interesting to note that red and white commonly appear on national flags. Most Islamic flags have a star and what people commonly think of as the moon but given its position relative to the star, it suggests mars, red mars. So, we see red and white, the colors of spirit and flesh commonly in Islamic national flags as well.

The Jewish Dietary Laws also make clear the common presence of spirit flesh or red and white structure in this tradition and its role in authoritatively commanding a dietary regime. Remember that the key quality of spirit is that it is whole and that flesh divides. In the kosher food regime, the basic idea is to separate milk and meat to make eating whole and kosher. Regarding flesh, the key to making it kosher is to separate out its red blood to make it whole and to remove its white fat, again to make it whole or kosher. Kosher food is properly separated to be made whole; after the blood and fat are removed, there is only properly separated flesh, made kosher through separation. Something, one thing, separated is whole. Separating and wholeness are the basic characteristics of spirit and flesh. By eternally eating according to this structural logic, eating inundates the brain, which comes to think that spirit and flesh and therefore wholeness and separation are good to think as well as eat. Kashrut is food for thought, inundating us with the common distinction of Jewish life, and distinguishing away in various ways both blood and fat, red and white, to make eating whole.

So, this is how or religious culture or the system of common differences works. There is a basic distinction which allows us to relate to God, which forms our family lives, which is replicated in religious and kinship domains, and which is endlessly repeated, in Biblical stories and popular religious symbolism and in our flag and in how many of us eat. It is voiced endlessly and repeatedly in our prayers and stories. It allows us to meaningfully relate (the term for relating in this system is love) and connect, and it is unconscious, like a grammar and it is there for us, to let us love and worship and live together, in the purity of spirit and the flesh. The essays that follow expand on the themes discussed here, making spirited sense of the substance of both the Jewish and Christian expressions of our culture.

• • •

A note concerning binary trees that needs to be written down but which doesn't fit neatly into any of these essays.

Here is a binary tree and I want to make a few points regarding it:

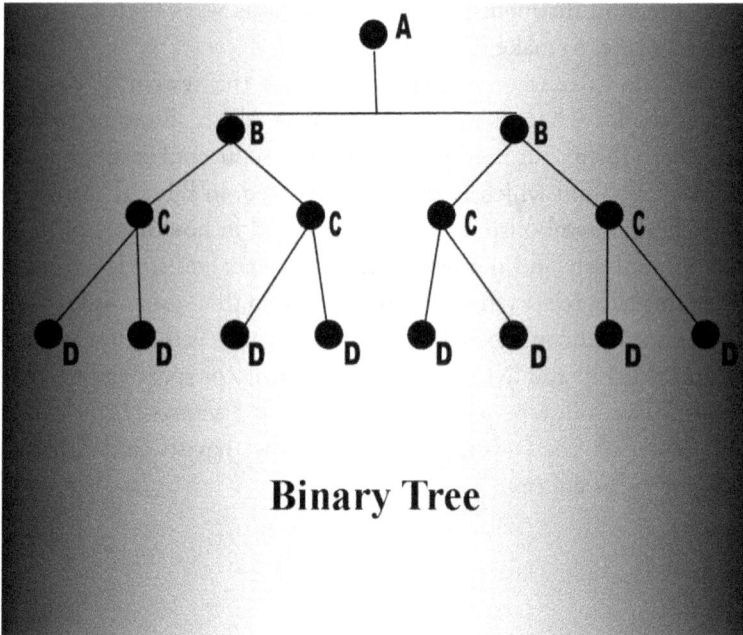

Binary Tree

ILLUSTRATION 3

The main point about the binary tree is that it appears to be a chart of differences only. But once you realize that it is a tree that has differences, it does comport to identity and difference. The tree is the identity or quality in which the differences occur. And it is about identity that I wish to make additional points. Namely, the total number of points on the initial line is one, on the second line the total, top and bottom, is three, and the total of points on lines one through 3 are 7. Each of these is a whole grouping of a tree, even the first. So, I want to note that 1, 3, and 7 can be viewed as whole numbers or a tree in a universe of binary differences. I want to emphasize this because 1, 3, and 7 are treated commonly in Biblical text as wholes or as unities. This gets pointed out throughout this book of essays.

Essay 7- Common Differences: Spirit and Flesh Aspects of Jewish, Christian and Islamic Traditions

There is a well–known joke that is told about a Jewish Robinson Crusoe who was left alone on a deserted island for more than 20 years. To keep himself busy, he built a house, a school, a hospital, a gymnasium and two synagogues. Finally, he was rescued, and with great pride, he showed his rescuer his buildings. The rescuer said, "I can understand the school, the house, the hospital and the gymnasium. But why did you build two synagogues?" "You see that synagogue over there", he replied: "That one I never go to".

This story is about something more than the sometimes-quarrelsome nature of synagogue formation. "I don't go there" says something about me and my identity. And, this is bigger than just saying that I am not a member of that synagogue or that church. It goes to the core of how identities such as Jew and Christian may have formed. They are formed from difference.

Yet, simple difference alone is not the whole issue here. Saying, "I am not a Jew/I am not a Christian" points to a wider identity that may be part of a system of related differences. In fact, in structural anthropology, the basic units that articulate distinctions are called binary oppositions and they are the essential building blocks of culture and cultural institutions.

These basic building blocks structure the character and relationship between Jewish and Christian religions. Understanding this constitutes an explanation of these religious tropes which is the aim of this essay and this book. The most basic building block that defines this

Jewish Christian relationship is spirit/flesh. Kinship likewise contrasts with religion as flesh does with spirit. This demonstrates that religion is a spiritual domain by contrast to the flesh domain of kinship and my focus here is religion. I will exhibit my method for discussing religion by first discussing kinship, which is also constructed from the spirit/flesh opposition. But first, take note that these two domains are distinguished from the outer world. That is, if the domains of kinship and religion are taken as the love or meaning domains of our social system, then these love domains are in the spirit. They divide, as religion and kinship do, by spirit and flesh and against the wider world by spirit and flesh. The wider, practical world, from this point of view, is not in the spirit, but is essentially in the flesh.

So, we have a common difference of spirit and flesh and it undergirds the distinctions of religion and kinship, and the distinction between love domains and the wider world. Other essays in this book also show that this opposition constructs distinguishing differences between Judaism and Christianity, as well as the difference in emphasis between Catholic and Protestant. In the Catholic and Protestant case, they are distinguished in their fundamental emphasis respectively on the Word of God (spirit) and the body of Christ (flesh). Spirit/flesh even dictates that there exist 3 major religions in a system dominated by spirit and flesh. So, a common difference, spirit and flesh, is key to constructing the major sociological blocks, kinship religion, and the different religions in the system under its sway.

The key thought here is that spirit and flesh provide an underlying structure that is used to build the domains of our culture. Since this way of conceptualizing may be unfamiliar to the reader, I will demonstrate my thinking by way of traditional American kinship followed by its application to Jewish and Christian relations. Hopefully, the kinship analysis will make the religious analysis easier to grasp.

Turning to kinship, the traditional, procreative family is defined for Americans by a husband and wife and their children. This statement is based on an older, normative idea of kinship as described by David Schneider in his "American Kinship". The cultural basis of his American kinship has not changed even if the empirical forms of family life in America have for many. For purposes of this essay, it is the traditional family and its structure that link to traditional religious ideas that are explored here. This traditional family has a husband and a wife who are married, and this married state arises out of an act of marriage. And as the reader knows, this marriage act occurs in the spirit; it binds the partners as one in the spirit even if they are two in the flesh. This flesh, however, can be characterized as gendered male and female. And of course, so is God, who in the Garden of Eden said that in the image of God He created them, male and female He created them. So, a married couple is like spiritual God, who as gendered is male and female united, and we can conceptualize the married couple as:

<u>God</u>
pre-marriage male/female

and with the marriage act:

<u>God as male-female</u>
the couple as male-female

So, with the marriage act, there is a clear identity of the couple with the spirit top or God portion of the structure. The united (not distinct) fleshly couple reveals gendered people together in the male and the female. Their union is just like the male-female in the God top portion of this triad. Further, the couple unites in the flesh through acts of intercourse in a state of marriage. So not only are the gendered flesh and spirit components of God and the couple identical in appearance as male-female, other structures like act/ state further enhance the character of the spouse's relations.

The point then is that marriage is constructed out of these oppositions: a union of two fleshly but gendered people in the spirit, so it can be characterized here as male-female. Again, the marriage act takes two different people and transforms them into an identity. As male-female, they are identical to spiritual God (male-female) even if they are in the flesh. Thus, the unity of gendered differences in this system is or matches the spirit of God. Elaborating on acts of intercourse, these are literally in the flesh. In the traditional view, these define the scope of the relationship of man and wife with a family because the product of intercourse, children, complete the family's scope. From a structural perspective, intercourse is an act defining a state of family relations, husband, wife, and male and female children, much as marriage defines or transforms a gender difference into an identity. Marriage is a spiritual union, created by spiritual acts and physical acts to give us a unified state of married relations between spouses - this leads to a state of relatedness between all the members of the family.

The consequence of intercourse between spouses includes children who express the shared flesh of the married partners. Their relationship to the parents does not depend on episodic acts of love but instead is founded upon a constant state of relationship in the flesh. This state of relationship to the parents and with one another shows that act/state combine with spirit/flesh to define the relationships composing the traditional family. The diffuse, enduring solidarity in family life has its scope defined by the biological facts of intercourse, which lead to the parent and child relationship (see David Schneider), all of which can be viewed as a state relationship in the flesh.

To repeat, the traditional family is a kinship unit. It is basically in the flesh. The spouses in the family come together as one in the spiritual bonds of marriage, have acts of the flesh that produce states of relationship to and between their offspring. Intercourse and its consequences define the scope of the family, showing that family life is ultimately of the flesh even if sanctified in the spirit. The family is composed of spirit and flesh, spirit by marriage, flesh by its descent into childbearing.

Furthermore, the family relative to the wider world is a spiritual refuge, an island of love, sharing and meaningfulness compared to the self-interested, selfish world outside it. This world could be described as sinful, which is to say it is in the unsanctified flesh. This is a traditional cultural scheme even if it not your view now. The oversimplifying point here is that a cultural unit such as the family may be defined in the flesh, but it also can be sub-constructed, so to speak, in the spirit. In other words, kinship as well as religion are in general in the spirit by way of their contrast to the outer world, which is in the unsanctified flesh. By way of marriage in the spirit, by its connections to God and His structure, this unit of flesh relations is entirely in the spirit. This is important to understanding Judaism, which is a religion whose concerns are defined by spirit, but these concerns are in the flesh, which it spiritually sanctifies.

Here is one of the main ideas: in western culture, kinship is in the flesh; religion is a domain of the spirit. Just as kinship is cross-sectioned by spirit and flesh as we have just shown, the religious domain is also. The religious domain can be conceived of as a spiritual religion (pure religions of salvation) and flesh religions (ones concerned with things like eating and procreating). The first would give us a religion emphasizing the unity of the Spirit, which we can take as Islam. And religions of the flesh ought to divide into two: one emphasizing flesh and the other spirit. As will be explained, this is Judaism versus Christianity. Please note that this is triadic, with one religion in the spirit, and two in the flesh.

Here is a mind experiment to explore whether this is true at a logical level. Examples follow later. First, imagine a purely spiritual religion. It would unify since this is spirit's first attribute. Next, it will stress ascendancy in the spirit, since spirit is up. Then it might emphasize words since words are immaterial like spirit. It might think of itself as spiritually encompassing, claiming as its own the prophets of kindred faiths and even placing its most Holy Temple above the most Holy Temple of a sister faith. Perhaps it would talk about individual salvation since groups of people are clearly in the flesh and individuals by themselves may be characterized as having souls. It could emphasize light and peace since peace is whole just as spirit is. It may want a spiritual encompassment of all people since the spirit is whole.

Now, this may describe Islam more than Christianity. Perhaps. But in such a simplified view, one can see a religion with radically spiritual concerns Looked at more closely, its branches may well reflect the triads we so frequently notice in the essays in this book. In any case, imagine a spiritual religion that profoundly emphasizes the flesh. What, logically speaking would its concerns be?

First, it might define a holy people since a people is in the flesh. Second, if it defines a people, it might think in collective terms rather than individual ones. Third, rather than think first of unity, it might think first of distinctiveness, of this people perhaps. Fourth, it would think principally in terms of eating and intercourse. These are acts in the flesh that a flesh religion would sanctify. And a flesh religion would be a religion of descendants, not a single ascendant since descendants go down in time in the flesh where an ascendant goes up in the spirit. Such a religion would think first with food rather than words, words being spiritual conveyers of meaning where food may convey meaning in the flesh.

All of this – the people, the collective, the eating and the descendants are sanctified in the spirit, in a religion of the flesh. Such a religion might ritualize or spiritualize the commonplace, like making blessings for waking, for returning from trips, for cooking and so forth. Ritualizing, which is concrete behavior and a physical act, is a spiritual act in the actual world. Ritualizing is tangible behavior; it is physical, even worldly and so is concrete. Ritual is of the flesh.

Now, the point of this is just to make clear that religion, a fundamentally spiritual concern in a system based on spirit/flesh, can emphasize the flesh. This does not diminish its spirituality; it is only a different kind of spiritual expression with a different, fleshly focus. But there is equivalence: a religion with ancestors like Abraham, Isaac and Jacob and their descendants can be as spiritual in its way as a religion with an ascendant like Jesus Christ. Only the focus is different.

This discussion may be too abstract -- we have only discussed possible spiritual and flesh expressions of religious sentiment. How are Christianity and Judaism related? Here, I am suggesting that Judaism is to the Flesh as Christianity is to Spirit.

And while they are opposed as spirit is to flesh, they both ultimately express flesh religion in the common, larger tradition in which they occur. To make this clear, it is necessary to explore a purely logical implication of the spirit/flesh opposition, remembering that the flesh domain is kinship and the spiritual domain is religion. Remember also that the spirit/flesh opposition can cross-sect a domain to structure it. This means that while kinship, a flesh domain can be structured by spirit and flesh (marriage and descent), religion, a spirit domain, can also be structured fundamentally by flesh and spirit to form a triad. Here is the triad: one Spirit Religion, and two flesh religions, one of these flesh religions being radically in the flesh and the other, being profoundly in the spirit.

Therefore, elaborating this logically, in the flesh versions of religion, one religious expression should be a flesh version, and another should be a spirit version. The flesh version should further divide into a flesh and spirit religion or subdomain. Adopting a macro point of view, this predicts three major religions in this system and they form a triad while within them there should be religious divisions of spirit and flesh emphasizing branches. That is, where spirit is one and unified, flesh is two and divided, hence logically two flesh expressions of religion: one sanctifying in the spirit and one sanctifying in the flesh.   The spirit version of religion could likewise be divided into a flesh version and a spirit version but these would be viewed as spirit-flesh differences, differences of unity in a common religion. Here is a chart of these logical possibilities which names the religions that correspond to what we should predictably expect:

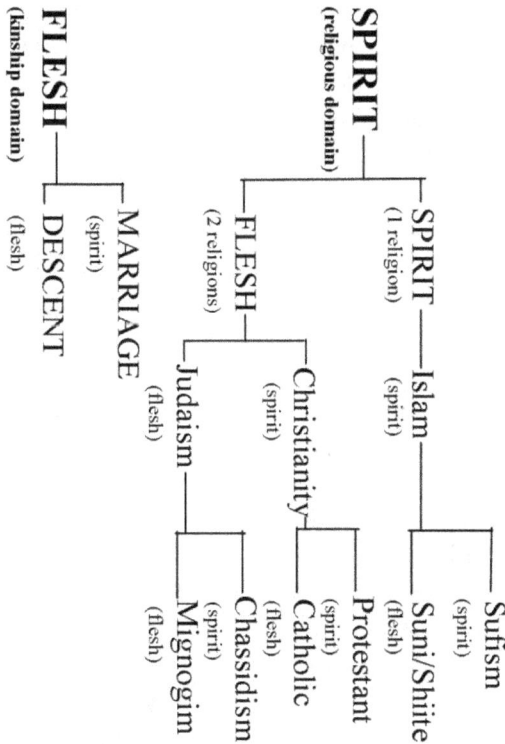

SPIRIT (religious domain)
- **SPIRIT** (1 religion) — Islam (spirit)
  - Suni/Shiite (flesh)
  - Sufism (spirit)
- **FLESH** (2 religions)
  - Christianity (flesh)
    - Protestant (spirit)
    - Catholic (flesh)
  - Judaism (spirit)
    - Chassidism (spirit)
    - Mignogim (flesh)

FLESH (kinship domain)
- DESCENT (spirit)
- MARRIAGE (flesh)

ILLUSTRATION 4

74

Why is Christianity viewed here as a flesh religion that emphasizes spirit? This is so principally because the body of Christ is the key to Christian salvation. His is a body whose blood saves. His flesh provides a likeness to the believer's own flesh, which makes possible their identification with Him which gives rise to the possibility of Christian salvation, the religion's main focus. Hence Christianity is in the flesh (as is Jesus's body). But its focus is His spiritual salvation.

This view is affirmed in the crucifixion. Remember that the crucifixion involves Jesus laying low his flesh to rise in the spirit; crucifixion is a passionate act which creates a state of spiritual salvation. It creates a family of God whose believers are in a spiritual state of relationship with each other and their Savior. One is a brother or sister in Christ if one believes. God is a father. These relationships come of a spiritual act in the flesh, namely crucifixion, that creates a spiritual family of God, containing a complete spirit/flesh contrast and recapitulation of the human, kinship family.

Therefore, this family of God has a construction similar to the one offered in these essays for familial kinship relationships but this family of God is in the spirit and the other family is in the flesh. But both have passionate acts that produce states of relationships, intercourse and crucifixion respectively. In other words, spirit/flesh along with act/state construct the meaningful qualities of the kinship and the religious terms involved, one in the spirit and one in the flesh.

Concerning the spirituality of Christ's salvation, it is individual, not collective, it is ascendant, and it overcomes the distinctiveness of the flesh to be as one with God. That is, it involves transformation, from flesh to spirit, a change in states, from separateness from God to unity. That is, from difference to similarity. All this is spiritual, of course, but it comes of crucifixion, from God's passionate sacrifice of His body. Hence, Christianity is a flesh religion in the spirit and if the spirit/flesh opposition holds its governing place, it would command the existence of another, or second religion. This religion would not be concerned so much with salvation but with sanctification (spiritualizing) things in the flesh. What might this look like?

First, as said previously, it might emphasize its distinctive identity by way of something in the flesh, like a people. It might say that it is a religion of descendants, from Abraham, Isaac and Jacob. It might emphasize concrete and lively things like eating, even drinking. If Christianity pursues everlasting life, addressing the problem of death by saving the individual soul, then Judaism might emphasize this life, incorporating death by way of the flesh of animals in a system which nourishes in this life. If this were so, it would make a life/death (which mirrors spirit/flesh) distinction critical to its food system, which it does in the kosher separation of milk (life) from meat (death). Milk by the way is white while most meat is red, the colors of spirit and flesh as another essay discusses. In any case, meat is divided by life and death, or spirit and flesh, by a distinction between blood and flesh. Blood is the spirit of the animal, according to Jewish Scripture; it is unlike flesh and cannot be eaten. In a system that separates, eating something full of life like blood is improper mixing. Flesh should go to flesh, as likeness to likeness as the essay on Transformation in this book shows. So only the flesh of meat and not its blood may be eaten by people in the flesh, but only once it is spiritually incorporated (double meaning intended) in a scheme supporting this life. In other words, the meat must be kosher.

This shows that likeness to likeness, not transformation of a difference is the key to Jewish thought. There is opposition or binary character in this. If Judaism represents a difference from Christianity, its basic intellectual movement would be different. The basic movement in Pentecostalism, the form of Christianity I am most familiar with, is from flesh to spirit – it transforms or moves from flesh to spirit. So oppositionally, Judaism separates, it does not move from spirit to flesh but instead separates things in the flesh to reach the shared goal expressed in Christian transformation, making things whole. Instead of flesh going to spirit, in Judaism, flesh goes to flesh. Judaism, therefore, divides rather than transforms but to a similar effect.

This is elaborated further in an essay entitled "Food for Thought" later in this book. But, Judaism divides to make whole; the distinction is the primary thing. This is apparent in the slit of kosher slaughter (which kashers or makes whole the meat), the separation of the fleshly foreskin in Jewish circumcision (which separates the baby' foreskin away to create a Jewish male, a form of wholeness), and even in the insistence that kosher animals have properly separated or split hooves (being kosher or edible is a form of wholeness). Here is a more important and central example: The Jewish people are separate, a people apart. It is formed literally by the parting of the Red Sea. (There is a death/life opposition here and the Israelite slaves were wearing white in a red sea – spirit and flesh colors -- but let's not go too far afield). By separating from others, the Jewish people form their unity, i.e., separation makes whole. Moreover, the Sabbath, the principal holy day of the Jewish religion, is a day separated from the week, giving a rest state as an alternative to daily activity. It is a separate day of rest which makes the week complete or whole as is the separated away Sabbath day.

Dividing to make whole is the very opposite of transforming to establish a whole state, i.e., a difference converted to an identity. The new state, its unity in the spirit not its difference in the flesh, is marked in Christianity while dividing provides the identity of the Jew. Broadly speaking, the relationship is oppositional, the terms formed of spirit/flesh and difference/identity are related and the spiritual outcomes which is sanctification, are almost the same.

But this might raise the question of how Judaism's spirituality sanctifies-- where is the spirit in Judaism? While it emphasizes eating and even encodes food to make statements about life and death as well as about the distinctiveness of Jewish eating, Judaism also has words. That is, to be a Jew, not only does one have to be born of a Jewish woman, one should also have Torah. The spirit/flesh opposition is present here: women in the Western tradition are more in the flesh than men, and the Torah involves spirit. The Jewish Scripture or Torah is God's revelation, and since it occurs in a concrete system, its spiritual words partly take the form of law, which is a concretization of spirit.

So just as a Christian is a person in the flesh who has given this flesh over to Spirit through the Body of Christ, a Jew is a person in the flesh, a descendant who practices the law of the Torah, which connects to life of this world and his or her people. There is opposition and similarity here.

From this, one can see that both religious identities are constructed by common differences in different ways to a similar effect.

They produce believers whose religious lives and identities are in the spirit and whose faiths support family life as well as ideas of salvation (which exist in Judaism even if minimized). What does this say about the historical relationship between the two religions? First, it suggests that a cultural process generated the basic structures of belief and institutional life in some systematic way. This is indicated in the previous chart which placed Judaism and Christianity in the flesh box of the religious domain.

This suggestion would be more powerful if it could generate additional insights into the spiritual domain and it does. First as discussed, the spiritual domain of religion should be bifurcated by spirit/flesh. The resulting flesh religions yield Christian-spirit and Jewish-flesh faiths which themselves may be bifurcated by spirit/flesh. This leads to an additional and seemingly predictable insight: I have suggested elsewhere in this book that this spirit/flesh bifurcation is the main difference between Protestantism and Catholicism (the Word of God/the Body of Christ). And here is another predictable insight. A spirit/flesh distinction seems to exist within Judaism, between traditional orthodoxy and its modern offshoots (the *mignogim*), and the Chassidism, who pick up on a fundamentally spiritual theme less literally connected to the Law.

In the purely spiritual version of religion in this system, moreover, the religion at the top of the chart which has been identified as Islam, something different should happen. One could imagine a purely singular, even mystical version of Islam and triadically at a flesh level, two other versions divided by spirit and flesh, but this division, consistent with the drive to unity should be contested. That is, if there is a spiritual expression of spirit religion, it should not split and believers should believe it does not split even if splits exist. It appears that Sufism does not split whereas Sunnis and Shiites split along a flesh and spirit dimension, though both Sunni and Shia claim theirs is the true Islam. In that sense, they are each saying their Islam is one. They contest their difference. Nonetheless, they split over the true nature of descent from the prophet Mohammed, one in the flesh and one not.

Second, since there is a cultural process behind the differences expressed in Judaism, Christianity, and Islam, there must be some historical connection and catalyst which established differences. Perhaps a group of spiritually minded Jews focused so strongly on the spirit that they paved the way for a shift in religious structure. This would still be a cultural process, albeit the result of group practices, the historical group setting the ground for Christianity possibly being the Essenes, and perhaps there was Jewish input into the Koran. However the emphasis in each religion occurred, it is clear that the possibilities for religious expression inherent in the spirit and flesh distinction were the basis for religious elaboration. Spirit and flesh give us a tripartite religious system, this common spirit and flesh distinction allowing each religion to systematically differ from one another. This serves the purpose of creating distinctive religious practices in binary comparison to one another, which brings us to the joke this essay began with. As part of a need to establish an identity in contrast with the Jews, both Christian and Islamic thought arose. Each creates a contrast using the spirit and flesh distinction to make its own identity. After all, differences establish identity, as anyone refusing to go that Synagogue could testify to.

It is unclear if our Jewish Robinson Caruso viewed the synagogue he did not go to as more in the flesh than the spiritual one he attended. But that distinction was available for him to think about the synagogues he could attend. And that distinction, spirit and flesh, is the difference that created all the major domains found in the broad religious-kinship system described here. This distinction likewise stands behind a division of this culturally created religio-kinship world and the secular world outside it. The kinship-religion domain contrasts as a spirit domain against the outside, sinful, and in the flesh universe. Kinship and religion likewise divide by spirit and flesh. Within kinship, we see spirit in marriage and flesh in descent. The same spirit and flesh distinction divides Christianity and Judaism, which are flesh religions. These religions are constructed first by a distinction between them of spirit and flesh and then within each, one finds spirit and flesh versions as well. The spirit and flesh distinction likewise forms a triad in the broader religious realm if it is declined as spirit as one, flesh as two, giving us the expectation of three major religions. And then Islam, although only discussed here briefly, shows us an internal division of Sufi and Sunni/Shia, which is a triadic version of spirit and flesh.

Common Differences Revisited/Common Differences

Flesh and spirit are the common difference constructing the various expressions of the entire system. They give us the system of common differences.

Essay 8- Food for Thought: A Cultural Account of the Jewish Dietary Laws

The great Jewish rationalist Maimonides expected Jews to seek the inner meaning and sense of the Jewish dietary laws even though to him these laws appeared beyond reason. For him, the kosher laws belonged to the category of *hukim*, religious laws whose reasons for being cannot be ascertained with any certainty. In contrast to Maimonides' opinion, various anthropologists have attempted to explain these difficult to understand customs and traditions, taking just such seemingly "irrational" practices and showing their inherent sociological and cognitive sense.

The anthropologist Mary Douglas and the scholar Jean Soler have attempted to find a cognitive basis for the kosher laws. Douglas believed that Jewish food prohibitions are a product of the way ancient Hebrews classified foods. Foodstuffs that did not fit into well-defined social categories were problematic, unknown and unclassifiable. Consequently, anomalous food, such as pork and camels, became abominations, loaded with pollution and dirt. Kosher laws banned such dangerous foodstuff as *traif,* or unclean. In Douglas's view, the kosher laws protect an ancient way of categorizing and classifying the world; the perceived uncleanliness of objects outside of that world affirms the perceived order and cleanliness within it.

Jean Soler's structuralist interpretation of Jewish food prohibitions is the kind of explanation that will be offered here. He writes that just as a language contains only a few of the sounds a human being can produce, so a community adopts a dietary regime by choosing among the many possible foods. No human community eats all possible food. Americans do not eat dogs, for example. Peoples choose their customary foods between a wide range of edibles. These choices have logic to them, and in the foods that are permitted and banned in the kosher dietary regime, we can see the characteristic logic of Hebraic culture.

For Soler, the dietary laws address a specific problem and offer a solution to it. The problem is that life belongs solely to God, yet man might consume and therefore take as his own the lives of animals by killing animals and eating meat. Meat-eating is tantamount to absorbing the life principle which risks making man God's equal. Kosher eating offers a solution to this problem by enforcing the opposition or separateness of God from man. It does this by permitting the eating of meat while excluding the eating of blood. God may eat blood, or consume life, but man may not. Blood is the life principle and without it, meat is distinct from God and appropriate for man who likewise is distinct from God. Soler says that this separation of God and man is extended to the separation of the Jewish people from others and this separation is expressed throughout Jewish cuisine in different ways. By saying that some foods are proscribed -- foods that other people eat -- foods that Jews find unclean, the dietary regime defines the difference between Jews and others, just as Hebraic thought establishes a separation between God and man.

Kosher laws, or *kashrut*, as a system of cleanliness also relate to the problem of killing or taking the blood of animals. Soler maintains that "Killing is the major prohibition of the Bible," so animals that kill are viewed as unclean and Jews may not eat them. The pattern of separation, the problem of killing and the restrictions of *kashrut* are linked together: most hoofed animals are herbivorous, not carnivorous. Because they do not kill, they are clean and edible. But since not all hoofed animals are herbivorous, other criteria arc introduced: namely the chewing of the cud. Cud chewers also do not kill. Together, these criteria restrict killer pigs as edible food: pigs have hoofs but do not chew the cud, and their exclusion is a hallmark of *kashrut,* (much as the refusing to eat dogs and cats is a hallmark of Western dietary custom).

This brief overview of Soler's ideas provides a departure point for a somewhat different structuralist analysis. First, to Soler's belief that killing is the major prohibition of the Jewish Bible, I agree: death is a major problem of the text. Death, of course, is introduced immediately outside the Garden of Eden and it presents a moral problem. Killing is outside the scope of perfection in Eden. That is, death does not exist in Eden and its wholeness. This wholeness is pre-historical: God did not create death in timeless Eden. Eden, without death, was created "good" and death is un-Edenic and bad. The oppositions structuring Eden and the history that follows is that of whole and separate. Eden is a whole place without distinction or separation. As noted in the earlier discussion of Leach in the Garden of Eden, Eden's rivers initially did not split, there is no nature and culture distinction between animals and humans, and gender distinction at first is unknown to Adam and Eve. It is a whole place and distinction gets introduced as Adam and Eve leave. This wholeness/distinction opposition is of course a precursor to spirit and flesh, which have as their primary qualities wholeness and separation. And this wholeness/distinction governs the direction of the story in Jewish Scripture. Just as we move from wholeness to distinction, from perfect immortality to life outside Eden with death and work, we can move from this separated, unwhole state back to wholeness again. The Biblical narrative, governed by whole and separate and then separate whole, will seek a historical (and a particular) perfection. Where Eden was ahistorical and for lack of a better word, unparticular or undifferentiated, the text, governed by binary structure, must seek something opposite. It seeks a particular perfection, as we shall see, dominated by separation that makes whole. The text then has a direction, given primarily by a distinction that latently has the quality of spirit and flesh. It will seek a particular, spiritual perfection in a historical world through the concepts of separation and wholeness that ultimately stand behind the Jewish dietary regime.

Now, the introduction of death outside of Eden presents a problem of restoration of perfection in historical time. The text makes this restoration the problem of the text by its movement toward Jerusalem and its killing sanctuary, The Great Temple of Jerusalem. Along the way, killing is dealt with progressively, initially from divinely initiated genocide to ever limited killing of people and to killers with ever-increasing moral character such as Moses. Its final Jewish textual expression is the full incorporation of death in perfecting Jewish rituals, in the expiating animal sacrifice in the great Temple of Jerusalem. For an historical perfection to once again exist outside of Eden, death must somehow be reincorporated into a new (if limited) perfection that supports life.

As stated, this problem, this killing that is outside the perfection of Eden, in my view, finds a first resolution in the Temple of Jerusalem. This great Temple, the destination of the Five Books of Moses or *Tanach*, is a place of killing. That is, it is a place of sacrifice where the blood of animals is consecrated to God to reincorporate killing into a Jewish religious system that supports life. Death gets its place in the sanctified relationship sacrifice builds between God and His people through their priests. This reincorporation likewise takes place in the kosher laws — dead food is made edible to support life. Just as death is incorporated in Temple sacrifice into the religious system, dead meat finds its way into the sanctified and life-giving eating of the Jewish people. So, in the killing acts in the Great Temple and in the movement from Eden to the Great Temple, a logic behind the dietary laws may be revealed since sacrifice incorporates death into religious life just as the kosher laws incorporate dead meat into life-giving, sanctified food.

A key distinction here is between life and death, which forms an opposition life/death and to a large extent it governs the Jewish Scriptures' themes and literary intentions. This theme connects Eden to Jerusalem and priestly slaughter to the kosher butcher's knife. To demonstrate this, let us envision the Temple sacrifices, its altars laden with the blood of animals. How do these altars express and resolve the problem of death introduced in Genesis? By making death not an act of sinful murder, man against man, but instead by prescribing death for animals, to sanctify a people and later to sanctify its food. (Death of a person — sin/sacrifice of animals -sanctification). Sacrifice overcomes the post-Eden murder at the beginning of history, it reverses the immorality of killing because unlike initial killing, it sanctifies and it can only happen in a better moral state like Israel. That is, the land of Israel is not the wilderness of Sinai; it is a land of a people with a law, a land of moral advancement. It is in this advanced place where further moral progress related to the issue of death in a religion that sanctifies life can be made.

So, the direction of the text is from Eden to Israel and to the Temple, all in the development of life sanctifying through killing or sacrifice.

But again take note: death does not belong in Eden, a land of ahistorical perfection. Death occurs outside of Eden, and it is a kind of foundational imperfection. Furthermore, outside Eden is not just a different place from Eden; it is a different time as well: Eden is timeless; outside Eden is historical. And it is in history that the problem of death can be reversed, from being the opposite of life to being incorporated in a sacrificial system that supports life. But immediately outside of Eden, death raises its ugly head in murder: an immoral act. Cain slays Abel.

The history that follows can be interpreted as an attempt by the text to recover a perfection in the historical world by reversing the consequences of murder. A "full" reversal of human murder might be prescribed animal killing for a moral purpose and sacrifice works here. Therefore, the text becomes preoccupied with the relationship of firsts and seconds to get to an appropriate place for animal sacrifice. Eden is a first, and for completion of the problems that come of leaving Eden, Israel is a second, but not fully until it has its capital and Temple.

Elaborating on the first and seconds theme in the text to get to sacrifice - first, Israel is doubly a second, following as it does both the Egyptian experience and the expulsion from the initial paradise. Of logical necessity, this second Eden must be a completion of a whole new world that encompasses the fact of death to restore a new perfection. This theme is expressed throughout Jewish Scripture.

In this theme, Israel and Eden are opposites, one being God's created perfection and the other being historical perfection, (though ultimately this overstates the perfection). Each is a Land. In Israel, the culminating place of wholeness is the Great Synagogue, just as the central place of Eden is the Garden. As similar places which are as different as time and space allow, their relationship within the Biblical text can be described as oppositional. But why is this point important to understanding Jewish dietary restrictions? The Biblical text develops the significance of this Eden/Israel distinction to produce the categories of thought behind the practices of *kashrut*. By going from Eden through Adam to Noah and Moses and back to Israel, the moral significance and character of the Jewish dietary regime are revealed. It is revealed through limited moral advancement in each of the important characters and their stories. Little moral advances presage the biggest one, which is dealt with at the end, which involves death into a system of life. We get to this point through small moral blessings in the text leading to Jerusalem and its Temple.

Beginning with Noah, the text treats him as a second Adam who is also heir to a new creation. Both Adam and Noah are ultimate ancestors to all peoples who come after them. Both are told by God not to eat certain foods; Adam is told not to eat of the Trees of Knowledge and Life; Noah is told not to eat the limbs of living animals. Where Adam is made by God, Noah is chosen by God. These similarities are accompanied by complementary differences. Adam is expelled from Eden; Noah begins the journey to the land of Canaan. The text makes this clear through the name of Noah's second son's child: Canaan.

A systematic binary opposition also exists here: Adam is denied a particular land; Noah is promised land, generally speaking (particular/general). Noah's inheritance is a moral step forward from the expulsion from Eden. His moral advance, however, is limited. This is expressed in the following description which again evokes his similarity or similarity/ difference to Adam.

After the flood, which was sent by God to destroy His wicked world, Noah emerges from his ark. He immediately gets drunk, and his sons find him in a stupor. They see his nakedness. Ham, the son of Noah, covers his father's nakedness. Where God covered Adam and Eve in Eden, the son of Noah undertakes this moral advance and there is a contrast here. Where Adam ate the fruit of the Tree of Knowledge and discovered his nakedness, Noah gets drunk by the fermented (or transformed or second) fruit of the vine and his sons discover his nakedness. First God acted to properly cover nakedness in Eden, now and secondly, humans do post-Eden. Neither situation is completely moral, since there was unwarranted nakedness and neither God nor a child should be the ones to correct and clothe another person let alone see unwarranted nakedness. So, even though there is moral advance, nakedness is modestly covered and clothed, that advance is limited; it is not complete nor is it the one the text is building towards. Here is a clue to where the text is going: the ark of the desert can be contrasted with the Great Sanctuary, the Temple of Jerusalem (which has an ark for the Five Books of Moses). This is the moral target of the text and we get additional moral steps in stories like this one along the way.

To clarify, let us look again at the end of Eden and the destruction of the world before Noah. When Adam and Eve leave Eden and enter the historical world, they are under the curses of God: a curse of the very ground they live on, a curse of pain in childbirth, a curse regarding the need to work and gain a livelihood by the sweat of one's brow. They are not blessed, they are cursed, but not completely so. Complimenting these curses was a commandment to be fruitful and multiply.

So, the situation is morally mixed; it includes blessings and curses. People are cursed and they are given a positive good to pursue, childbirth with marriage. This moral possibility allows humankind to move forward toward the moral world God wants. God himself is similarly mixed and not fully formed from a moral standpoint. (The text affirms this by His self-attestation: I am what I will be!) He has allowed Eden to end and then He later destroyed a world and kills his living creation. He knows this is not good and a truly good God, like truly good people, would not arbitrarily kill. They would (by contrast) procreate. Therefore, just as He begins to right His evil creation by destroying and undoing it through a flood, God tells Noah to bring forth all the flesh that they may swarm the Earth. God lifts His curse upon the ground, a curse made at the time of mankind's expulsion from Eden. And then God grants his great blessing to Noah and his sons: "Be fruitful and multiply and replenish the Earth." God then repeats his first commandment to Adam and Eve to procreate, but this time for a second world beginning anew with Noah. It is a world whose earth is no longer cursed by Him– God too has taken a step forward by giving us a moral ground as a blessing

The text then has moved us from God and cursing and destroying to Noah, in which there also are blessings and curses. But it is Noah, not God who curses, so it is a curse with a historical difference.

While God lifts His initial curse and provides His blessing after the flood, Noah is not as magnanimous. His reaction to his sons' dressing him is to curse his grandson Canaan. The curse is significant to

87

understanding the text. It is the man Noah and not God who curses the next generation, a proxy for the land of Canaan, at the outset of a new history. Therefore, humans have advanced in moral character: the moral culpability implied in a curse is issued by a mortal human instead of by God. While the new creation is still dominated by sins at its outset, human responsibility advances by human recognition of and culpability for sin.

This suggests that one purpose of the text is to work out curses like these from history and to fully restore the blessing of God to mankind. This is the blessing of life: to be fruitful and multiply, and this blessing is made against the backdrop of mortality and death which can be taken as the opposite of blessings. It is also made against the backdrop of land because while God lifts His curse on the ground, which He made early in Genesis, Noah curses Canaan with the snake-like curse of subordination. And Canaan becomes the name of a particular ground.

So, there is a system established here through binary oppositions: blessed/cursed, God/human, death/life, firsts/seconds. The text uses these oppositions to develop blessings in history. These can be established principally by people since the curse to be overcome is an historical as well as a human one. This represents moral progress because the responsibility for moral action, as we have seen, falls to man, not to God, whose actions, such as the destruction of the entire world, are beyond human moral comprehension in any case (and in need of moral progress as well, but that is another story).

Moral development, then, begins with an initially blessed world that is later cursed by God. The end of this development is also constructed from these semiological elements and through the completion of Israel, which they orchestrate. This is accomplished through Land and in terms of another opposition that applies to land-particular land such as the Garden of Eden and land in general. All this leads not just from Adam to Noah but also from Noah to Moses and then to an explanation of *kashrut* through the ultimate aim of this history: The Temple of Jerusalem, which is a particular place in a particular land called Israel.

Noah begins history anew by landing his ark in a dry place, which represents a movement from wet to dry though the landing is marked by drunkenness and a curse. The text must reverse or transform this, and the person of Moses does just that. Like Noah, Moses has his ark but his is on dry desert, not wet sea. Like Noah, Moses aims for land, but unlike Noah, his land has a particular name: Israel. The place where Noah landed had no name. Like Noah, Moses is chosen for a moral purpose, but where Noah sins, Moses commands through the word of God. Moses is the first leader of a newly formed Jewish people just as Noah is the first person in a recreated world.

With Moses, we witness a particular people going to Israel through the blessing of another covenant, that of Mount Sinai. Of course, for the continuation of the world, Noah had a covenant which was marked by a rainbow and that was received on the mountain where Noah's ark landed. Moses received the collective covenant of God and the Jewish people on a mountain. This covenant also involves the ark, but it further involves human rulership over their moral lives. God commands moral behavior which Jews must follow. The resumption of moral behavior is a correction of the evil stemming from the generations of Eve and the curse of Noah. Significantly, Moses arrives at Mount Sinai from Egypt and since the text has proceeded by contrasts in so many ways, one expects contrast here also. Now, Egypt is a land; its Hebrew meaning is "narrow place." The text contrasts this place with the destination of the Jews: a land flowing with milk and honey- so narrow Egypt contrasts with full Israel.

As a "full" place, Israel is a place of fulfillment for the Jews. It marks their freedom as a people and their reception of the moral law. Here they build their ark and sanctuary: The Temple that stands as a monument to freedom as contrasted with the pyramids, monuments to slavery built under Pharaoh. This temple is the high point of the movement to Canaan. Indeed, it is on Mount Sinai that the architecture of the Great Synagogue is announced, and it is on Mount Sinai that Israel is called the land of milk and honey.

The movement to Israel marks a great transformation of Jewish history in that it allows Jewish distinctiveness to change the slave mentality of the Jews, who must now wield a moral law. This move represents a classic transformation, a movement from one status to another. It is a new collective identity founded, as Soler notes, on the difference between Jews and others, as the memorialized recollection of the Exodus from Egypt demonstrates.

From its emergence from Sinai, Israel stands in full opposition to Eden, signifying that there are fundamental similarities in which basic differences are expressed and resolved. The differences are obvious: like Eden, Israel is Land, a promised land of milk and honey. It is not like Egypt which though a land is a narrow place. Israel is instead a place of wholeness and completion. It is where the Jews may practice the Law. Israel is where Jewish national life can continue unhindered, unlike in Egypt where they were subject to lawless oppression — so the issue of law and lawlessness exists in both places. Israel is where the Jews can have their priests and temples. Eden also is a whole place. In Eden, man, made in God's image, is the king of God's good creation. Eden is a place of harmony between all God's creatures; it is without death and fully in relation to God, who freely is present and freely in communication with Adam.

By contrast, Israel's wholeness is through moral law, which it wields to sanctify life. This lawful sanctification is so complete that it incorporates life's opposite: death. By using the death of animals in their sacrifices, the priests of Israel establish their relationship with God, once again paralleling Eden and its God-man harmony, by establishing a difference. That is, after Eden, Cain's murder of his human brother marked the separation of God and Man; in Israel, the priestly killing of animals renews the tie between them. Now, humans are not animals, so there is another contrast between Cain's murderous acts and the animal sacrifices by the priests. In both acts, death is deliberately caused, but where the first separates God and man, priestly slaughter reverses the moral distance between God and murderous man by creating a whole or worshipful relationship between the people of Israel and their Lord. So, the sacrifices "complete" a relationship with God on the model of man's initial relationship to God in Eden, but this sacrifice takes place in history. This completeness is undertaken by the moral action of men in a particular time and place. It is done by priests.

Elaborating further on this last point, Israel is a land of milk and honey, a land of life which, in its completeness, can accommodate the problem of death. The priests in the Holy of Holies, in the inner sanctum of the Temple of Jerusalem, make the bloody incorporation of death into Israel's celebration of life. That is, in the holiest place in the holiest city in the holiest land priests handle death by the sacrificial and life sanctifying spilling of blood. This reverses the murderous history coming out of Eden, where we begin history with murder. Now we have High Priests whose sacrifices (killings) are acts of moral, ritual purity. Now we have an opposition: immediate post- Eden which is at the beginning of history (which itself reversed Eden by giving us death after Edenic life) and the inner sanctum of the Temple, which reverses the initial murderous presence of death at the beginning of history. Again, this reversal is ultimately formed through the moral, ritual actions of priests, who are the principal wielders of divine law and the instruments who relate Israel to God. At its most holy, through its priests, Israel is most Eden-like. It returns historically, to the wholeness of pre-historic Eden. Its opposition to murder, its sanctification of life, makes the Temple most Eden-like. In other words, the incorporation of death into a system of life is accomplished by sacrificial acts, not murderous ones. Moreover, Priests separate blood from the bodies of animals by cutting and spattering it around the altar. It is the blood that has the life in it. Wholesome Life is affirmed. Blood covers the altars. And this wholeness is accomplished by an act of separation much as the Jewish people became whole by separating themselves from the Egyptian slave experience. Sacrificial separation transforms death from a curse of history into a key religious act by men, which restores a whole and spiritual relationship with God, much as the separation of Exodus transformed Jewish slaves into one free people.

Thus, the land of milk and honey is the place where death becomes part of a perfected scheme of things through the cutting of animals and the spilling of blood. With this, the text has accomplished two things. It has shown us how death can be incorporated into a scheme of life. And it has told us how to slaughter animals for moral purposes through a separation of a fleshly, animal body and blood through cutting. This is an act of separation and it occurs for purposes of life sanctification, making its sacrifice spiritually whole. This perfected killing of animals for sacrifice in the Torah was available for the Rabbis when they thought about the slaughter of animals for food. Like the

Priests, the Rabbis wanted to incorporate dead animals and death into a system that supported life. Of course, dead animals inherently present a problem if they are consumed for purposes of life enhancement. Eating dead meat is an intellectual inconsistency of the first order in a life-sanctifying religion and it required much thought. Again, these Rabbis had to know that the Temple and its animal slaughter brought death into a system that sanctified life. They wanted to further develop the tradition here. With a religious perfection at hand, with death properly brought into the Temple of Jerusalem, with this high point in Torah, Jewish Biblical thought shouted out a new way forward to think about food. In this regard, Rabbinic thought adds to Torah by way of its advances. And as they considered Judaism as a life sanctifying system, and realizing that eating is essential to life, they thought about meat like the Priests conceived animal sacrifice. It is worth restating: the perfection of the temple in terms of bringing animal death to help sanctify life was there to think about food, which is faced with the problem of dead meat that gets eaten. The Rabbis needed to sanctify this food and solve this problem and incorporate dead meat into dietary cleanness, which is at the heart of a life-sustaining rabbinic religion.

And the Rabbis had another Biblical tool to use as well, the distinction of milk and blood. In Exodus 23:19 the reader is told not to boil (mix) a kid in its mother's milk. In other words, the text calls for a separation of life (milk) and death (the killing of the kid). From a structural point of view, milk and honey are the opposites of blood, much as the life they represent is the opposite of death. This indicates that the drinking of milk sustains life and the spilling of blood ends it. While both milk and blood are essentially full of life, this similarity contains a difference in that the spilling of blood is also a killing act. In this sense, milk and blood despite or perhaps through their similarities, are opposites. So, along with the sacrifices in the Temple, we get a complete framework of thought. We get the separation of the sacrificial animal into flesh and blood, sanctifying life through this separation in death, and we then have from the text an opposition of milk and blood which become available to think about food.

Later in its history, the Jewish thought once again puts blood and milk together as an opposition - blood/ milk, to form a wholeness or purity of food in which blood is separated from milk. Here is how this post-Biblical rabbinic tradition thought about blood to create a dietary regime. First, blood is divided from milk, and then blood is separated from flesh, a double separation.

Now, initially, blood has contact with meat and we can readily see that meat can be dissected from the blood, blood which gave life to the dead animal and is the life-principal of the animal. Once separation occurs, this leaves bloodless meat, which by itself is unmixed, not containing life. The absence of the now drained blood, the blood which when spilled kills, leaves the meat removed from death. Separating the blood from the dead meat leaves properly separated-from-death or sanctified (kosher) flesh. It is food that can be eaten in the flesh by others – by people in the flesh. Separation makes it consumable and pure; it is no longer dead meat but properly separated flesh. It does not mix death and life.

In other words, *kashrut* has decided to "think" about meat in relation to blood. Jewish thought developed through the Temple, and importantly, it develops beyond. Using a proxy for spirit and flesh, it uses separating to make whole, not only in sacrifice but in a dietary regime as well. Since distinction or separation is the way Jewish thought transforms or makes whole, it follows that Jewish thought not only bans the mixing of flesh and blood in meat, it also wants to ensure that death in the flesh does not mix with life in the milk. And the meat, though drained of blood, is still in the domain of flesh and death, not life, wholeness, and spirit. But milk is life-giving, it is whole and it is squarely in the domain of life. Where the spilling of blood kills, the consumption of milk sustains life. Therefore, just as death should be separated from life, blood and milk should not mix. Furthermore, since blood once had contact with meat -- they once shared a commonality, then meat should not have contact with milk. Rabbinic thought differentiates meat and milk domains to insure separation of blood and milk.

The Jewish Scripture, then, proclaims a developing scheme of thought whose elements, such as milk and blood, death and life, dry and wet, cursed and blessed, particular and general, separated and whole, historical and transformed are available to understand what is established by the Temple of Jerusalem in the wake of the Exodus from Eden and

Egypt. These elements are used to develop other aspects of Jewish dietary laws. The key elements of *kashrut,* for example, are the notions that milk and meat must be separated and that animals that have cloven hoofs must chew the cud to be kosher. The separation of milk and meat is based on the principle of separating milk and blood.

Again, the key to this discussion is the theme of the completion of Israel, whose wholeness allows separation of death and life to be incorporated into the dietary regime of the Jews. Death and life are united by separating the life force of blood from the flesh so that dead food can nourish just as life-giving milk does. The system does this in a double act of separation: not only is milk separated from blood in the shape of an opposition between dairy foods and animal foods but within the category of animal foods, blood is separated from the carcass. In other words, blood and the death associated with its spilling are removed from the sustenance the food offers and so it becomes kosher-pure-and fit to eat. Here we have wholeness through separation doubled, and we see Jewish thought, as Levi-Strauss might say, "thinking" its food so that it can be eaten.

This wholeness/separation dichotomy (which the reader must see as a spirit/flesh proxy) explains the split hoofs requirement: a split hoof is a divided or separated hoof. This division helps make an animal whole or kosher. The theme of transformation, which is essential to the completion of Israel, also explains the requirement that a kosher animal chews the cud. Chewing the cud is an act of transformation. The cud is processed, so to speak. Its state is changed, and this is an act of transformation. This transformation of the cud is part of a binary principle: separation or distinction is not transformation or change. The opposition of separation/transformation follows the opposition of separate and whole. This general opposition is manifested in the naked use of separation and transformation in the importance of cleft hoofs and chewed cuds in the designating of kosher animals. Separation and transformation appear as a direct principle in defining meaning in eating just as they are the underlying principles of Jewish and Christian semiology.

The theme of wholeness also relates to the banning of the sciatic nerve, which must be removed from animals and never eaten.

Conventionally, this prohibition comes from the incident in which Jacob wrestled all night with an angel of God. Two results are recorded: Jacob limped, and his name was changed to Israel. In tribute to the recollection of this limp and this incident, the sciatic nerve is prohibited. That Jacob gained the name Israel, however, links the prohibition to Israel's wholeness. As the name Israel is claimed, the sciatic nerve is injured-wholeness on the one hand, injury on the other. So, the sciatic nerve is not whole and cannot be eaten. Wrestling, moreover, is an act, and if in Jewish thought we can find an opposite to acts that complete, then the prohibition can even more obviously be related to wholeness.

As in Christian thought, we discover the clear opposition: acts/states. Acts related significantly to the working week which is crowned by the Sabbath, a day of rest or inactivity. Sabbath peace is a state of rest. This day completes the week even while it is separated from it. It shows that as Sabbath completes the week, a state can complete acts through an act of separation. Separating the sciatic nerve is similar in form or homologous, therefore, and not only because it evokes the name Israel. It is homologous because a nerve responsible for movement or acts is separated to create wholeness or a state of purity. The sciatic prohibition, then, not only memorializes the text; it signifies the completeness of making kosher or transforming food to sanctify it.

Having given the structural foundation of the basic rules of the Jewish Dietary Laws and having shown how these structures arise from the Torah, the next step is to account for all the detailed prescriptions and proscriptions of kashrut. This returns us to the Biblical text. And first, we must remember yet again that Judaism through *kashrut* sanctifies by separation. Sanctification, of course, is a change of state, a result of the moral action of men. The kosher laws are human laws formulated by people; their moral character, then, continues the theme of moral transformation through law, as Jewish Scripture preaches. Second, kosher laws ban certain foods as impure and correspondingly create a category of pure food. This is sanctification (transforming) by way of separating. And third, the Torah enjoins *kashrut* in but a few passages, a key one being, "You shall not boil a kid in its mother's milk." (Exodus 23:19, 34:26 and Deuteronomy 14:21) Here, we have both the idea of separating milk and meat and the notion that life-giving substances like milk should be kept separate from the slaughter of animals. A life and death separation defines the meaning of the Biblical significance of boiling, in mother's milk. Life-giving milk and dead infant, extreme differences must not mix.

Another key passage on food prohibitions is: "It shall be an everlasting statute throughout your generations in all your dwelling-places: all fat and all blood shall ye not eat" (Leviticus 3:17). The word for fat in Hebrew is *heleb,* while the word for milk is *haleb.* The similarity of the words for fat and milk relates them meaningfully to one another through a difference. That is, the text is making, or ruling, a distinction or opposition between these two substances. Blood is banned as is fat; both are opposite of milk. Rabbinic thought elaborates this; not all fats are forbidden, just those that form in blocks in the body of animals. This indicates that fats that can be readily separated from flesh are banned just as the blood that can be drained is banned. Fat is an equivalent of blood and an opposite of milk. It is separated away, and this separation is not only the basis of purity and impurity in animal foods having fat; separation is also the structural basis or meaning-giver of the practice. In this regard, the Torah gives more details that must be examined and explained: the Torah states that blood carries the *nefesh* or life-spirit, of the animal and as the carrier of animal life, it is in a mixed state when that life is dead. This mixing violates the system's separation of life and death, of spirit and flesh. Thus, the key point here is that the *nefesh* of the blood once was alive but when it is dead, its state is mixed in its dead form. Differences cannot mix, blood being different from body as spirit is to flesh, mixing is banned. It is banned for eating "Only remain firm not to eat the blood, for the blood, it is the soul, and thou shalt not eat the soul with the flesh. Thou shalt not eat it." (Deuteronomy 3:23-25)

Jewish scripture defines *kashrut* principally in Leviticus 11:1 with a rule requiring that edible animals have parted hooves and that they chew their cud. Leviticus 12 specifically eliminates pigs and camels from a kosher diet. The text then indicates that God permits the eating of "whatsoever hath fins and scales in the waters, them may ye eat." However aquatic animals lacking either fins or scales may not be eaten and are a detestable food for the Biblically minded Jew.

The elementary form of religious significance, to use Durkheim's language, that gives rise to this proscription is the opposition of separation/wholeness which was introduced in the Garden of Eden and is now available for cognition in *kashrut*. Animals with fins and scales are whole in this view, by definition; those that have not are incomplete, and are separated away and defined as abominations. Fish, moreover, do not pose the problem of blood. The Hebrew word for blood is *dam* and only terrestrial animals have it; fish have *tzir,* what we might call the blood of fish. Yet it is not *dam.* So, we see how important classification is to the rules of kashrut, which are not troubled by the "blood" of fish.

Leviticus takes on the whole domain of living things, defining as it does animals on land, in the sea, and in the air. Again, the theme is completion and the text echoes the order of Genesis and the beginnings of created things to establish the wholeness of the food it allows. This reaffirmation of the order and the domains of originally created things is reminiscent of original perfection in prehistory and helps establish kashrut as a second-order event which also creates wholeness. Additionally, the text develops its death theme. When it comes to fowls, an interesting if obscure array of animals is viewed as detestable: The great vulture, the bearded vulture, the osprey, the kit, the falcon, the raven, the ostrich, the night hawk, the sea mew, the hawk, the little owl, the cormorant, the great owl and the homed owl, the pelican, the carrion vulture, the stork, the heron and the bat.

Once more, what elementary forms of religious significance give rise to these proscriptions? In his commentary on the unclean birds (from the text's viewpoint), Yosef Hertz, the editor of the traditional *Chumish* or Jewish Scripture studied in most American synagogues, writes that all the birds listed are birds of prey that live in dark ruins or marshland. Thus, these birds are associated with death and darkness. They are like spilled blood: living humans cannot mix with death. The principle of separation prevails, and these animals, classified as they are, are banned as food. Moreover, many of these animals mix domains: the cormorant, for example, hurls itself from the sky to snatch fish from the water. Mixing is forbidden. The ostrich, a wild animal, is noted for living and wailing in human ruins. Not only does this mix domains, but the wailing also mixes human and animal behavior. Thus, this mixing is separated away or banned. The great owl in Hebrew signifies a dweller in twilight, a mixed time, and so, like the ostrich, is banned as food. The stork, though an animal, is associated with human fertility and kindness to its young. It lives primarily in marshes and along riverbanks, areas that mix land and water. Perhaps this mixing bans it as a food. Or perhaps, since it is an animal linked to human behavior and life, it mixes animal and human domains and so cannot be food.

The text also states that all winged, swarming things that go upon all fours are detestable. But detestable, winged swarming things that have four legs which are jointed and whose gait involves their use in leaping about the earth, these creatures may be eaten. Unjointed creatures of this type are inedible and even untouchable, bringing the peril of pollution through any contact. Again, how does one interpret this in light of the elementary units of religious signification isolated here? Of course, these elementary religious significations are the oppositions we have found structuring religious texts and practices within the system of common differences and perhaps they will tell us something about swarming things. Now, swarming things of this kind are destructive of crops; they cause famine. Swarming things of this kind are the opposite, in a sense, of human fertility; they cause people to die because they blight the food supply. Since being fruitful and multiplying is the first blessing and commandment of the Bible, swarming things that threaten human survival are opposed to the central theme -life or reproduction- of the Torah. This invites the binary separation along the theme of life and death, and swarming things are banned.

What about the exception? My guess is that swarming things that leap on all fours and have jointed legs are the kinds of swarming things that plagued Egypt during the Exodus. They played a part in the birth of the Jewish people, so the text bows to them and permits their inclusion as food, detestable though they might be. Perhaps there also is opposition here to the snake that seduced Adam and Eve into sin in the Garden of Eden. This snake, of course, went from living in a tree to slithering on the ground. The jointed grasshopper or swarming thing, by contrast, leaps constantly from the ground into the air. He is not frozen into the air as the snake is stuck on the ground. He has acts of leaping while the snake has a state of being grounded. They are act/state opposites. The snake moreover provoked the basic immoral condition of humankind; outside of Eden, the jointed swarming things presaged the passage of Jews back to Israel and its moral law. And the grounded snake is not edible while swarming grasshoppers are. Winged swarming things that leap and are jointed at the leg are allowed as a foodstuff through association with Exodus and fit semiologically by their textual and act-anatomical contrast to grounded-state snakes.

Following the discussion of winged swarming creatures, the text states that whoever touches the carcass of unkosher animals shall wash his clothes and be unclean until evening. Of course, since mixing of unlike things is prohibited, touching non-kosher carcasses likewise is impure. If not-mixing separates, touching joins. Therefore, touching the carcass of impure animals pollutes. Once polluted, one not only is unclean, one must wash. But why is a person dirty for only a limited period of time? Just as contact is fleeting, apparently so is the pollution. From a cultural or performative standpoint, a period of time by definition separates the polluted from the pollutions.

The text reiterates its injunction against animals that neither part the hoof nor chew the cud, this time naming animals that go about on paws. Of course, animals with paws are predators that are associated with death. Contact with the carcasses of these animals also pollutes and requires the washing of clothes. Again, improper mixture or contact generates impurity and requires separation.

Interestingly, unclean animals do not defile through contact while alive. For this to fit into the semiological scheme we have developed for *kashrut*, the code must define an animal first as dead or alive, then as either edible or inedible. In other words, an animal, if considered as living, cannot bring with it the pollution associated with death, especially with the death-loaded carcasses of nonkosher animals. The rule not to eat the limb of a living animal makes this definition certain. Living animals are not edible, only dead ones are. Living and dead are kept completely separate. Only contact with impure dead animals pollutes. Radically separated, live animals cannot be associated with the stigma of impurity.

Having discussed how the contact with the carcass of banned animals pollutes, the text returns to swarming animals, listing those that are not kosher: the weasel, the mouse, the great lizard after its kind, the gecko, the land-crocodile, the lizard, the sand lizard and the chameleon. Why these animals specifically? The weasel is a predator: both the weasel and the mouse are mammals that neither chew the cud nor have split hoofs. The mouse may be associated with an infestation of human habitations, a state of impurity, and a mixture of wild-creature and human habitat. The great lizard, gecko, land-crocodile, lizard, sand lizard and the chameleon are all land animals that have scales, but no fins, and while they have the characteristics of sea dwellers, they are land creatures. Hence, they improperly mix and have the indices of incompleteness. Given significance within a kosher semiology, they are defined as impure food. Leviticus then repeats the prohibitions against contact with their dead carcasses, saying that should these make contact with vessels of wood, raiment, skin or a sack, any vessel whatsoever, the contact makes the item impure and unusable. Clay vessels must then be broken. This reaction to mixing makes cultural sense; the breaking of the clay pot dramatizes the opposite of wholeness, which *kashrut* proclaims. For this reason, the text seemingly interrupts itself to state, "Nevertheless, a fountain or a cistern wherein is a gathering of water shall be clean." Cleanliness is the opposite of mixing, and water cleanses-it rights dirty mixing. Therefore, water or pools of water are properly counterposed to the pollution described in this part of Leviticus.

Hertz interprets this passage to mean that these carcasses may be put into a fountain or a full cistern without defiling the water, which cleanses. It rights improper or dirty mixing and so water cannot itself be defiled. In any event, the text clearly states that impure vessels cannot be eaten from: again, the cultural impulse to separate governs meaningful behavior or meaningful eating.

The text further states that if any of the carcasses of these animals fall onto any sowing seed meant for planting, the seeds remain clean. But if water be put upon this seed and any of these carcasses fall upon the wet seed, then the seed is unclean. This prohibition has to do with mixing and the character of water. Dry seed could have substantial contact with the carcasses since no mixed contact occurs, whereas moist seed could not. In this case, water seems to be considered as an agent of mixing as well as a purifier, a characteristically binary view. However, this passage provokes a deeper question: Why is seed mentioned in the text?

It is mentioned presumably because seed is a source of life and food. In a system that promotes life and incorporates death by way of separation, seed necessarily should be separated from the carcasses of the impure. Conversely, harmless mixtures or contact that does not involve mixtures of essences present no harm. But it is appropriate for the text to discuss such contact since seed is highly signified in this system of thought. Above all, from the text's point of view, seed, like milk, is full of life.

The text then states that if "any beast of which ye may eat" dies a natural death, the carcass may pollute even if the flesh may be eaten. Touching the carcass temporarily infects the person, but only necessitates the washing of clothes. Thus, the text distinguishes between dead carcasses and prepared meats. The carcasses are associated with death, which pollutes by touching, unlike the butchered meat which is without fat and blood and so is transformed from naked death to kosher food.

It is worth noting that in the Bible contact between carcasses and clothes pollutes; these clothes must be washed. Why should clothing be signaled out for comment? From the standpoint of the *Pentateuch*, the wearing of clothing is a singularly moral act. Adam and Eve were dressed by God as an act of moral modesty; Noah was clothed by his children for the same reason. Clothing shields us from the nakedness of our condition, which since Adam and Eve is a mortal one. Clothing, therefore, stands in moral opposition to the (mortal) nakedness of our natural condition and so it clearly cannot mix with or touch dead carcasses. Contact makes impure, and the text commands washing.

The text then repeats one of its injunctions about swarming things. Leviticus 11:42 states, "Whatsoever goeth upon the belly, and whatsoever hath many feet, even all the swarming things that swarm upon the earth, they ye shall not eat; for they are a detestable thing." The connection between these creatures is that all are associated with the ground. The context of this association is the curse laid upon the snake in Genesis, which was to locomote on its belly on the ground after having caused Eve to sin and after having helped to introduce death into the world. The ground, associated with a curse-the place where people are buried and the very dust to dust to which bodies decompose, gives rise to a prohibition against eating animals profoundly associated with the ground. These include animals with many legs, animals which locomote on the belly, animals on all fours which also are predators, and animals which swarm on the earth.

Yet Israel is a land which is composed of ground, but it is a land of completeness whose wholeness gave full expression to the separation theme of Jewish thought that stands behind *kashrut*. And in *kashrut*, animals are banned because of their association with the ground. How can this be interpreted semiologically?

For one, Israel is a transformed-through-separation ground, so in *kashrut,* it follows that special rules must apply to the transformed land of Israel itself. This is the case, though these kosher rules are not examined here. Second, if *kashrut* is a wholeness it should be able to incorporate the ground through acts of separation. This is what happens: the ground and the animals associated with it are included, like death, by being separated away as abominations. The code mentions them; they are interpreted as potential foodstuffs that are rejected.

Finally, in terms of discussing the details of the *Pentateuch's* dietary regime, the commandments concerning pure and impure foods end with the commandment to sanctify oneself and be holy, for God is holy. Of course, a principal characteristic of God is that He is totally other, so sanctification and separation are clearly connected.

Now that this discussion of the Hebrew Scriptures dietary laws is completed, several other issues require investigation. First, if other aspects of Judaism can be constructed through such themes as life/death and separation/wholeness, then is *kashrut* an especially distinct and fixed aspect of Judaism, unique from other Jewish practices? The answer, of course, is no. Themes surrounding food, for example, are expressed throughout many Jewish practices. Holidays such as *Hanukkah, Rosh Hashanah and Purim* all have their characteristic foods, to say nothing of *T'ubishvat,* an Arbor Day, and Passover with its bread of affliction (which is unleavened or untransformed). These foods are readily interpreted within our framework for the dietary laws. Apples and honey, for example, characterize Rosh Hashanah; honey, like Israel gives life or sweetness to the apples of Eden. These remind us of our mortality and raise the question of the holiday which is answered in its Book of Life: who will live and who will die?

The omnipresence of food as a symbolic medium, moreover, may say something fundamental about Judaism, especially in contrast to Christian semiology. Judaism, judging by its holidays and its dietary laws, uses foods as a language as opposed to Christian practices, where verbal expression of belief is critical. It is what goes into one's mouth, not necessarily what comes out that allows this food language to make its Jewish statements. Even its most solemn days, such as Yom Kippur, are marked by fasting - days without food. Judaism like many other traditions but uniquely uses food to make fundamental statements of personage and sanctification.

Why should this be? First, food is essential to life. One cannot live, let alone procreate, without food. And Judaism is a religion about life. Choose life that you may live, exhorts Jewish Scripture toward its conclusion. The entire journey from Eden to Israel, from Egypt to the land of milk and honey, is about choosing the moral life and propagating Jewish (and other) people. This is expressed literally and figuratively - an opposition that is key to the ritual and textual statements of Judaism. Eating is literally a life-affirming act; it is elaborated by webs of symbolic meaning in *kashrut* which makes of dietary law a culinary life in the spirit. In other words, the spiritual life of Judaism, to use Christian-oriented language, creates its salvation through the moral separations and life sanctifications involved with eating, an act of the flesh. Again, why should this be so? One answer involves what I term the binary relationship between Judaism and Christianity.

Let us accept for the moment that "Religion in the West" means a life in the spirit, just as kinship is about relations in the flesh. The key opposition is spirit/flesh. If religious life is constructed through binary oppositions, then life in the spirit would have at least two positive forms: We could imagine a spiritual life expressed principally in the spirit, though directed at the flesh (Christianity); and we could imagine a spiritual life expressed mainly in the flesh, focused on living, eating, child-bearing and community life, but which also worshiped God spiritually even if its religious services today are modeled after sacrificial ones in the Great Temple. This is Judaism. A spiritual life expressed firstly in the flesh naturally would focus on the eating of food since this is a basic act and requirement of the flesh. It also would focus on procreation, a key act of the flesh which can be conducted in the spirit of matrimony.

If such an opposition between Judaism and Christianity exists, the first being a spiritual life in the flesh where the second is a spiritual life in the spirit, then we should expect this to be systematically expressed. Germane to *kashrut*, we see this in the meanings given to blood in both religions. Blood at the cross of Jesus saves the Christians who are under it, a spiritual act since physical blood should stain, which it does only to those who are not spiritual believers in His blood. The Jewish religion, by contrast, does not focus on the blood of one human but on the blood of many animals its followers eat. This is a fleshly, not a spiritual religious concern and the point of blood for the sanctified living is to separate themselves from it. Here is a systematic opposition: saved Christians want to be under the blood of one God/man, Jesus, while kosher Jews want to be separated from the blood of animals.

So much for blood! Let's return to the overarching difference between Judaism and Christianity and an arbitrary/systematic distinction which this examination of Jewish dietary laws inspires. I am suggesting an arbitrary Jewish/ Christian systematic distinction that is revealed through kosher food. To elaborate on this, the place to begin is contained in a Levi-Strauss observation about semiological systems. I am not referring here to Levi-Strauss's theories about how related peoples, such as the Indians of the American Northwest coast, establish differences of customs and symbols to create their own identities in the face of their cultural similarities, though this does apply. Rather, I am referring to his observations that these semiological systems systematically elaborate arbitrarily chosen chunks of meaning. *Kashrut* at the level of its practice, at the level of its lived, day to day experience, expresses the fiat or the arbitrary nature of its exclusion. It says without apparent rhyme or reason what may be eaten-hence Maimonides' inability to find a rationale for *kashrut* at the level of its practice. But this dietary system does contain an underlying logic. It offers arbitrariness to its believers and conceals systematically the basis of its spiritual resonance with the flesh. Christianity, on the other hand, systematically offers a way, a light, a truth that directly transforms in the spirit. It systematically conceals the arbitrariness of its terms, such as spirit/flesh, which could be replaced by any other principle, for example, wholeness/ distinction or pure/impure. Hence Judaism is arbitrary (though secretly systematic) while Christianity is systematic (and equally arbitrary). *Kashrut* may concretize the character of Christian spirit and in its rules-for example, the rule about the exclusion of fat- we see arbitrary difference determined by an underlying cultural logic powerful enough to elaborate the entire scope of all traditionally Western religious thought.

This brief discussion emphasizes a recurring theme: religious practices and beliefs such as kosher eating are products of an underlying "grammatical" or semiological code, expressed here in a religious language rooted in the texts of the Jewish tradition. What more can this observation add to our discussion?

Levi-Strauss attempted to show how such semiological codes worked to construct the symbolic worlds of indigenous peoples. One of his major points was that these codes often had simple but incompletely stated hidden messages which these codes fragmentarily but endlessly expressed in the rite and myth and kinship relationships of daily life. His term for this was polyphonic: messages are partially but repeatedly expressed. *Kashrut*, as a symbolic form of eating, is such a code, or expresses such a code, and has a message expressed fragmentarily but repetitively throughout its proscriptions and practices. The message is that life should be sanctified, that eating should be moral, that being alive means a worshipful relationship toward Him who grants this blessing, that moral action comes of human choices, that eating is a fundamental act of communion with life, and that the source of life, even animal life, is sanctified. This life requires consideration, even when it is edible food, and eating is a signified event that should be sanctified and made whole. In kosher eating Jews express their choice of life over death, just as they express their separateness as Jews. This unconscious message is present in each kosher meal, though fragmentally and in a way that, over time, repetitively constitutes a Jewish mindset.

Now, my principal purpose in this essay is to characterize the Jewish dietary laws: these are cultural in character and they are a product of language and literature. *Kashrut* has a message. Now, given that it is a cultural product, what does this say about the validity of the Jewish Dietary Regime for believers or for simple observers? For those with literary faith or just plain religious faith, it is a fundamental form of signification. Just as Jews mark birth and death with circumcision and burial; adolescent and adulthood with bar mitzvah and marriage, just as Jews cover the body with clothes, and just as they adorn time with the Sabbath, Jews signify the food they eat by making it kosher. Jews move from being death eaters to food sanctifiers. Saying that *kashrut*, like most religious practices, is an artifice of culture or language does not falsify it for believers or even undermine any faith-based approach to it. It only shows that kosher practices occur in a world of human language that can be understood in part as language. It probably is fair to say that this author practices *kashrut* in a largely traditional way in his life.

    Kashrut is a particular, not a universal way of handling food, though any food regime is based on non-utilitarian choices about what is edible and what is appropriate and in what manner. Eating is always signified, a point made by Levi-Strauss, himself the grandson of a rabbi. He wrote that natural species are chosen as food "not because they are good to eat but because they are 'good to think.'" Jewish thinking about food allows Jews to live the text and their tradition, connecting them to the great literary and moral traditions of the Bible and asserting, through food, that life is sanctified, kosher eating sanctifies life, and that this is how we eat.

Essay 9- Firsts and Seconds in Biblical Texts: Embedding People in its Terms, Leading People to Different Places

Jewish Scripture wants its readers to think in terms of certain contrasts or oppositions, such as life and death, up and down, slave and free. Here, another binary distinction is explored, first and seconds to show how Jewish Scripture uses it to tell its story. And briefly at the end of the essay I suggest how the Christian tradition took the distinction in a different direction.

First and second suggests a triad, which previous essays have explored. In this case, however, we have only a proxy for the non-triadic opposition flesh/spirit, the one indicating something separate and the two indicating something whole. This is of course the opposite use of one and two analytically derived from one spirit and two flesh in Common Differences Revisited. But this is our triadic analytical observation about flesh and spirit as we discern it in the text and in the traditions. In my view, this is not the Bible's use of one and two at the level of Bible's self- presentation. The number one is viewed Biblically as separate and two as whole. The question is whether this is true and a second question is how this opposition governs the direction of the text, if at all, like separate and whole did beginning with the Garden of Eden.

To answer the initial question, we might speculatively put ourselves in the mindset of a religiously/culturally embedded believer, perhaps Leach's 12-year-old shepherd boy living somewhere before the middle ages. Leach believes, and I agree, that this fellow might have an unbiased and clearer view of the meaning of the text. How would he approach first and seconds? My guess is that for him, second means a magnification of a first. Perhaps this can be heard in religious statements like, "Magnify the Lord with me". A magnification easily could be a doubling of a one, and therefore a two. This makes the two bigger than the one, it is whole where one is separate, and as magnified, two is spiritualized in the sense that it is complete.

On this theory, two marks completion. Therefore, when we see two of something in the Bible, it is something that the text wants to see as complete. For example, twos' mark a direction in the text in the story regarding Ruth and Boas where two women and a second marriage direct a future and important line of descent. In this story, elaborated below, a female line of descent is established as a second, and it leads genealogically to King David. This may be true as well for Jesus. And twos highlight an important, completed view of God which is given in an important text in Genesis: In the image of God, He created them (Adam and Eve), male and female he created them. This image of God as male-female (because distinction doesn't exist in Him) is repeated twice in Genesis. The text marks its significance through a repetition. In the Rabbinic literate, this same point is emphasized: when something is repeated it is being marked for special signification. Here, it is taken as a second, as something of complete importance.

Regarding the second question, it seems unclear whether firsts and seconds govern the direction of the text in the same way as complete and incomplete govern the Biblical text. This last opposition gives us Genesis as complete, and certain main portions of the Bible as ever-increasingly less incomplete in that perfections or high points of various kinds are established. It further describes the beginning of a new completion at the end of the text, with the Jewish people without a Kingdom re-establishing itself with a law and a military. Now, firsts and seconds do lead to the end of the text with First and Second Chronicles in Jewish Scripture and to the New Testament in the Christian Bible in Christian contrast to the Old. And as with complete and separate governing the text, there are highpoints or seconds or various completions along the way. But it is not certain if first and seconds are as systematically present as whole and separate are in the overall structure of the text. Better to think of first and seconds as weaving the text together, first and seconds being used to magnify or highlight certain tropes, and embedding the reader in its ever repeating, first and second distinction.

Now, like twins and pairs, firsts and seconds abound in Jewish Scripture. And the text uses them to address its main problem. This problem is that people, like God at the beginning of history, are murderers. While Cain murders Abel just outside Eden, and God destroys His first creation in Genesis, at the end of Jewish Scripture, not only is a lawfully bound community established, but there is also a full commitment to this community's Jewish life, even if it is not in a Jewish state. This beginning is the opposite of the end I am describing, much as death is to life. The Jewish scripture gives a tale of moral achievement or progress that reverses the moral wrong of the murders it begins with. It does this by steps, steps previously described through the structure whole and separate and now in this essay by firsts and seconds, using these to get us from the beginning to the end, which of course is another opposition.

This discussion begins with Genesis where there are two creations, clearly a first and a second. In a sense, the second story completes and repairs the first one. Next, there is Adam and then Noah. Adam clearly is a first who stands at the beginning of human history. He also stands at the beginning of creation, where he was the initial man in a non-historical place called Eden. Noah, on the other hand, is the first person in a new or second creation. Therefore, he is a second Adam who begins the story of humankind anew after the Flood.

The next obvious first is Abraham. He initially stands at the beginning of Jewish history, which is not the general history begun by the non-Jewish Noah. In that sense, Abraham is a second to Noah. Abraham as a name is also a second: his initial name being Abram, which is changed to Abraham in the course of the text. He is a second, moreover, in the sense that Jewish history is a second to the general history that precedes it, yet he is clearly a first. Abraham is the first Jew.

Turning next to Isaac, it is apparent that he is also a first and a second. Although Isaac is Abraham's second-born son, he is the first-born of Abraham's wife Sarah. Ishmael is merely a first-born; he does not come from a marriage but from a consort. He does not come from a triadic union. Isaac, on the other hand, is clearly a legitimate second child who is assigned a status as a first. He continues the line of descent, where he as the first-born is a second to Abraham.

In the course of these firsts and seconds, the text provides a moral lesson: human sacrifice is wrong. This is a moral step in a continuing moral story about killing.

Isaac in turn produces a first and second. Isaac sires Jacob and Esau. Esau, a hairy, red and rough hunter, is the first-born, while the smooth, white shepherd of a brother, Jacob, is second. They are twins, of course, and the issue between them is that of birthright which ought to go to a first-born. Esau though first-born trades these rights for food at one point and Jacob later supplants Esau before Isaac on his death bed. The issue clearly is about first and seconds: who should rightfully have the first-born line of descent and the blessings that come with it. Jacob, a second, becomes a first, secures the blessing of a first-born, and continues the lineage.

Jacob, as we know, marries Leah and Rachel, who was the youngest or the second sister. Here we see firsts and seconds in full triadic display. Rachel was the pretty one of this pair and was originally the wife Jacob desired. Jacob offered her father Laban his labor for seven years in exchange for Rachel as his wife. When he completed his years of work, Laban was to give her in marriage. But at the time of the marriage, the first daughter was covertly switched in place of the second. Jacob marries Leah and then later marries Rachel. Rachel is the first desired second daughter who is a second wife. She is both a first and second while Leah is only a first.

The story is meant, I believe, to get the reader to unconsciously think in terms of firsts and seconds. The triadic structure in play is:

<u>spirit</u>
flesh

as:

<u>male</u>
female

as:

110

<u>male (single)</u>
female (double)

• • •

<u>Jacob (first)</u>
Rachel/Leah (first or second)

or:

<u>Jacob (second-first)</u>
Leah-Rachel (first and second)

The top line is a one, and the bottom a two. Perhaps the structure convulses from one expression of it to another. With Rachel and Leah, the fact that they are presented twice by way of switching is meant to doubly impress the readers and embed them in the text's use of one and two. Imagine this as a convulsion, as a turning of the structure, as a generative use of structure, as a transformation. As for Jacob being a single when he was a second child who became a first, we discover a structure similar to the Godhead. Jacob is represented as a second-first (like flesh-spirit) and Leah and Rachel below similarly structured as first-second. This use of identical structure top and bottom in relationships also appears in both the Jewish and Christian Godheads, as later essays hopefully establish. Thus, all these entities have the same structure. Here, in the development of early Jewish Scripture, this basic if changing first and second structure continues with Rachel's children; the text makes her children seconds to Leah's, but then again, there are just two of them.

Jacob sires many children but only Joseph and Benjamin came through Rachel. Joseph was the eldest; Benjamin the youngest of the pair. Benjamin is therefore a second from a line of seconds through his mother. Judah, the fourth son of Leah, continues the Biblical theme of first and seconds. He comes from a line of firsts through his mother. He sires children while acting as a lever, and they are twins: Perez and Zerah.

Given the back and forth between firsts and seconds that have been identified thus far, we should expect more of this from these twins and we do. From the womb, one sticks out an arm, a crimson thread was put around it, and it returns to the womb. The other twin completely breaches the mother first. Perez is the first-born but arguably he is a second.

There are other twins or pairings along the way but the personage the text wants to lead to is Moses. Having oriented the reader to firsts and seconds, we find a new leader who is unlike any other that Israel has produced. While first in Israel, Moses is initially a second. He is the younger brother of Aaron. These two are clearly paired in the text, the younger Moses becoming the first lawgiver and the leader of his people where Aaron assists him, as a second, as his public voice. Aaron appears in front of Moses and before the Jewish people as a spokesman when he is behind or second to Moses, who is actually the receiver and teacher of God's commandments.

Further, as the leader of the Hebrews, Moses is a second to Abraham. That is, where Abraham was the first Jew, Moses is the first leader of the Jewish people. He is a second to Abraham as a source of the tradition. Yet "none was like Moses": he is a second who was a first. Moses, moreover, is a second to Adam also. This is true in the sense that Adam stood at the beginning of human history without laws and morals. But Moses stands at the beginning of Jewish history with a sanctified law (which was given twice by the way and which comes to us as two tablets). He proudly gives us a moral advance, sanctifying life with the commandment: Thou shalt not kill. He is a high point to Cain's low. He begins the Jewish religious tradition much as Adam began the human lineage. Moses, therefore, is twice a second: the person paired with Adam as well as Abraham. As a lawgiver, he is complete, and seconds imply completion (as do two in marriage!) His law, of course, is literally a high point and it is perfected on Mount Sinai. His law is written in stone a second time, this last time by a man and not God, and even the Ten Commandments, which Moses received on the mountain, appears as two tablets. Sinai itself is a second, mirroring the mountain that Noah's ark landed upon after the flood.

But the story does not stop here because Moses himself was imperfect or not complete. While he is our best, as the tradition describes him, he is nonetheless guilty of the crime that began the Biblical tale.

Moses, though God's lawgiver, is a murderer, having slain a taskmaster in Egypt.

So, the story continues, and the major pairing becomes one of prophet and king. Moses is the first prophet and Saul is the first King. Kingship is introduced in Jewish scripture by the first Samuel – there is a second –and its moral character is immediately made clear. Samuel says that the Jewish people's desire for a king is evil. Why should this be?

A king replaces God as the chief, everyday authority for the Jewish people. In the Torah, this is God's view of kingship and He did not like this prospect. God, who was a first, could not only not become a second, he also could be supplanted, his authority and law ignored. This possibility is evil, according to the prophecy and kingship is immediately suspect. But God approves of a King nonetheless and the Bible gives Israel King Saul.

Saul is obviously the first King. He is a first and second: he leads Israel but the tribe he comes from is not a first. He also is very singular; his son fails to succeed him but dies with him instead on a battlefield. He is succeeded by David, who is from the tribe of Judah. Judah comes through Leah and therefore is from a first tribe. David then is a second King from a first tribe. He is moreover paired with his son Solomon, who also is his second.

Before examining David and Solomon, note that Saul, who is the first of a potentially morally evil set of rulers, is also a moral failure according to the text. While he tries to follow God's command to utterly defeat a foe, he fails to kill them all, their animals and women included. He used a human judgment, supplanting God's (less than moral) command to slaughter everything and everyone and therefore is rejected by the prophet Samuel as a worthy King.

The Biblical text asserts the primacy of God's authority here however immoral; this is in contrast to Saul's good judgment. Regardless of God's moral, genocidal failings in this, the text asserts that good Kingship requires complete submission by the King to the divine will. Saul, while trying to do good, fails at this. (Clearly, God needs moral improvement too and this comes later in the text and in the traditions, though I don't discuss it here. I just note that moral progress actually fell to a human, King Saul who refused to commit genocide alongside his military victory. The text actually sees this and despite this, it wants to highlight God's ultimate sovereignty.) But, if Saul could be unworthy at this juncture in Biblical history, a king submissive to God's authority could be a moral triumph. David is such a second King and he is the first of his line. He displays the moral character God wants in a Jewish king. Full completion would come with David's second and this we see in Solomon.

Therefore, my argument is that David, while a first in his line and a second to Saul, is a first to Solomon. They are a pair of first and seconds, making them like all things that come in pairs, complete from the standpoint of the text, in at least important ways. David is a first second, Solomon a doubled second. One was a warrior King who united (completed) the Kingdom and who wrote psalms (very complete spiritual praise of God); the other was a builder of the Great Temple in Jerusalem. Solomon's wisdom was legendary: he was the complete or wise man. The will of God and the message of the prophet found a home in each King. The moral path of the Torah led to the Temple of Jerusalem, the path only being marred by Solomon's penchant for foreign and non-Jewish wives. Therefore, kingship (The Torah separates the political and the religious and deals extensively with the relations between them, an amazingly modern thing to consider!), which supplanted the authority of God, achieved its fullest form: the religious led the political while the political ruled.

Yet the path of Jewish Scripture continues until all Jews are committed to full religious practice and full Jewish family life. Religiously, it means following the moral laws of Moses. And from a family point of view, this means Jews marrying one another and raising Jewish children. And the text shows us that Kingship, at least in this time, is the evil the prophet originally said it was.

Solomon gave rise to kings that split the kingdom into two. What was whole or seemingly complete became divided in half. One became two (rather than two being one). The political intrigue that follows is a lesson in the failure of political authority and its Jewish kingship. The virtue of David and Solomon was that they followed the Torah and the prophets for the Good but the ones that followed them generally did not. Instead of uniting the Jewish polity, these kings perpetuated its division, giving us just separateness without political wholeness. This ultimately destroys Israel's political life and by the end of the Jewish Bible, we get a very interesting pairing of people.

They are Ezra and Nehemiah. The first was a priest, the other a military man who rebuilt the defensive wall of Jerusalem. Neither was a king, and neither was a prophet. They achieve two things. They were able to defend the Jewish people even though no state existed. And the priest was able to renew fidelity to the Torah and to Jewish life. Ezra unearthed and taught the people Moses's law and rediscovered Jewish practices. He also corrected what he perceived as an abomination: the intermarriage of large numbers of Jews with the native population. Unlike Solomon, who maintained large numbers of foreign wives, the Jews under Ezra abandoned their non-Jewish spouses and collectively fulfilled the statutes and ordinances of a newly re-discovered Book of Moses.

In terms of the text's development, this separation of Jewish men from non-Jewish woman advances the story to its Biblical (and not post Biblical) finale. That is, David and Solomon are not the end of the story. They are not a perfect completion of the themes of first and seconds because they had foreign, non-Jewish wives, Solomon especially. Despite their greatness, they were in this sense and from a Biblical point of view, morally flawed. But Ezra ends intermarriage not just for the leadership of Israel but also for the people as a whole. The only sin Solomon exhibited shamelessly is cured at the end of the text. At the end of the Biblical text, Israel is left with an unmixed or whole, religious people that has a priest or rabbi; we are not left with a prophet. Israel is left with a militia, not a kingdom's army. Ezra and Nehemiah are a pair, first and seconds, and they display a moral progress that leads into the post-Biblical period. They are similar to the relationship of David the warrior King, and Solomon, the builder of the Temple. However, it is also different because the political kingdoms of Israel are now past. We are brought to the beginning of the rabbinic period. In this light, Ezra is a first like Abraham and Noah, with more to come. Yet the text has brought us by way of first and seconds to an understated and incomplete end of the story. It is a new first, a new beginning that takes us out of the Biblical period and into something new and developing, hopefully without a God who commands the death of defeated people but with one that champions justice and peace and a Jewish ethic that supports the same.

Underlining my theme of first and seconds weaving the text together and highlighting the moral and other achievements of its Jewish history, the final two books of the Jewish scripture are First and Second Chronicles. These books recall the lives of King David and King Solomon. The names of the last two books of the Jewish scripture make the key point: the text has proceeded by way of firsts and seconds to tell its story.

It is a story of Biblical heroes, morally flawed though they are. Adam was the first man, Noah another first, Moses another first, and all of the kings were firsts. The Jewish Scripture is establishing a lineage of firsts with firsts and seconds, a theme that gets taken up again in the essay here on the triadic stories of the Bible. The Bible goes from one character to another to achieve moral advance. It comes to near perfection in the Kingships of David and Solomon, and it lays the foundation of the rabbinic period by giving us a Law, and a Jewish people as a community engaged in self-defense. It reveres its heroes in the end: and since Jewish Scripture reaches its high point in Kingship, it finishes by recapping the lives of its two greatest Kings, who are a moral model for the new rabbinic period to come. Jewish structure proceeds by first and seconds and it is a complete book on its own terms, ending as it does with a first and second chronicle. This is so even if the neighboring Christian tradition disagrees about how the Biblical story ends. Christianity forms its first or Old Testament and its second or New Testament from the same structure.

Essay 10- Pentecostal Patterns of Culture

Cultural patterns have been important historically in American anthropology. In books like Ruth Benedict's Patterns of Culture, the anthropologist interpreted her data to show how an overarching theme weaves together a society's myth and rite, its method of trading, its domestic ambiance, and its social interactions. But despite a fascination with pattern theory, there was never a satisfactory explanation of how a pattern of culture was constructed. Nor, in my opinion, have the way cultural idioms weave a patterned unity into the 'social', 'economic' and 'religious' aspects of society been shown by most modem anthropologists. But in the revivalist tradition described here in the essay entitled "Moralizing the West", a pattern of religious enthusiasm seems pronounced. Revivalist religion is spirited; it comes from the heart, and it is shouted for others to hear. We see a stylistic consistency: robustness. And this robustness connects to cultural elements like sound as opposed to silence, heart versus mind, the spirited contrasted against the rational. Do these building blocks provide a basis for a description of a pattern of culture which we can specify? Can we describe an entire religious/social complex in terms of such building blocks?

Can the analysis be complete enough so that all the "meaning" or social character of the complex be derived from the building blocks that construct it? If so, we would have an explanation for a pattern of culture, especially if all the building blocks of the system were teased out to show how they construct all the religious tropes of believers. The focus here is the crucifixion as Pentecostal believers discussed it to discover how it is constructed from elementary cultural forms like spirit/flesh. This essay locates a pattern of human Christian relationship at the cross and finds its similarities to kinship relations. Finally, general social/economic differentiations which are also patterned by Pentecostal building blocks will be identified and discussed.

The hope is to discover a deep Pentecostal structural pattern of culture and we may begin to see this at the cross. But first a preliminary comment: These data that form the basis of this study are the result of prolonged participant observation in a single Church of God located in Chicago in the mid- 1970's. When I use words like "Christian" and "Pentecostalism", these refer specifically to the Christians of this church and to their practice of Pentecostalism. The Pentecostal idea of the crucifixion discussed here is theirs and the idea of Pentecostal brotherhood comes from them.

In Pentecostalism, crucifixion is crucial to human spirituality and again, its structure may give us a key to Pentecostal patterns of culture. It is at the cross where life in Christ is defined. Crucifixion is where Christian salvation is made possible, and His death gives new life to otherwise mortal believers. Crucifixion displays the following binary oppositions - up/down, individual/collective, Jew/Christian, act/state, and spirit/flesh. Eternal life through Jesus's death at the cross is possible through religious language and at the least, through the way these binary oppositions define this event.

First, consider the Jewish/Christian opposition at the cross, though it immediately leads to others, like individual/ collective. Informants say that where the Old Testament time or history was a time of the Jews, after the crucifixion a new and Christian age of grace began. This division of history into a Jewish and Christian dispensation involves other distinctions: wild/ordered, collective/individual and old/new. That is, the Jewish dispensation was a time of the Jews-a collectivity or people who are the biological race chosen by God (in Pentecostal, not Jewish terms). They spend much of their time in the wild, that is, the wilderness or desert. They experienced the disorderly vicissitudes of Old Testament history without the certainty of orderly messianic salvation. By contrast, with Christ's death, all people-not only Jews-can be individually grafted into the family of God. Grace is assured to all who personally (not collectively) submit to Christ's submission.

In the old dispensation, collective Jewish life is characterized by a people in the flesh whose priests conduct animal sacrifice. The new Christian age is characterized by people individually in the spirit. Jesus's divine crucifixion or human sacrifice, in contrast to priestly animal sacrifices, shows a new and individual exchange relationship between Christian believers and God. This replaces the one in the Jewish disposition.

This opposition of priestly (Jewish) and divine (Christian) sacrifice involves exchange relationships as well as contrasts of private/public, animal/human, particularistic/universal, indirect/direct, periodic/eternal, imperfect/perfect, and of course, collective/individual. Put simply, in the crucifixion God comes to man as a perfect sacrifice for the salvation and forgiveness of everyone, whereas in Jewish priestly sacrifice, a few men come to God indirectly on behalf of a particular people. These men represent this people and offer God imperfect animal sacrifices intended to benefit only the Jewish people. This priestly sacrifice was private, Animals, principally sheep according to informants, were sacrificed in an isolated sanctuary in the High Temple, the act being hidden behind a veil and the animal, while as excellent as an animal could be, nonetheless was flawed. In this sacrifice, the priests went to God to ask His forgiveness for the sins of the Jewish people. God was not present to receive the offering of animal flesh and neither were the people who received forgiveness through these acts of ritual animal slaughter. Thus, the temple sacrifice can be characterized as indirect, imperfect, private, and non-human. In it, an exchange was affected: in return for animal sacrifice, God collectively forgave Jewish sins although this forgiveness was only asked for and granted annually. In this sacrificial complex, animal offerings were exchanged for forgiveness primarily on a fleshly basis. Spirit, in the form of priestly prayer, was secondary to the carnal effectiveness of the ritual.

Continuity between Jewish priestly sacrifice and crucifixion exists. It is established clearly by common terms: the crucifixion is called a supreme sacrifice and Jesus is referred to as a Lamb, the animal of priestly slaughter. Further, Jesus is Himself the High Priest who sits on the Lord's right side as man's mediator before God. Nonetheless, the differences between priestly sacrifices and the wider meanings of the crucifixion are as instructive as they are systematic. Not only does a new age or dispensation emerge from the grace that Christ's suffering brings, but the crucifixion also shows God approaching man. In Jewish ritual, man approaches the Lord. With the coming of Jesus, God has chosen to meet man personally on his own turf.

With crucifixion, the new relationship with God is direct and personal and the historical concept of a Jewish chosen people, as previously presented by way of Pentecostal believers, changes as well. Jews, though remaining God's people, must now choose their choseness if they are to be individually saved by the personal God who has chosen all people. This choice is posited on an individual basis in contrast to the chosen-people status which Jews collectively share by birth rather than by individual will. Thus, the indirect and collective nature of priestly, Jewish sacrifice is replaced by the immediate and personal qualities of Jesus's sacrifice. The old sacrifice ineffectively attempted to ameliorate the sins of the people; the new one demands that individuals actively turn to God for their effective sanctification. The divine sacrifice becomes the source of an eternally new relationship between individuals and God. God, by way of Jesus, now saves all individuals at the cross; there is no need for the indirect, collective animal sacrifice of the priest. Now there is direct salvation for all believers at the cross.

Further, the elevation of Jesus at the cross and the separation of His spirit which is also elevated, from His flesh, which is lowered, enables individual humans to undergo a parallel process. God's crucified flesh is lowered to man, who is of the flesh and associated with that which is below. (Man is destined to be buried in the ground after he has produced descendants who will also be buried and who descend further down in time.) Thus, Jesus offers and lowers His flesh to man. Just as dust goes to dust and ashes to ashes-similar cultural elements freely associate. In other words- the lowly flesh of Jesus's nature goes to man's flesh. Like goes unproblematically to like. Humans in the flesh receive the gift of Jesus's flesh and in this flesh can experience his separation from it. The believer then becomes elevated in the spirit, just as Jesus' spirit was liberated in crucifixion. Thus, the crucifixion is about the triumph of the spirit. Jesus's sacrifice, unlike that of the Jewish priests', is basically of the spirit and through His flesh, he brings the human believer into his sacrifice and its spiritual uplift.

Thus, for Pentecostal believers, the crucifixion, despite its oppositional relationship with Jewish sacrificial rituals, nevertheless involves the collective aspects so important to the priest's sacrificial activity. Collectively, it is a sacrifice for all people and all believers who, identify with the flesh of Jesus, collectively form the new church. But clearly, at the cross, these fleshly and collective aspects do not relate directly or specifically to the Jewish people. Rather, the body of Christ through His self-sacrifice becomes universally available to all people collectively for all time as the means by which they may individually through their faith enter the spiritual way of salvation and form the church. The church, which is the body of believers, is at one with the body of Jesus, one male, the other a female, churchly body. This is a united relationship, and it is described as a marriage of the church and Jesus.

Here is a collective marriage of church and God, united in the Son of God's body. This union establishes the family of God in which all God's children, no matter their age, are siblings to one another in the Lord. The individual believer, because he or she is in the spirit, is fully identified with the Church and the body of God, but as an individual, still can be considered an offspring of this relationship. And so, as offspring of the church and its marriage with Jesus, these individuals are siblings. This siblingship is made possible through Christ's passionate act of love on the cross, where God the bridegroom unites with His wifely body, the church. So, a passionate and divine act of love involving spouses produces Christian brotherhood and sisterhood, but with a great difference from those found in kinship, which is fundamentally in the flesh. These religious relationships are in the spirit, which needs equality since it is all equally high or elevated. Therefore, Christian brotherhood is ageless and without (physical) generation. It does not have generational differences with children down in time from the initial spouses. In the church, though the marriage of Jesus with this church, brotherhood and sisterhood are at one equally with God and one another in the spirit.

Together as one in the body of Christ, these Christian siblings also remain as individuals, each sharing in a common spiritual nature.

Their spiritual siblingship is as much a social relationship as kinship relations, semiologically constructed in the spiritual domain as much as kinship is structured in the flesh. And these spiritual social bonds are established from a passionate act of love at Jesus' crucifixion much as in kinship siblings are created through an act of love. All the bonds in the Christian family are built of love and are composed of spirit and flesh, which, of course, was Jesus's essential nature. It seems paradoxical that a fleshly act of crucifixion establishes the spiritual and loving state of relatedness found in the Pentecostal religious realm. Yet the Pentecostal idea that humans are principally of the flesh necessitates just such a foundation. That is, Jesus initiates a spiritual path by separating his spiritual and fleshly aspects on the cross, which permits fleshly people who identify with God in the flesh to follow His spirit. This identification is not symbolic but real for my informants. By being in God's flesh (from an anthropological point of view, this is a performative posture which is real by the saying of it) believers may personally participate in His sacrifice. By identification in the flesh, believers separate and uplift their spirit while they submit (again performatively) their bodies as Jesus did. For people who are in the flesh, this initial identification with Jesus is established in His flesh. Through the flesh of Jesus, God and man are linked. And in the spirit of this crucifixion, through this passionate act of the flesh, Christians are likewise linked in the spirit and in His love as brothers and sisters in the Lord much as children are linked in the flesh to their parents and their parents' union.

A union of opposites-divine spirit/human flesh-is established by what humans and God have in common. Again, this connection is made principally through God's flesh, which is obviously (and seamlessly) in the spirit. Through His flesh, the latent spiritual possibilities of mankind may be realized. In a general sense, then, we see the founding of relations in the spirit. These relationships are cast in kinship terms (brother and sister in the Lord), involve a common dichotomy (flesh and spiritual relations are a part of crucifixion), and result from a transformation: Jesus's crucifixion, which again is a passionate act. In this founding of Christian relatedness in the spirit and body of Christ, we can see rule-governed structures at work.

Here is how structure is rule-governed: a transformation from one (different) state to another (such as damned to saved) involves a rule of likeness. Movement from one difference to the next involves a continuity or likeness between the differences. (See the essay on Transformation and Formation in this book for more on this rule) This rule, amplified in the history surrounding crucifixion, for example, is expressed in many ways including the significance attributed to Jesus's appearance in the time of the Jews. The new age, which His transformation establishes, begins in the collective character of the old Jewish time in which Jesus, the Jew, appears. That is, the old age links to the new through a commonality: Jews, their time, and Jesus in that time. Secondly, the rule of likeness is displayed not simply by virtue of Jesus's Judaism but also by his body. These elements, Jesus's body, his Judaism and the time of the Jews are all "like" or similar elements, they belong in Jewish history. And in Jesus, these elements through the likeness of his fleshly body to them make contact with or created a new difference in the spirit. This difference is established by the character of Jesus's spiritual body. In the diagram below, likeness and difference in the elements involved crucifixion are charted so that the way similarity establishes difference is obvious. Likeness and difference focus on Christ on the cross and he is the link between dispensations. He is the spirit in the flesh and His flesh founds an age of spirit on the cross: Jesus's historical mediation is necessary in this system, not only because informants say it is, but also because of the contiguity with the Jewish dispensation and with Jewish and other humanity which His particular human flesh provides. This contact permits His spirituality to prevail. It creates a spiritual transformation or change to historical time and to the possibility of spiritual salvation through Christ's spiritual nature. This occurs as we have seen, through His spiritual body.

1. Jewish Dispensation	2. Christ on the Cross	3. Christian Dispensation	4. Age of Grace
down → up	down→up	down–but–up	up/down→down/up
flesh → spirit	spirit→flesh	flesh→spirit	spirit→flesh
(animal sacrifice) (God)	(God) (Man)	(Man's ongoing sacrifice for God)	(God's eternal sacrifice for Man)
state → act	act(s) → state	state→→spiritual acts	acts→→states of grace
(of people in the flesh) (in the flesh conducting ritual slaughter)	(of God's sacrificial flesh) (of spirit in initial human conversion)		
collective→individual	individual→collective	collective→Universal Church→universal	→individual
(Jewish people) (God & High Priest)	(High Priest Jesus)	(Christian people)	(believers on Earth)

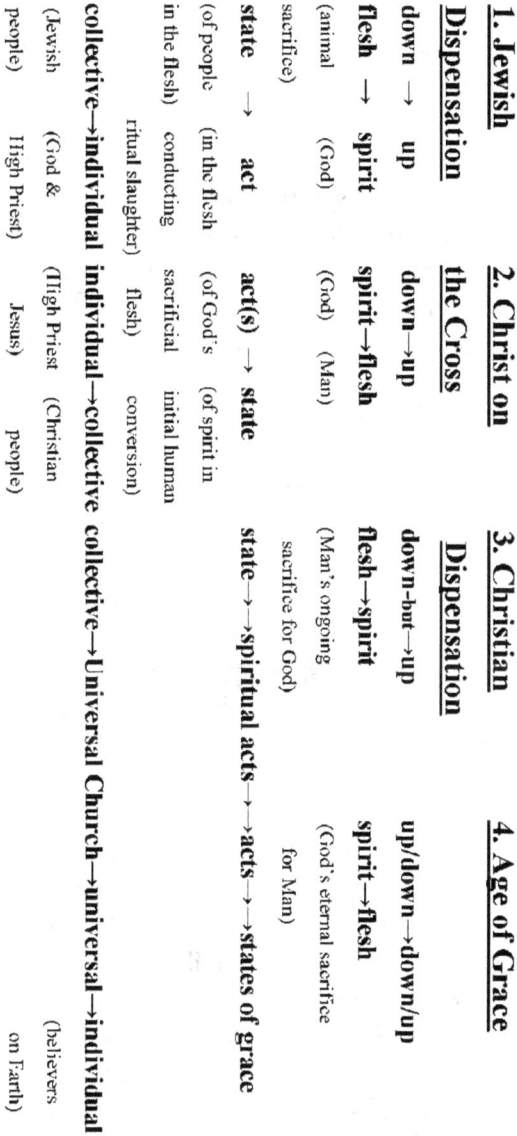

ILLUSTRATION 5

This illustration is a structural accounting of the passion of the cross and it is not a religious statement. It shows how like elements in the crucifixion line up with other like cultural elements to bring about a difference, in this case, a spiritual transformation from a time of the flesh, from a people of the flesh, and from a religion of sacrifice. Through likeness, through fleshly sacrifice, it affects a change. This change is to a religion in the spirit, a time of grace, and a universal path to salvation. All this occurs through the spiritual body of Christ.

Therefore, in this Pentecostal scheme, spirit consistently reigns and this is true in Pentecostal kinship understandings as well. Marriage, for example, is a spiritual act of two people in the flesh. The spirit/flesh nature of marriage is present in the union of spouses, which is conceived of both physically and spiritually. Thus, acts in a state of marriage involve a spiritual and fleshly union of the two partners. Marriage includes a spiritually sanctioned physical relationship involving the act of getting married and the ensuing sexual act, which is the distinctive feature of the relationship. (This discussion owes much to Schneider, 1968.) Intercourse, a passionate act, produces offspring in the flesh who share states of relatedness with each other and with their parents in the flesh. These offspring concretely manifest the spiritual union of their parents by their joined physical states, composed of both parents' substances. Children are part of the family unit, which is defined as spiritual, according to my informants.

Significantly, the scope of the family is defined by the results of the spouses' intercourse. In this regard, the spiritual unity of the family unit is marked by the fleshly acts and states with which familial kinship is substantially and primarily concerned. Though in the flesh, the family results from a spiritual union; its form of relatedness is constituted from the dichotomies that compose the family of God. Each of these two families-Godly and human- are scoped out of a central "symbol", crucifixion and intercourse respectively. (Schneider, 1968, for kinship). These symbols are themselves constituted by the spirit/flesh and act/state dichotomies. The key is found in this statement: Crucifixion involves Jesus, the spirit in the flesh who passionately acts to produce spiritual states of Christian relatedness; while intercourse, although spiritually dominated by marriage, is primarily a passionate act of the flesh, which also produces fleshly states of familial relatedness.

Again, the notion of love is important: Jesus's crucifixion and human sexual intercourse are both passionate acts of love. Love, then, involves spirit and flesh, and acts and states (of produced relations). It also involves the up/ down contrasts; informants say that love is submission. Certainly, Jesus lovingly submits His flesh for spiritual uplifting. (How this up/down structure works in intercourse and sex roles is discussed in another essay here.) This spiritual connection to man through the flesh is crucial to understanding love because such fleshly acts produce states of relationship in both the kinship and religious domains. The family of God is fashioned at the cross while kinship or familial relations are structured and created through intercourse. Thus, connection or association in the flesh creates love relatedness and these creaturely or fleshly, low forms of relating are dominated by the spirit. This spirit not only has an above aspect because it dominates; it is organized by a collective (or social)/individual opposition. Spirit is collective, involving the interrelatedness of individuals. Love is first a product of several parties in relation such as man/God or husband/wife; and again, we see a collective as opposed to individual aspect. This collective/individual element is clearly oppositional; the opposition, present throughout the Pentecostal cultural scheme, gives love a diffuse character, which is often known as a state of loving-relationship.

Nonetheless, this diffuse or collective structuring of love is counterposed by an acute and individual quality of love relations organized by another opposition we have studied here: act/state. In other words, love's diffuse expression correlates with the place of act and state (passionate versus daily love, for example) within social relations composed through the spirit and flesh. Acute love seems marked in contrast to the general backdrop of love relations because Jesus's passionate act produced general states of relationship and generally stands for God's (spiritual) love or relationship to mankind. In kinship, acute love is also marked because the married state is not as passionate as lovemaking nor is the state of parent-child relationships in family life as intense as the acts that produced them.

To summarize, love generally is the cultural meaning which fixes relations formed in the flesh but of the spirit, either in terms of acts or states. These relationships exist in the domains of kinship and religion.

Love, then, is a specifically structured term for meaningful relationships in kinship and religious spheres, the term's meaning being itself composed of features or attributes set by the constituting dichotomies found in the general cultural pattern.

Even love as submission is possible only through an opposition orchestrated by the underlying culture. The decisive fact here is that Jesus was crucified as a result of His submission to His father's will. The cross was the altar for Jesus's love of God. An analysis of this fact shows that God's highness compared to human lowness is enacted at the altar. Jesus is below God and Jesus is raised high in contrast to mankind whose members bend the knee and bow the neck to worship Him. This theme is more generally present: those who worship God and who bend the knee and praise His name express submission through service to God, especially in following His will. Such acts of service and submission not only follow the contrast between Heavenly God and lowly or earthly man, as articulated by the up/down opposition, they also follow the contrast between spirit and flesh. Man, in the flesh, should love God who is spirit, going low before him in order to relate with Him and share His uplifting.

This cultural patterning of man's submission to God extends to human relationships. Specifically, a man should relate to his wife, according to informants, as Jesus does the church. Obviously, the church is the bride of Christ; she submits to Him by identification with his flesh. Man in the flesh should love God who is spirit, man bowing low before Him in order to relate with Him and share His uplifting. Love then implies submission.

Thus, the man in a marriage should rule, his spiritual submission and will dominating the woman who, at the logical level, is the fleshlier and ever more submissive partner (just as spirit should dominate flesh). In this context, wives perform a supportive role while husbands make decisions. Nonetheless, the Christian submission of the husband to God ideally tempers and makes benign his privilege of rulership. In fact, while sex roles are a point of religious and social friction for some, and while informants stress different aspects of Pentecostalism to support arrangements between spouses in the home, it appears that ideally a man's Christian submission enables him to acknowledge his wife's feelings and this tempers his authority.

127

Admittedly, this brief summary of culturally organized sexual differentiation is abstract. More concretely, informants have specific ideas on the roles of the sexes in this world. Husbands are oriented first to the work world and their financial obligations toward their families. For women, the concomitant orientation is to domestic duties like child-rearing, house cleaning and cooking. This differentiation is generally maintained in the behaviors as well as in the cultural conceptions of the Pentecostal Christians I studied.

How is this dividing up of the world culturally constructed? First, (as we have noted) the love relationship between spouses is in the spirit; love is displayed by the fleshly partners and in a home dominated by spirit. So, the love domain of the home not only has an initially collective aspect; it also has an internal quality. Again, the home and its Christian love are in the spirit, which means rooted in Jesus, in whom the Christian spouses essentially live. Consequently, the domestic, like the religious, sphere is internal compared to the extra-domestic and nonreligious realms. The two meaningful love domains are internal while the excluded domain of the practical work world is external and, to overstate for the purpose of making a point, is perceived as being involved with the filthy lucre of this sinful world. Love thus perceived becomes opposed to money (Schneider 1968) and this division is embedded in Christian domestic sexual roles.

Therefore, Pentecostalism assigns women domestic duties and men the worldlier, economic concerns. This ordering of work and love domains reverses the spirit/flesh assignments given to each sex, in my view. The fleshlier female partner remains at home in a love domain whereas the more spiritual man works in the wider world. Seemingly, the more spiritual man is less tempted in a world filled with temptations, while the woman, whose nature and history are that of temptress, is more safely secured in the sanctified domain of love. In this arrangement, the wife serves her husband in domestic duties, thereby submitting to him in the realm where submission is required: the spiritually dominated domestic unit. Thus, a wife's submission to her husband may meaningfully occur in the home. Here it is important that this division of meaningful and not meaningful (or practical), of love and work domains compartmentalizes and separates the external world and economic action in general from the areas of life which Pentecostalism and spirit especially develop.

The Pentecostal system, then, provides space for economic, worldly action while maintaining boundaries between it and spiritual concerns. Spiritual growth may result in material blessing as well, but for the most part economic practices are distinct from all but the most general moral and spiritual control, just as spirit is secured against economic intrusion. Ideally, the family and the church are divorced from worldly things even while the system provides a link, through sex roles into the economic sphere. One responsibility of a loving husband is that he financially supports his wife: if he does not, he weakens his Christian testimony. The obligation to support the family is essentially an unselfish obligation that a Christian husband has towards his Christian wife. On the one hand, a man pursues self-interest in the work world, and on the other, he is selfless, sharing or loving in domestic life. This sharing at home is as thorough a way of life as selfishness or self-interest is in the economic domain. Self-interest/Collective love is clearly a culturally encoded opposition and an extension of other elementary forms composing the Christian person. In the field of economics, this love or selflessness is a widely recognized theoretical problem because it does not arise (clearly) from self-interest. In Pentecostalism, it is an expression of the Christian or western-cultural definition of the person. This person pursues economic self-interest and by cultural contrast, domestic sharing. Each motive may be "properly understood" by the social actor, but in any case, domestic behaviors are meaningful and not purely natural as economists, psychologists and others would have it. In a sense, self-interest/sharing as encoded aspects of the Christian person shape a natural bent toward survival. This includes shaping a perhaps inchoate "natural need" for personal gain and for the protection and enhancement of one's spouse and offspring. Thus, we see religious, kinship and economic conduct patterned within a system that has a cultural logic. In other words, this Pentecostal pattern of culture exhibits an ordered set of binary relationships constituting the nature of and connection between family, religion, sexual roles and economic activity.

This Pentecostal pattern may relate to American culture as a whole and is possibly a key to the cultural basis of a variety of social arrangements, movements, and new developments in our society such as various feminisms. Such developments could arise from the principal structures found in Pentecostalism (by their being combined in different ways). Or such developments could arise from structures and distinctions closely related to Pentecostalism. These may represent shifts away from Christian dichotomies, as witnessed in various women's movements conception of love and work. Specifically, the division between inner, meaningful, love domains and the external, practical economic domain could be recast into new patterns of work and love. Perhaps work might be organized by an inner/outer dichotomy rather than work being defined by a contrast with love. Such a definition might produce two types of work, one domestic and one not, and this changing of relations between "domesticity" and economic life might bring a concomitant switch in sex role definitions. In this scenario we might see significant changes in cultural ideas about who is responsible for family income and the family's physical maintenance. In this cultural possibility, domestic labor is simply work, like any other form of work; it is not defined as a labor of love. Such work could loosen its association with the feminine and the inner world; such labor has nothing gender-determined or especially meaningful about it.

Another combination of cultural elements could produce a different pattern of love and work where the meaning of each is changed. Imagine the love and work domains each being structured by an underlying distinction of practical and meaningful as illustrated in a simple diagram:

LOVE
practical/meaningful

WORK
practical/meaningful

In this structuring of love and work, each is organized through both poles of a meaningful/practical opposition. This organization might imply shifts away from the family as the exclusive love unit within an economic system where occupations and jobs support homes. Since the home is a practical as well as a meaningful unit the family could be as

130

much a consumption unit as it is a meaningful one with a component of love.

Patterns of work and related community organizations could change as well if a cultural pattern dictated that meaning is as much a part of economic life as it is the foundation of domestic life. In such a scheme, we might see the kinds of claims for work that early Marxist-Leninists made in the 1920s: new demands for socially meaningful work might be complemented by the development of communal organizations which are craft or labor-oriented. Such cultural thinking may have no connection to economic realities even though such thinking may drive revolutions to state-imposed reorganizations of everyday life.

But returning to the point, this Pentecostal church and its members exhibit social and cultural patterns of love/money which may be general to the culture. Its patterning of everyday life may relate to the principles structuring new and varied developments in the parts of the American social system. So, the relationship of these Pentecostal religious-structures to the social organization it produces may be helpful in constructing a grammar of variance for other developments in American social life.

In any case, the binary organizations built into the crucifixion and its related religious terms are clearly present in the Pentecostal patterning of everyday life. This patterning has an underlying structure and it gives us a profound pattern of culture, and it is centered on the crucifixion and the structures it expresses. As for the pattern of Pentecostal robustness, this is explored in a separate essay here entitled "Moralizing the West".

Essay II- Christianity/Judaism: A Study in Cultural Contrasts

In this essay, the reader is introduced to an attack on Jewish particularism via an academic writer's structuralist analysis of Jewish dietary laws. It is, of course, instructive to see another writer's take on the kosher laws; it is a gateway to discussing how Judaism compares at a structuralist level with Christianity. At the very least, Soler's attack on the Jewish dietary laws is instructive about the nature of anti-Semitism, which a comparison of Judaism and Christianity as a study in cultural contrasts can address.

Jean Soler's article, "The Semiotics of Food in the Bible"[3] left me with a sense of disquietude. The article uses a structural analysis of the kosher laws to conclude that the distinction "Jew" in the Western tradition has been transcended in Christianity and that it was "stiff-necked" on the part of the Jewish community to assert itself as a distinctive entity, whether in culinary rite or political stance. The author contends that such distinctiveness is an inflexible assertion of an unmediated and uncompromising difference. Jews, he believes, assert this uncompromising distinctiveness just by existing even as they assert that the distinction God/man, so fundamental to Old Testament thought, is uncompromised. This God/man distinction is rigidly adhered to in the Old Testament's kosher laws and stands behind the difference of pure and impure as it is applied to food. Some foods are consistent with the sanctity of God (are kosher) and as the distinction God/man implies, with its God, not God exclusion, some foods are not.

Soler writes that just as Jewish notions of purity are arbitrarily oppositional, the identity "Jew" is rigidly divisive from others by its very nature. This divisiveness is apparent in the fact of non-hybrid Jewish existence, revealing itself in the ways Jews cook, eat, worship God, and act in political life, and even by the endogamous way in which they insist on their survival through in-group marriage. Soler comments specifically on Jewish culinary practices but makes most of his case against Jewish particularism by innuendo:

> By contrast, whatever variations the Mosaic system may have undergone in the course of history, they do not seem to have shaken its fundamental structures. This logic, which sets up its terms in contrasting pairs and lives by the rule of refusing all that is hybrid, mixed or arrived at by synthesis and compromise, can be seen in action to this day in Israel, and not only in its cuisine.

Soler's view has its strengths: he shows how a basic organizing structure, God/man, could be used to define what kinds of foods are kosher and what kinds are not. From here, he extrapolates the dichotomy God/man into the culinary distinctions made in Genesis between vegetable and animal, and into the later distinction between flesh and blood. In this light, his discussion of the history of food proscription in the Bible is especially interesting, though perhaps Soler has missed the role of imbalances in Biblical accounts of this kind. As Soler's Biblical materials reveal, we find two polar and extreme situations of food restrictions under Moses:

1) Vegetarian restriction (excessive limitation)
2) Total license in dietary matters

These are resolved (perhaps one could say mediated) to a third condition-*Kashrut* rules-which provide workable dietary restrictions for Biblically minded Jews. The kosher laws are neither vegetarian nor do they provide complete license in what people eat. In that sense, they represent a compromise, which is counter to Soler's interpretation of these laws. He focuses on the strict dichotomy which undergirds them: God/man.

Soler goes on to illustrate how religious thought is constituted through such dichotomies. He shows how such dichotomies form a system of interrelated concepts, symbols, practices and beliefs that make logical or cultural sense when treated as an interrelated whole. His analysis is systematic and binary, follows from the work of Levi-Strauss, and has the virtue of taking structuralist analysis, which has principally focused on myth analysis, into Western religious thought.

But despite the article's many theoretical strengths, Soler makes a fundamental error in the presentation of his symbolic discoveries. He confuses his role as a critic and cultural analyst. Soler uses structuralist analysis, which discerns the intersubjective and deep structural forms of socio-cultural systems, to judge a particular cultural posture, namely the stance of the Jew in Western society. Soler claims for his value judgment the validity of structural analysis. His assertion of Jewish intransigence ("stiff-necked") shows his dislike of what he thinks is an overly rigid cleaving to Jewish distinctions. This may be seen in the analysis of the kosher laws, which the author dismisses as the working out of oppositions that are too rigidly enforced, too rigid in his eyes even for unifying the Jews who revolted at Sin in the desert. These Jews rebelled against the vegetarianism of Moses and instead sat "round their flesh pots and ate". The initial dietary rigidity enforced by Moses, Soler intimates, required compromise even within the Jewish food system. Soler notes that a third regime of kosher dietary restrictions replaced the initial vegetarian ones.

Yet this new system of dietary purity, per Soler, continued to assert the God/man distinction which underlay the vegetarian distinction between animal and non-animal food. Hence, in the final kosher laws, the initial and main distinction of vegetarianism is only displaced. Yet the author's wish is not so much that the God/man distinction should be displaced, as that it should be resolved. A mediator between God and man -Jesus- is, in his view, the resolving factor. Since the Christian Son of God is capable of reconciling the separation inherent in the God/man opposition, He can end rigid dietary distinctions and can universalize the relations of all people in God through His medial being. Jesus overcomes the distinctions of the flesh that the Jews rigidly cleave to, as seen in their kosher laws, and this makes them irrelevant.

In brief, Soler points out an interesting series of oppositions: God/man, pure/impure, Jew/other, etc., which help organize a variety of dietary regimes. But he goes beyond analysis to assert that Judaism is corrected, its rigidity is overcome, by the coming of Jesus. He uses the medial character of Jesus to apply a Christian solution to the distinctiveness found in the Jewish kosher laws. Yet, and this is what I argue here, Jewish and Christian systems have different ends. Christianity takes on the problem of death and tries to transform it to life, where Judaism takes on the question of life and tries to sacralize it. One transforms -- Christianity goes from difference in the dying flesh to sinless identity with Jesus on the cross, from death to life. The other, in sacralizing food and in establishing things like the identity Jew, it separates rather than transforms. It maintains distinction to make food holy or kosher. Jew is a separated identity that is made whole or sacralized through Jewish practice. The Jewish and Christian religions do different things here (transform and separate) and there is no one correct religious process, as Solar implies, only difference. Jesus transforms; kosher separates (even if both elements - transforming, separating- exist in both religions).

Taking on this last point, Judaism concentrates generally, but not exclusively, on this life and the requirements of daily living. One such requirement is eating, hence the Jewish, cultural organization of culinary activity,

Now, the issue of eating in Judaism does not promote a preoccupation with the difference between God's immortality and man's mortality. Instead, it represents an interest in the life portion of the life/death distinction that each religion elaborates. In other words, Judaism elaborates life by sacralizing it (while not ignoring death) and Christianity overcomes death while not ignoring life. As such, Judaism's interests include reproduction as well as personal righteousness and daily rite. For these main purposes, the Jewish system posits *mitzvoth*, that is, transformations by good deeds. These deeds alter the culturally conceived human condition in a structural manner equal to (though differently from) Jesus's transformation. Where Jesus transforms death into eternal life, *mitzvoth* -- while broadly including acts of kindness, mercy and justice -- these *mitzvot* regarding food consumption simply sacralizes (an equivalent to transforms; it separates to make whole) this life-giving activity.

In the "this life" (as against next life) orientation of Judaism, it is the Jew, collectively and individually, whose task it is to improve a fallen world. This takes the form of religious acts and often these are acts of separation, separation to make holy. That is, the observant Jew acts to reproduce a better world by doing *mitzvoth.* In eating, this involves endless acts of proper separation, separation to make kosher or whole. Jews sacralize food and its connection to life by separating or dealing with separation to make whole. This is true throughout the branches of Judaism, and it is especially true in the mystical Jewish tradition, with its emphasis on gathering earthly shards of the *Shekinah,* a quality and earthly expression of the mystical Godhead, and bringing those shards together. The mystical Jew deals with fragments in the world to make them whole. The theme is separation to make whole, not transformation.

By this contrast of Jewish and Christian transformations/ formations, I make no value judgment. Juxtaposing the two simply indicates that an oppositional and distinctive difference exists between Judaism and Christianity, transformation occurring differently in both. In Judaism, transformation occurs often as formation or as the establishment of difference, not the overcoming of it. (See the essay on Transformation in this book.) It is incorrect to assert as Soler does that there is only one proper mediation of the distinctions underlying the kosher laws. Separating food does not require transformation; it is simply a way of making food holy and incorporating animal death into a system that supports human life. Soler does not accept this difference-making, and he elevates his favoring of Christianity into a cultural judgment against Judaism.

To repeat an earlier point, Soler criticizes Jewish structures and their religious signifiers for their binary distinctiveness. For him, Jewish particularism is itself an isolated division which has not been universalized. But all identities within this Jewish/Christian scheme depend on distinction, even one that seems beyond distinctiveness, such as religious universalism. Take a particular/universal distinction and say even that Judaism is a particular religion, but Christianity is universal. This universalism contrasts, in a binary way, with Jewish particularism. Universalism is one term in an opposition, particular/universal, not an end to all opposition or distinction. It is a distinction in a common quality, religion, even when it calls itself universal. This works in the same fashion as particular Judaism, just differently. Indeed, a Christian identity reveals the same logic of cultural distinctiveness that Soler holds to be peculiar to the Jews, past and present.

So, if one views Christianity and Judaism side by side, considering the logic of their ideas, terms, symbols, practices, and injunctions, then this synchrony further reveals an identical binary cultural logic in both. Put into binary relation, Judaism and Christianity, establish each other's distinctive character.

This suggestion invites a general examination of the widespread contrasting patterns existing between Judaism and Christianity. For this admittedly exploratory and sketchy enterprise, I rely on my studies of Pentecostalism and my Jewish background for much of what follows below.

· · ·

In examining the contrast between Jew and Christian, it is convenient to begin with the concept of sin. Both the Judaism I know and the Pentecostalism I studied have notions of sin. For Christians, sin is an omnipresent condition of life and a consuming religious concern. For Jews, sin is not an omnipresent state but instead consists of unethical or immoral actions. In Pentecostal Christianity, people are naturally sinners in the flesh; the carnal state inevitably gives rise to actions reflecting the sinful conditions of fleshly life. But for Jews, sinful action is hardly inherent in human life. Jews may be sinners, but only because of improper actions; and the status of "sinner" may be changed if personal conduct alters to conform to ritual and ethical prescriptions. Thus, sin is understood differently through a different emphasis on acts and states. Sin for Pentecostal Christians is a given state, reflected in naturally motivated action. For Jews, by contrast, sin is founded not in existence but in action. A Jewish sinner whose being or state is thought of as a sinner is so because of his or her repeated disposition to sinful acts. In Pentecostalism, a sinner is a sinner; in Judaism, a sinner sins. Thus, an act/state contrast creates or structures a difference between two notions of sin. Other differences between Jews and Christians also have a similar, binary organization.

Yarmulkes (skull caps) furnish a simple example since they illustrate the systematic use of differences or contrast that define these separate cultural entities. A yarmulke is a ceremonial hat which is worn in a ritually observant manner by Jews. It is especially common for male Jews to wear yarmulkes in the presence of the Torah, the five books of Moses in scroll form -a practice that indicates respect before God and things sacred. This contrasts with the Christian patterns of hat-wearing and doffing where an uncovered head indicates respect. Thus, an obvious contrast may be drawn. Hat-wearing shows respect before God and Torah for Jews; hat-doffing show respect before God and is appropriate to worship among non-Jews. Hat on/hat off is an oppositional contrast. Now the extent of the use of one or the other difference may vary, as it does in Jewish culture or even in the Catholic tradition with its crowned bishops and skull capped popes. The point, however, is that a difference of custom between Jewish and Christian cultures takes an oppositional form. The difference suggests the same thing: a hat worn; a hat removed shows respect for God.

Differences in concept and custom extend to even more fundamental areas, such as Bible interpretation and self-definition. Genesis, for example, is interpreted differently in the Christian and Jewish frameworks. For Christians, the central consequence of the Garden of Eden is that sin is introduced into the world, that Adam and Eve and all their descendants exist naturally in a state of sin and, in a word, the condition of man is fallen. But for Jews, the consequence of the expulsion from Eden is not a state of sinfulness but the opportunity to act morally. After Eden, people may act to transform the condition of man into a state so just and so merciful, so righteous and so pure, that the kingdom of God can be established on Earth and the Messiah can receive and be received in the world. Thus, for Christians the consequence of Eden is a state of sinfulness; for Jews, it is a precondition of moral action.

The act/state opposition as it structures sinfulness dominates the essential Jewish and Christian interpretation of Genesis. This distinction is complemented by a systematic use of another; here Christians emphasize the fall of man, Jews emphasize the possibility of his ascent. Christians address the issue of ascent in their system by way of the fall: it takes place in the context of a Christian notion of sin and a need for transformation. To reiterate, in Eden, the Christian sees the consequence of a fall; the Jew sees the possibility for a historical uplifting. Where "down" is generally emphasized in Christian interpretations of Genesis, "up" is chosen in Judaism. The association of cultural elements in Genesis breaks down in the following way: Christian interpretation is to state and down as Jewish interpretation is to act and up. Thus act/state and up/down are the logical elements that organize these interpretations; different emphases give radically different meanings to Genesis.

But where is the "down" aspect of the up/down dichotomy in the Jewish interpretation of Genesis? Where is the "up" aspect in the Christian version? Jews acknowledge the lowered status of humankind after Eden, but Jewish practice emphasizes the opposite of this condition by stressing uplifting activity and historical tasks. Christians likewise recognize the original, sinless condition of Adam and Eve; they are cognizant of the "up" against which the downward fall of humankind occurs. The up/ down opposition, then, exists in both systems; proof enough that the presence of such oppositions may be found in these different interpretations of Genesis.

This occurrence of a common opposition to define and give value to Christian as well as Jewish ideas deserves further comment. As previously discussed, the notion of *mitzvah*, for example, contrasts with (and is homologous to) the Pentecostal notion of transformation and may be understood by using oppositions common to both Judaism and Christianity. In other words, the notion *mitzvah* is consistent with the Jewish interpretation of the post-Eden condition of man, in which the historical task is to transform the world by action into a renewed, moral state. *Mitzvah* is a principal term for moral activity in Judaism; it implies a change of condition and can be described as an individual activity. Here, the Jew spreads moral light into a darkened world. Hence, *mitzvah* is a transformational notion that links together Judaism's emphasis on action and a concern for "upness".

The Pentecostal notion of transformation is a Christian equivalent to *mitzvah*; transformation applies to the special moment of conversion in the Christian scheme. Here, the individual's natural and sinful state is switched or converted to a saved state. Where *mitzvah* in the Jewish scheme is often an activity on a state of affairs, Pentecostal transformation is an act that produces a new state. This act is of the spirit (Pentecostal informants say that only God transforms) and the of-the-flesh sinner must submit or go low before Jesus's corporeal transformation. Thus, Christian religious language defines a state of human affairs after Eden that is low and of the flesh -a state of sin- and then transforms this state into a new state by acts, both human and divine.

The oppositions up/down and act/state, are used differently in the notions of *mitzvah* and transformation to shape the distinctive ends of each religious system. Yet the underlying oppositional similarity between Christianity and Judaism uncovered so far seems inadequate to the scope of differences found between these two religions. Are there other common oppositions that are also used differently? Again, do oppositions such as act/state become more differentiated through other oppositions shared by Judaism and Christianity but used differently? This should be the case and it is explored below.

• • •

The identity 'Jew,' for example, not only concerns tradition and following the God of Abraham, Isaac and Jacob; it also concerns, in a fundamental way, transmitting that tradition and lineage down to the next generation. A Jew passes on his heritage down in time. The tradition is a collective and timeless remembrance of things past, whose living history, such as the Exodus story, provides the collective liberation that confirms the special mission and place of the individual and collective Jew in the present. The Jew, then, carries a tradition that he reproduces not only in moral action and not simply in ritual practice, but also in literal reproductive fact. It is not spiritual rebirth that is essential to his tradition but the continuing birth and development of the House of Israel. The opposition here is (Jewish) birth/ (Christian) rebirth as well as Christian and timeless up and Jewish down in time. The Jewish mission includes not only the objective of historical transformation through mitzvah but also a continued historical existence down in time. The reproductive unit, like the Jewish tradition in its totality, is a collective one - the family is the bedrock of the tradition, the sub-stratum of cultural transmission and collective identity.

Can we elaborate on the oppositions or contrasts in this? We can when we examine the fundamental task of the Pentecostal Christian. The Christian aims not at the reproduction of a shared tradition through the continued existence of a people down in time but instead is interested in spiritual uplifting. He is interested in individual salvation, in ascending to heaven as a pure being in the spirit. Thus, his task does not relate to the collective reproduction of the past but to a new and personal rebirth in the future. He is not concerned principally with the flesh, for in his viewpoint it is associated first with death and sin. As a religious first principle, the Pentecostal seeks the spirit and heaven.

While the individual Christian wishes to go up to heaven, the collective Jewish tradition goes down in time. Up/down and collective/individual are key organizing principles here; opposing uses of these identical principles (common differences) are systematically worked through in the identity of Jew and Christian. These identities, for example, involve concepts of identity and faith, which are homologous to each other and yet have opposed orientations. Where Christian faith looks to the future and the spiritual conditions in the afterlife, Jewish remembrance faces backward to an earthly, historical, this-worldly, and fleshly tradition. Faith and remembrance may be taken as binary opposites, though they are also functional equivalents since a practicing Jew remembers (observes) his tradition and a practicing Christian has faith.

This difference, Jewish looking backward and Christian looking forward, is consistent with the bigger differences between the two systems. Judaism focuses on the issue of reproducing life (though it does not ignore salvation) while Christianity wishes to save people from death (though it does not ignore reproduction). Hence a life/death opposition differentiates these two religions' identities. This opposition is related to the ones previously uncovered, and it helps reveal another important contrast between the two religions, and this may be the most important.

Here is a suggestion: within the domain of religious spirit, Jew is to Christian as flesh is to spirit. To reiterate, within the spiritual domain of religion, Christianity is to Judaism as spirit is to flesh. Judaism is a flesh religion.   From the standpoint of the underlying, generative ideas of the Western religious tradition, Jews and Christians part company along the most deeply set opposition of all: spirit/flesh. Each elaborates its dignified position from the spirit or flesh dimension of the spirit/flesh opposition that each stress.

Let's flesh this out, so to speak, using ideas we have already introduced. Judaism, as we have said, stresses purity of the flesh where Christianity emphasizes purity of and in the spirit. Jewish purity is made clear in the kosher laws, though it is also illustrated in the *mikva* (a ritual bath principally for women after their menstrual period but also undergone by men during the holiest of Jewish holidays). The *mikva* also stresses a spiritually oriented cleanliness primarily in the flesh. In *kashrut*, however, the particular dietary restrictions are ultimately explained; the injunction is clearly on the side of purity with regard to foods consumed, especially regarding pure and impure meat. This meat is referred to as flesh.

Purity in the flesh-and this could refer to the purity of the eater as well-is to be maintained by command of divine Law. The point is that kosher laws are meant to prevent defilement in this life, defilement of a living this-worldly person before God. Kosher is meant as a modality of purity for humans, it sacralizes the life-giving food Jews eat, and the meat and food substances people consume in the flesh. This emphasis on physical purity points to the overall importance of flesh element of spirit/flesh in the Jewish religion.

The emphasis in Judaism on descent - the God of Abraham, Isaac, and Jacob, for example, or even in personal Hebrew names like David, the son of Henry- likewise shows the fundamental flesh dimension of Jewish life. Generations are in the flesh and generational names underline its importance in Judaism. To be sure, this fleshliness has little of the freight that Christian systems attach to the flesh dimension of the spirit/flesh dichotomy. Yet this dichotomy is essential to the cultural definition of the Jew who as a descendant is primarily though not exclusively in the flesh.

For Jews, as I understand it, two facts are essential to a person's Jewishness: that one is born of a Jewish mother, and that a person studies or follows Torah. The first is a definition by natural substance or flesh;

it is the general condition of the Jew. If a person does not follow the Torah that person is still a Jew; being a Jew is a natural unalterable fact of the flesh. Yet from the standpoint of the relatively observant Jew, it is Torah that distinctly transforms a person into an observer of the historic tradition. Torah is law, a moral guide to a way of life sanctified by God, a code for conduct and as such, it analytically corresponds to spirit. But it is a spirit in the flesh, spirit as law; and as concrete law, it is yet another flesh dimension in the flesh definition of the religious Jew.

By contrast, Pentecostal Christians may define themselves as spirits in the flesh (as Jesus, the model Christian, defined Himself) and this major statement is huge for Christians and is so clear that it hardly needs elaborating. But the use of the spirit/flesh dichotomy is different for Pentecostals. Flesh, for example, can never be pure, in the Jewish sense, for Pentecostals. Here it is relevant to note that the task of the religious Jew is customary rite and personal righteousness. To put it differently, spirit is expressed in an opposition between rite/righteousness; this is made apparent in the Torah and Haftorah readings on Yom Kippur- the holiest day of the Jewish year. The readings focus on the ritual slaughter of animals (flesh) and sublime ethical injunctions (spirit) and are central to worship on this day. The point of this brief discussion, then, is that Spirit is elaborated in Judaism by oppositions such as rite/righteousness that are different from Pentecostal contrasts and lend different meaning to spirit in Judaism. Rite/righteousness is a concretely fleshly distinction in the spirit, and this is distinctly Jewish.

Additionally, clearly, both Jewish and Christian identities are composed of common differences such as the spirit/flesh opposition which are put to dissimilar uses. The varying contrasts of custom and belief -*yarmulkes* and hatlessness, *mitzvah* and transformation, remembrance and faith-indicate that contrasts between related systems play a part in determining the distinctive content of each religion/subsystem.

Soler, then, perhaps shows prejudice in the way he juxtaposes Jewish particularism and Christian universalism, stating that Jewish distinctiveness is rigid, and contrasting it with the transcended difference manifested in Jesus, the God/man mediator. As this essay shows, Jewish distinctiveness is simply a different use of the spirit flesh and other oppositions within a common system of differences. It is not less or more flexible; Jewish constructions just use the spirit/flesh distinction in the system of common differences, differently. And identities are always distinctive, as this contrast between Jewish and Christian religions shows even if the identity is defined culturally as non-distinctive or whole in the spirit. There is only opposition among cultural elements (even among the distinct and indistinct, the two and the one, flesh and spirit) that confer systemic meaning. Even Jesus and the universalism of Christianity reflect an oppositional position in the logic of culture.

Universalism contrasts against particularism and the transcendence of particularism in Christianity is a particular process involving many distinct oppositions (up/down, spirit/flesh.) It is not something beyond cultural logic and difference. It is composed of differences and these create something distinctively universal, not actually universal. Universal is the particular idea of a particular tradition that is composed of its distinctive differences. This judgment raises the point I made against Soler in a new way. I criticized him for confusing his role as cultural analyst and cultural critique when he suggests that the cultural distinction Jew has been transcended by the crucifixion and the Christian relationships to God that it establishes. My analysis here has led to the same problem in that it uses cultural analysis to attack the truth of universalism. This argument here says that Christianity is no more universal than something particular, just uniquely different. Universal here is a different quality contrasting against particular, nothing more, and this would seem to be a critique of Christian universalism and its claim to truth, since all things are particular, even a claim to be universal.

So, what to make of this, especially in light of my desire to use anthropological analysis to promote tolerance in the world and to dignify all cultural traditions? First, we should clarify that all western religious ideas are in the spirit and we can establish that by first distinguishing domains: religion in the spirit and kinship in the flesh. Next, this spirit domain or religion is itself divided by spirit above and spirit/flesh below. Since spirit is whole it is singular; the flesh below divides and it divides into two, in this case by spirit/flesh. If this illustration of religion and its various domains is correct, it would look triadically like this:

spirit
spirit/flesh

This illustration then predicts three major traditions using these common differences. This is so: first above we have Islam, a religion preoccupied with the oneness of God. Below, we have established Judaism as the flesh religion. As for the spirit religion in the flesh denominator below, it would have to be decisively based on the body of God, which in Jesus it certainly is. Proof enough, in my opinion, that this triadic structure for the religious domain is real.

In discussing the flesh religions, we would have to show that one was particular, which Soler and I agree is Judaism. Since this is a system of contrasts, the religion next door would have to contrastively claim itself to be universal. It does. But then, how to evaluate this tolerantly, instead of just dismissing universal as an equivalent, contrast to the particular? Here is a suggestion as to how: the universal is particular but different, it is Christian. This is what universal means here, nothing more. Universal here means Christian - the universal does not need to be dismissed as the basis of an intolerant and false claim just as the universalism of Moslem spirit should be viewed as Moslem, it also being a particular universal. This way of thinking makes each expression of spiritual faith equivalent and it invites people to look toward them depending on whether their concerns are salvation-oriented, or their concerns are simply with meaningful daily living within this tradition.

On the issue of tolerance, a sticking point for many is the claim that the Jews are a chosen people. It seems as profound a claim to uniqueness as the claim that one's religion is universal, so it requires examination. This status, this choseness, relates to Judaism being in the female slot of the triad constructing the three great religions. In other words, the male spiritual or religious domain contains within it a female or more expressly fleshly religion and in this system, in the logical complex composing it, females are chosen. That is, in the Western tradition, while men choose, women are chosen, and a female people in the flesh then easily become chosen (by God), which is affirmed by the Jewish people being frequently described as the bride of God, a chosen spouse! (And in the system of common differences, God is not

145

monogamous in that he has many brides). This is the meaning of chosen people within the Jewish tradition. A male God chooses female and fleshly Israel as a bride. And in the western tradition, it is men who uncover and women who are uncovered. Now, in circumcision, we see Jews being marked in the flesh, a cut or separation that makes the male child a wholly Jewish person (a separation to make whole of course and it is separation in the flesh). More to the point here, we also see a penis publicly uncovered in circumcision. This is a feminizing treatment of a very male, and continuing to be male organ. This is something a female religion does: its masculinity, like something female, is uncovered. The broader point is that Judaism as a spiritual religion in the female flesh demonstrates a logic relating to female flesh. This logic gives meaning to Jewish concepts of a chosen people, with circumcised males, that should in no way invite parochial chauvinism or untoward hostility. It is only a cultural system working out its logic in the flesh versions of the system of common differences.

Following on the discussion presented thus far, a further word on religious tolerance and structuralism is in order. Along with Soler, I hold that binary analysis may do much to uncover the cultural logic of Judeo-Christian symbolic forms. But the implications of this possibility are many, and it is always possible to use structural analysis as a kind of hostile unmasking of the binary arbitrariness basic to any system. Since such a possibility is not a tolerant use of the limited knowledge obtained through the structural understanding of a system's signifiers, it might well be avoided. Structural analysis is especially helpful regarding the character of symbolic vehicles; it does not provide any special insight into the nature of the entities being referred to by the symbolic system. The Trinity, for example, could be understood in terms of a triad of spirit over divided spirit/flesh, with each of the lower terms or persons being made up of spirit flesh themselves. Then the commonality of spirit and flesh may provide the unity of the personages of the Trinity (they are all composed of spirit and flesh) and of unity of the Trinity overall - so the Trinity is composed of (common) differences. But what does this tell us about the truth?

Such an understanding of the Trinity reveals nothing about the Christian God itself or the rigidity of a system of differences though one can see that *kashrut* and the Trinity are composed of them, equally. It only tells us something about how humans view their God from within this Christian perspective. Since reference is traditionally not at issue in the study of semiological signifiers, structuralist thinking might pause instead to praise the religious genius-its human sense-making- which allows cultural agents to live socially with meaning, dignity and cultural distinctiveness. This view might explain my surprising emphasis on Jewish culture in these essays. I am not extolling its virtues compared to Christian ones; these essays attempt to dignify the tradition and show it as an equal to its sister religions. Furthermore, these essays demonstrate that the religious traditions studied here are cultural and are at the root of Western thought and society. The Biblical traditions (and its sister Moslem ones) are a credible basis for meaningful social life, they are cultural conveyers of significance, and they deserve respect and intellectual credibility in a world of secular doubt and growing prejudice.

Essay 12- Priestly Sacrifice

Why should secular-minded people think about why Leviticus permits priests to eat certain portions of the sacrifices and why other portions must be burned and smoked? Surely, sacrifices, even Biblical ones, are inherently pre-modern and beyond the intellectual scope of contemporary people. But is this really true? Is it possible that the animal sacrifices in Scripture contain the same structures that allow people to express relations with one another through the idiom of kinship or that enable people to eat meaningfully through *kashrut* or that permit people to think of God triadically or that encourage people to join together in socially significant communities?

The sacrifices of Leviticus, it is often politely said, are only of historical interest, but I think instead that its sacrifices show the Jewish Scripture to be a cultural text. This text consistently exhibits a structure which it deeply and unconsciously conveys to its readers by its repetition through a variety of stories and practices. This structure is based on spirit/flesh, which forms a variety of cultural sentences or permutations that often take a triadic or three-part form. The most common triadic expression of spirit/ flesh is:

<u>spirit</u>
spirit/flesh

This triad is a permutation of:

<u>spirit</u>
flesh

where the flesh in the bottom portion, unlike spirit which does not divide, separates into two parts, one being spirit, and the second being flesh.

148

This triad organizes the practices of sacrifice in Leviticus, particularly the sacrificial practices in Leviticus 6:1-8:36 which is our focus.

How does this structure work or underlie the eating prohibitions in this portion of Leviticus? First, imagine that Jewish scripture defines food as flesh and imagine further that food is divided into spirit and flesh. That is, fleshly food is constructed by spirit/flesh since flesh divides. And the spirit or life-giving foods are vegetarian-like foods and the flesh foods are meat. Further imagine that spirit and flesh divides meat: the spirit in flesh being blood and the purely carnal meat, flesh. On the theory that spirit goes to spirit and flesh to flesh (see Pentecostalism and Transformation in this volume) only flesh portions of food could be eaten (by people in the flesh) and spirit portions would need to go to spirit (or God) So, in the kosher dietary laws, only flesh portions of meat may be eaten; the blood, which Jewish Scripture explains contains the life or spirit of the animal, may not. The same distinction is identifiable in these Levitical sacrifices. Blood and fat portions of sacrificial food may not be eaten by the priests as they contain the spirit and purely meat (or its grain equivalent) or flesh portions can be consumed.

But ordinarily just by priests. The sacrifices are in the spirit, or are a ritual or concrete expression of spirit; they take place in a holy place, the Tent of Meeting whose special organization was replicated in the Holy Temple in Jerusalem. This is the domain of the priest. In this spiritual realm, spiritual food may go to God; flesh food goes to the priest. The "temple" domain does not extend to the people outside. Sacred space governs the pendency of spiritual and flesh food and who may eat what.

Does the text confirm these expectations? Leviticus 6:3 begins with priests in priestly garb being told that they must maintain a perpetual fire in the Temple for purposes of burning and smoking sacrifices. The ashes produced may be brought outside the Tent of Meeting to a pure place beyond the camp. The ashes, therefore, must remain holy, or in the spirit, wherever they are placed, which is not in ordinary space where the people are. They are to be properly separated. Meanwhile, the priests must maintain a perpetual fire in a properly separated sacred space. The red fire gives sacredness to the space; the fire is an encompassment of the spirit, perpetually smoking and consuming and encompassing the space with its white light and white smoke evoking the spirit or the lofty spiritual.

This space is the locus of ritual, and the first Tent of Meeting ritual described is the grain offering. The text reads, "A handful of the choice flour and oil of the grain offering shall be taken from it, with all the frankincense that is on the grain offering, and this token portion shall be turned into smoke on the altar as a pleasing odor to the Lord" (Leviticus6:8) What remains may be eaten by Aaron and his sons, but only in the Tent of Meeting, and it shall be eaten in the form of unleavened cakes. Only males may eat of it and anyone that eats the food must be holy.

The grain has come from a supplicant, not a priest, and so the grain and its sacrifice invoke a set of relationships:

<u>God</u>
<u>priest</u>
common person

which is triadic:

<u>spirit</u>
<u>spirit</u>
flesh

This gives the grain an ordinary flesh character with the priest and the sacrificial burning sacralizing the grain. The smoking and transformed grain relate to God, it is in this respect spirit, it is life-giving and concrete food and its untransformed flesh is edible for spiritual but fleshly priests. Smoking is transforming, the untransformed remains are flesh so we have transformed/untransformed. Its spirit portion is white – the frankincense, (which our theory predicts should be white like spirit), is white. Oil likewise is like spirit (pure and transformed) and it also is part of the inedible portion. This portion is turned into smoke, clearly like spirit, like to like, to become an (ethereal) odor which is (spiritually) pleasing to spiritual God.

The next offering of grain described in Leviticus comes solely from the priests. Priests are in the spirit, they are not like fleshly commoners, their sacrifices are then purely spiritual and the grain, reflecting its priestly giver, is a spiritual offering and only a spiritual offering and cannot be eaten. Their sacrifice is inedible to them. It is turned entirely to smoke: the spiritual priest produces a purely spiritual sacrifice that lofts its way to a spiritual God.

The next sacrifice permits priestly eating but only in the sacred space of the Tent of Meeting. It is called a purification offering (for inadvertent sins which make a person impure). The offering shall be slaughtered before the Lord where burnt offerings are slaughtered in a space immediately outside the inner area of sacred space. The priest who makes the offering may eat of it but only in the sacred precinct of the Tent of Meeting. Only males may eat of it (the priests were exclusively males). "But no purification offering may be eaten from which any blood is brought into the Tent of Meeting for expiation in the sanctuary; any such shall be consumed by fire (Leviticus 6: 23).

The sacrificial animal once slaughtered and then later burned, had to have been drained of blood before it was brought into the sacred precinct of the Tent of Meeting to be edible. If its blood is present, if its blood is brought into the Tent of Meeting, the sacrificial animal had to be entirely consumed by fire and turned to smoke. If its spirit is in any way present, it is a spiritual object, spirit encompasses; blood animates the flesh, making it spiritual, inedible for the priests, and something to smoke completely.

Yet the sacrificial animal can be eaten by priests if it is totally and properly separated from its blood. But, the eating of the flesh of the sacrificial animal must occur in a holy precinct for structural reasons, meaning that the flesh has been separated from its spirit or life, or blood. As separated flesh, it is holy, to be eaten in a holy place by holy people. Spirit to spirit, flesh to flesh, and sacralized flesh to fleshly people in the spirit in a sanctified or holy place. The likeness rule of structure makes the sanctuary the only place where sanctified flesh could be eaten by sanctified people in the flesh. (See the essay on transformation in this book).

The next sacrifice is the ritual of the reparation offering. Again, what is purely spirit is smoked, what is exclusively flesh may be eaten. It must be eaten in a holy precinct. This is followed by the ritual of the sacrifice of well-being. What is edible here and who may do the eating? If the sacrifice is for thanksgiving, then it consists of leavened cakes and unleavened wafers spread with oil, cakes made of flour and oil. One leavened and unleavened sacrifice is required. The priests shall receive it and then dash blood around the offering of well-being. "And the flesh of his thanksgiving sacrifice of well-being shall be eaten on the day that it is offered" (Leviticus 7:13), If it is not eaten on that day, it must be burned. The text does not say but the person who eats it is the priest.

The question now is only what sacrificial foods are edible and by whom. Here we have a sacrifice that is edible on the first day but not thereafter. This appears to challenge this essay's thesis but in fact, it is sustained at least in part because the edible sacrifice is referred to as flesh. But problematically for this essay's thesis, the sacrifice is both edible and inedible. One possibility that may overcome this is that a sitting sacrifice, surrounded by blood, may encounter the blood as it sits over time. The contact may make the sacrifice inedible but when proper separation occurs, the sacrificial food may be eaten.

The next sacrifice the text describes is the votive or free-will sacrifice. This sacrifice may be eaten on the day of the sacrifice and on the next but not on the third. "If any of the flesh of this sacrifice of well-being is eaten on the third day, it shall not be acceptable; it shall not count for him who offered it. It is an offensive thing, and the person who eats of it shall bear his guilt" (Leviticus 7:18)

Perhaps our thesis has been overcome by what is in the text. However, we argue that sacrificed foods that are spiritual in character, those portions consisting of (white) fat, (white) frankincense, (pure) oil, or (red) blood are inedible and only flesh or things purely in the flesh can be eaten. The text says that it is on the third day that the food becomes inedible. Therefore, is there something about 3 that might spoil the flesh with spirit?

There is. Three is a complete number in this system. For one, a triad is composed of three's obviously and not only is:

<u>God</u>
<u>Priest</u>
People

a triad, so is:

<u>God</u>
Israel the land/ Israel the people

a triad composed of three's as are a host of other significantly related elements in the Torah:

<u>God</u>
Adam/Eve

or:

<u>God</u>
Abraham/Sarah

or:

<u>Abraham</u>
<u>Isaac</u>
Jacob

Etc. . . . .

The list goes on and on. Each is a whole unit of relatedness. 3 is a whole number. And it is therefore spiritual or whole. And, since it is spiritual, the third day spoils this sacrificial food with its fullness, which then cannot be eaten. Flesh that is edible is first separated, not whole. Therefore, it is at least arguable that sacrificial food that otherwise is edible cannot be edible in the third day in a way that sustains our thesis: edible is wholly in the flesh and not mixed in the spirit.

Of course, for the third day to convey its purity or wholeness upon otherwise separated flesh, the text must say this is so and it does by saying eating such (spiritual) food is offensive. This is a matter of signification, it is something the text points to and defines in its own terms, it is not something in nature, and the text makes its meaning plain. It must ban the edibility of a sacrifice on the third day; if it is not banned, the significance of three is not there and three becomes insignificant.

If our thesis is correct, aspects of food that suggest the spirit should always be inedible in the text, and what follows next is God telling Moses that fat surrounding innards cannot be eaten. This fat is white like spirit. Blood is also banned as food: again, blood is the spiritual life of an animal, it must not be eaten. Leviticus then commands that priestly sacrifice must turn the fat into smoke, and only then can the sacrificial breast of the animal yielding the fat be eaten by the priests. The text distinguishes flesh that can be eaten from spiritual foodstuffs that must be smoked.

So, despite the dearth of clarifying hermeneutics, it appears that sacrifices, at least in this Leviticus text, are in sync with the spirit/flesh structures prominent in Jewish Scripture. The same forms that structure so many stories of the Bible (see the essay on "Storied Triads in the Bible" in this book) are crucial to sacrifice. Spirit and flesh abound here. Moreover, it seems obvious that sacrifice, as it was replaced and reformed in the Jewish tradition over time, divided into prayer (spirit) and kosher laws (flesh). All this shows how the essential structure of the system exists not only in the text but also in the post-Biblical tradition that grew and developed from it. Arguably, this helps establish the Jewish Bible as a central text of an evolving, particular tradition, one that contains the vital structures that inform a more developed Western life.

As argued in earlier essays, these include the structures of kinship, of religious community and of sacred rite. (and these earlier essays have entirely understated the importance of law and justice which the Bible brings to us). To establish the undiminished centrality of Jewish Scripture to the Western religious tradition (which of course is a Middle Eastern import), it is important to analyze the most obscure and pre-modern, and seemingly irrational practices the text displays. If these are cultural constructs made of the same cloth as the great traditions that developed from them, then the Jewish (and Christian) Scripture should have the exalted position, the foundational position it is given in the Jewish and Christian traditions. This is so even if it is read as a cultural text and not as a historical account. It retains its central position, even though it contains the merely apparent religious barbarism of priestly sacrifice whose basic structures as shown in this analysis here comport with the text as a whole.

But this may not be fully convincing to strictly secular people. It is one thing to say that the Biblical tradition should not be diminished for contemporary believers even if it contains unacceptable and pre-modern practices. But for purely secular people, Biblical barbarisms like animal sacrifice are not something to think through, they are something to reject. For secular people in the Bible's sway, structure and not the story or the practices may be the main thing and there is little reason for them to abandon great traditions based on premodern barbarisms in the otherwise shining, signified and possibly developing text. But it is another to say that the cultural character of this text should rightfully command centerstage for secular students of the Western tradition. For these people, what place should they give to Biblical meanings, when spirit/flesh seems to be made of whole cloth? Spirit/flesh is an arbitrary distinction that is apparently not found in nature, one that is likely hostile to individual freedom and practical action since it anchors people in families and communities. It restricts sexual and perhaps even economic appetites. Spirit/flesh gives us stories, moreover, like Genesis that are contrary to scientific knowledge and wisdom. A secular case can be made against the importance of the Bible as revelation, as literature, and as a foundational book for our society. But I would not ignore the importance of the Bible as a source of culture, as a central source of meaningful relatedness in the West. Without it, perhaps we only have our nation, our politics and our jobs.

Essay 13- The Trinity: Its Cultural Definition

Pentecostal Christians at the Church of God in Chicago that I studied for several years never distinguished between the Trinity as the true God made up of three persons, which is the term's referent, and the Trinity as an idea connected to a linguistic unit (or a word). But I wish to distinguish between the two and set aside the actual God that the Trinity refers to and study instead the collective or shared concepts associated with the term Trinity that believers carried in their heads.

This Trinity, viewed as the term or word that describes a religious or cultural concept of God, was one of the Church's most central concerns. This concern was principally for the individual personages of the godhead, especially for Jesus and the Holy Ghost, yet church members never forgot that they worshipped God and that this God in total was a Trinity. Their idea of the Trinity was in most respects a conventional one for an American Protestant church. In this essay, their conventional ideas of the Trinity are connected to the Pentecostal system and its deep structures and binary distinctions. Hopefully, this will lend insight into how the term Trinity is composed or constructed. In other words, this essay shows how the Trinity term takes its meaningful character from the system of Pentecostal belief and practice. In particular, the Trinity is a singularity (in its tri-part form) that stands as a unity against the distinctions used in other Pentecostal terms and practices. These distinctions are unified in the Trinity to give the godhead concept much of its intellectual character.

Specifically, The Trinity as a representational idea takes its character from the major binary oppositions that construct Pentecostal

156

belief and practice. Oppositions such as spirit/flesh, act/state, up/down, male/female, Jew/Christian, inside/outside and collective/individual are the building blocks of Pentecostalism. These oppositions or elementary forms of religious significance are the basic structures that organize and are organized within the Trinity. They are all differences that lodge as indistinctions in the identity of the Godhead, taking the form spirit-flesh, or male-female, for example. These differences are common throughout the Pentecostal system and they lodge together to construct the quality of the Trinity. They are the common differences that build the system of common differences.

While these oppositions lodge differently in the Trinity than they do in other Pentecostal constructs, it is instructive to examine the concept of baptism, if briefly, to show how these oppositions (here expressed as difference) work to give religious concepts, like the Trinity and baptism, their significance. Simply put, baptism by water involves immersing an individual in water; a person must go *down* in the *flesh* so that he or she may come *up* in the *spirit*. These actions or *acts* lead to a new *state* where the individual was a *sinner* he now is *saved*. The relationships constructing the meaning of the term baptism are up/down, spirit/flesh, act/state, sin/salvation and damned/saved. These distinctive oppositions or relations are lodged in the term baptism, giving it its representational qualities, which then permit it to refer aptly to events of baptism, which is also so constructed.

What we see in the Trinity, a quality, are distinctive relations or oppositions, like up/down and spirit/flesh being expressed as unities, spirit-flesh, up-down and these unified distinctions construct much of the content or identity or quality of the Godhead. The Trinity's resolution of these structural differences into unities also shows that a binary or "dualistic" scheme like Pentecostalism is consistent with a logical requirement of epistemology or knowing. That is, for distinction to be known there must also be identity against which distinction exists because distinction by itself is incoherent and identity by itself without distinction is not knowable – it is indistinct. Therefore, a system of terms composed of difference—as our analysis of baptism shows (and as many essays in this book demonstrate)-- requires a quality or a unity or a term like the Trinity against which differences can be lodged in or even be established by. In the Trinity, we see a union of opposites into an identity – a unified Godhead in this case -- that contains the summarized and unified main distinctions of the system. This unity in God is a logical requirement of a system of common differences. Without the quality of God, without His unity, the distinctions would be less than fully coherent. As is illustrated later in this essay, the resolution and unification of these Pentecostal binary oppositions in the character expressed in the Trinity do more than show the Trinity's structural definition and representational qualities. They make possible a meaningful (or related) system of differences and different terms by providing identity in a system of differences.

The religious reality of Pentecostal informants, their language of belief and their understandings, must be the basic grounding of this discussion. The people studied were regular churchgoers and the church was in a poor neighborhood on the Northside of Chicago. The congregation was mostly southern white, though blacks joined the church and there was racial intermarriage. Most of the members had moved out of the neighborhood. Their blue color occupations had led them to better housing in more affluent neighborhoods. Most had no more than high school educations. Most had families that were single generational. Their children did not aspire to college. They had a loyalty to the neighborhood church where most had come to God, a life experience that liberated many from a family history of alcoholism. They believed intensely, and most had internalized the meanings of Pentecostalism into their very bones. They spoke its religious language and knew when something was a true, religious thought and when a thought was outside their belief system. They were good examples and teachers of their beliefs and their structures. Surely, there is no structure without believers! It is the Christian thinker who expresses the Pentecostal, intersubjective religious concepts that are analyzed here. What informants said and did; the connections they made and their characterization of religious terms like the Trinity are the starting point of this analysis.

Congregants viewed the Trinity as a singular godhead (my term) or "God", composed of three distinctive personages who nonetheless are one. These three personages of the deity are variously described by believers: Jesus and God are referred to as male as is the Holy Ghost –

the godhead is a masculine entity. The Holy Ghost and Jesus do the will of God the Father (which could be taken as female or submissive behavior). Jesus and the Holy Ghost are thought of as agencies where God is a director. Jesus is the Father's son. The Holy Ghost has no kinship or obvious generational characteristics unlike those of the Father or Son. The Holy Ghost does, however, impregnate Mary. He also impregnates believers in moments of religious fervor, giving rise to their glossolalia. Jesus is called the spirit in the flesh. The Holy Ghost also is spirit who is made known to people through human flesh. God is characterized in many ways: this term is described in statements like "God was, is and always shall be".

God always is in Heaven while Jesus and the Holy Ghost go up and down from Heaven to Earth. Other descriptions used principally for God include all-powerful, merciful, immeasurable, infinite and eternal though these adjectives apply as well to the two other terms. God is also love, Jesus is "my all and everything" and Jesus is a "mediator". God is principally called the Creator, Lord and King. Jesus is further described as Master and Savior as well as by "sweet Jesus".

The church's believers made thousands of references to the godhead during the time I attended Church, and these varied endlessly. Yet, these few bits of data generally reveal what the Trinity is to believers. A certain terminological ambiguity exists in the word God who is both a personage of the Trinity and the Trinity in its entirety. So clearly, God may be the equivalent of the Trinity as a whole. Believers stress the words God, Jesus, and the Holy Spirit but they rarely talked about the Father or the Trinity.

And certainly, God is great, mighty and exalted!

One problem with this brief description of Pentecostal belief is that the adjectival descriptions – like great or glorious – do not uniquely describe the essential Jesus, Holy Ghost or God. These adjectives say what the divines are like, but not what their true nature is. God is not greatness even though the godhead appears as great; while God is might, mightiness is not intrinsic to the character of God. While these adjectives must be accounted for, they do not define distinctive features for any one person in the Godhead, or even for the Trinity as a whole.

Certain predicates have greater importance. Statements like "God is love" and" Jesus is a mediator" are more fundamental to the structures constructing the Trinity. Why? The terms love and mediation are significantly situated in the system, likely expressing something basic about God. In analyzing the Pentecostal godhead's qualities, moreover, a difficulty exists in finding distinctive descriptions for each person that apply in some fashion to each of the others. Therefore, the problems of identity and its relation to the distinction in the Trinity must be solved so that appropriate relationships of terms and characteristics of the Divines can be discerned. While this problem is logically prior, its solution is discussed later; a less difficult task confronts us.

That task involves uncovering the structures or binary oppositions expressed in believers' descriptions of the godhead. The first opposition is singularity/plurality since God is both one and three. Male/female is a second — all three members of the deity are male and can be contrasted with Man, who in this scheme is female, especially in his role as a believer who is receptive to spirit and submissive to God. Director/agent is third since Jesus and the Holy Ghost do the will of God. Act/state is a fourth because God as a director is static while the two agents act to do God's stately will. Also, God is conceived as a state. That "God is, was and always shall be" confirms His static quality in contrast to His agent's acting character. Up/down is a fifth contrast, since God on earth also is in heaven. He is up where Jesus and the Holy Ghost are sometimes found in the world, which is below or down from Heaven. Furthermore, God as the father is generationally above His Son; again, the up/down contrast is relevant to the Trinity. Finally, Jesus is both spirit and flesh, an obvious opposition.

So far, then, we find a variety of oppositional elements within the godhead: Spirit/flesh, act/state, up/down, singularity/plural, and male /female. Act and state establish differences between the Lord and the two other godly persons. Male and female at the least imply a difference between the whole godhead and man, who exists in the female flesh. Spirit/flesh distinctly characterizes the Holy Ghost and Jesus in that both are spirit- flesh with an emphasis on the flesh in each. But Jesus, a corporeal person, is marked in the flesh while the Holy Spirit, an impregnator (of flesh, thus primarily of flesh), is marked in the Spirit.

160

The Lord is also composed of spirit and flesh, His personage is principally spirit in the above portion of the Trinity while also unifying with the two other personages through the flesh level below. He then is spirit and flesh and this distinction is itself a quality, God. He further connects with the flesh aspects of the other two personages through their common spirit and flesh nature even if they are both essentially of the flesh. God above is spirit, and His flesh is in the flesh below and the two below personages are spirit and flesh. The unity of these personages can be confirmed in the common differences of spirit and flesh each share together.

That is, God is composed of Lord and Jesus/Holy Ghost. Spirit is expressed at the level of the Lord, and flesh at the level of Jesus and the Holy Ghost. Hence, we have:

<u>spirit</u>
flesh

in the overarching structure of the Godhead and this is repeated in the personages of Jesus and the Holy Spirit, each being composed of spirit and flesh while differing as spirit and flesh. So, again to repeat, their unity in the Trinity can be confirmed in the common differences each express. Moreover, these differences are not differences in the Godhead, they are identities.

In other words, a spirit and flesh distinction takes the form of spirit-flesh, for Jesus and the Holy Ghost while the top and bottom of the Trinity likewise are linked to God in the spirit, who is constructed of spirit with the (spirit)-flesh of the personages below. Still, issues remain undescribed in this binary construction of God's characteristics. Why are Father and Son terms used? Where do the oppositions analyzed so far come from? And how do they work together to characterize the Trinity (apart from seeing the distinctions as identities working together as described above)? Finally, are there more binaries constructing the characteristics that the godhead expresses? If so, how might these join in concert to characterize the Trinity?

A preliminary answer to these four questions must consider the Pentecostal conceptions of the Trinity in the context in which God is known to believers. This context is historical and spans the events believers describe in Old and New Testament times. The events at Jesus's crucifixion are most important here (described elsewhere in this book) but the appearance of various divine personages in eschatology cannot be disregarded. This history reveals an underlying, analytically discernable, binary oppositional relationship of Jesus and the Holy Spirit. This history shows their structural identity by way of a "reversal" of one another's structure, and it shows the fullest view of oppositional relations (including several new ones) in the character and organization of the Trinity.

Our starting point is Mary and the virgin birth, which involves an important spatial opposition: up/down or above/below. Mary is the mother of Jesus on Earth. She is, moreover, a virgin and without sin. She has been impregnated by the Holy Ghost who has come to Earth from above. This downward, earthly movement of the spirit is a divine act that will be reversed by the heavenly movement of divinity as the cosmology unfolds.

As a virgin, Mary is in the flesh but is not drawn to it and so is without carnal taint. Thus, the Holy Spirit can impregnate her, since the Holy Spirit can only go to an appropriate vessel, a pure and sinless body in the spirit. The Holy Spirit moves towards its likeness in Mary so that Jesus is born without sin or carnal relations. He, therefore, is in the spirit even though He exists as a man in the flesh. He lives, teaches, suffers, and dies. More important here is His death and resurrection. These events are crucial according to believers since Jesus' sacrifice is central to a great historical transformation. With Jesus's sacrifice, man's relation to God changes; the time of the Jews ends, and the possibility of grace now exists in the world for all people.

According to believers, after Jesus died on the cross, His body was placed in a cave. Caves, interpretively speaking, are neither above nor below ground, just as the cross was in the air, but is neither fully above (like Heaven) nor below (like ground or earth). In the cave, He was enclosed, while on the cross He was exposed, although neither state was complete: Jesus never went below ground but He was raised from the dead on a Sunday morning and was seen by women, among them several Mary's. Upon the Resurrection, Mary Magdalene tried to touch Jesus, but He would not let her. She, of course, had been very much in the flesh but Jesus only said that He must return first to his Father since He had not yet been glorified. Jesus then ascends to heaven.

He goes, then, from Earth to Heaven, from the down to the up, but He returns, though uniquely transformed. When he returns, His flesh is spiritualized – it is flesh but spirit also, immaterial yet real. Jesus can walk on water and eat food. He is seen periodically by the apostles who used to see Him constantly and it is not clear where He is all the time. Sometimes He is in two places at once, and possibly He alternates between the above and the below. After forty days of these appearances, Jesus goes straight up to heaven. Ten days later, the Holy Ghost comes down into the world, greeting the faithful in an upper room. In this event, known as the Pentecost, He evidences His acceptance in the believer's heart by way of glossolalia. The Holy Spirit is the only earthly agent of the godhead for Pentecostals today, and He has initially descended to Earth from Heaven. This series of divine events reveals a crucial Pentecostal opposition.

The series of events leading to Jesus's ascension involves overcoming the bondage of the flesh and receiving the liberty of the spirit within a system where untransformed flesh naturally goes to flesh – normal mortals in the flesh die (dust to dust, ashes to ashes and human flesh to dust and ashes in its decomposed nature). But Jesus is saved and transformed at the cross and this is the key to seeing the most important structural process of Pentecostalism.

Thus, the aim of this recomposing, transformational process is nothing less than the Christian answer to the question of death and the problem of immortality. Death is an end to life, and since this system wants to establish life beyond death, and sainthood after this sinful life, it must posit that a mortal, fleshly person can have creaturely immortality only if the opposition between the flesh and the spirit is resolved. Jesus illustrates "the way" this transformation is affected.

At the cross, Jesus the man puts his flesh down to be spiritually uplifted. He bleeds and dies to be transformed and enters heaven in an appropriately "fleshly" state of spiritualization. Jesus is both flesh and the mediating spirit (flesh-spirit); He goes up to heaven where His flesh must be glorified or spiritualized yet again in the Spirit. The rule of spirit to spirit permits this (the process of transformation and its rules of like going to like are discussed in the essay on "Transformation, a new approach"), the fullest spiritualization of His flesh. Jesus in his forty-day return is spiritual and real. He is fully or perhaps doubly transformed: flesh to spirit and spirit to flesh.

In the new dispensation of grace, moreover, the Holy Ghost is below, mediating through the flesh while Jesus is above, sitting at the Lord's right hand, pleading to God on man's spiritual behalf. The Holy Ghost is on earth to impregnate individual souls (be they men or women) though in the flesh, they have a speck of spirit, and so can be soulfully impregnated) and to begin the personal cycle of spiritual growth which Jesus undertook.

Both Jesus and the Holy Ghost are mediators, but their historical and spatial positions in the cosmology are appositionally related. In Jesus's case, He is a man in the flesh. He can lay low the flesh so that His spirit (as a man he is composed of flesh and spirit – He is the spirit in the flesh) can rise. By giving believers the cross and his fleshly sacrifice, others can do the same, and follow in his way so to speak, to lay low to rise high. In this, He is a mediator, showing others who identify with him how it is done. By way of human identification with Him, through their similarity in the flesh/spirit, He acts as a mediator, bringing his structure and transformation to believers through their likeness to him. Through their likeness, they affect a difference, a transformation.

In this regard, the Holy Ghost, by being down (on earth) when Jesus is up (in Heaven), shows his oppositional character (up/down). The Holy Spirit also is a mediator in the sense that He amplifies the spirit in the new believer, by bringing his spiritual insemination to bear while the believer lowers his flesh. Between Jesus and the Holy Ghost, the believer is immersed in structure; he or she is immersed in flesh and down, spirit and up.

While both Jesus and the Holy Ghost are mediators, their historical and spatial positions in the cosmology are oppositionally related. In this regard, as oppositions, one going down while the other is up, one marked in the flesh while the other is marked in the spirit, their difference does two things. First, it expresses the basic transformation Pentecostalism wants of believers, to go from flesh to spirit. Secondly, since they are different, it is this difference that needs overcoming in the

164

unity of the Trinity. Thus, the problem of being in the flesh, which believers in the flesh overcome, exists in the Trinity as well. The different Jesus and the Holy Ghost must become one in the spirit; the fundamental problem undertaken in conversion exists in the Godhead as well.

So how does the Trinity resolve this difference? It expresses a third term, God, who also exists in spirit and flesh, spirit above undistinguished from flesh below:

spirit
|
flesh

Here the flesh below is divided/united by Spirit or rather Spirit over flesh to the right and Flesh over Spirit to the left. In other words, the Holy Spirit exists at the flesh level of this Godhead, itself composed of flesh and spirit. It emphasizes the spirit where Jesus is on the left, Himself composed of flesh and spirit, emphasizing the flesh. Both Jesus and the Holy Ghost are likewise composed of spirit and flesh in a way that expresses their unity. They are not spirit/flesh but flesh-spirit, or spirit-flesh. So, the entire Godhead is composed of an identical difference expressed as a unity, which establishes the common difference or unity of the godhead. The whole complex is God and, to repeat, we see a difference in the basic structure of God repeated as spirit and flesh in both Jesus and the Holy Ghost below. We see common differences, first in the overall structure of the Trinity and then in the individual composition of Jesus and the Holy Ghost. These express an identity of unified differences. Hence, we have a monotheistic Trinity, a singular God. And it is a God composed of identities and differences – common differences!

But this isn't all and I would like to further explore the character of Jesus and the Holy Ghost, using the up and down distinction previously mentioned to better understand their placement in the Pentecostal story of salvation. As has previously been established, these two persons are dynamic reversals of one another. In other words, despite their opposition within the cosmology's diachronic, these two entities are identical. Both are spirit and flesh as they are known to people. However, they are distinct; and this is further expressed by way of the above/below opposition. For example, the accompanying chart characterizes Jesus' birth and death. The direction of the Holy Ghost and Jesus are in opposition, just as birth/death are opposed.

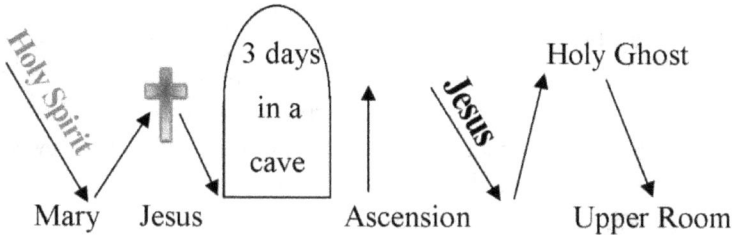

ILLUSTRATION 6

Jesus's rise from the dead, His giving His flesh over to spirit, His initial and major transformation of His and humanity's possibilities reverses the Holy Spirit's mediation of flesh and His impregnation of Mary. Where the Holy Spirit descends to impregnate flesh, Jesus ultimately rises to be glorified in heaven. Proving reverse, Christ's final ascent is complemented by the Holy Spirit's descent.

The opposition between these two entities, then, uses the above/below distinction and others to establish a spirit/flesh antithesis. Jesus as the fleshly representative of spirit is the opposite of the Holy Ghost as the spiritual representative of spirit. Yet the opposition between Jesus and the Holy Ghost can be written to show identity: The Holy Spirit is the spirit in the flesh (when He is known) while Jesus is the flesh in the spirit.

One condition of this identity that asserts difference is that as mediators, both Jesus and the Holy Spirit act on behalf of God. Where Jesus and the Holy Ghost act for God, the God term, which is distinct, gains the unique character of a state. Further, Jesus and the Holy Ghost transform for the Lord: God Himself is not an actor who transforms personally for humankind. Thus, God in contrast with the other divines takes on the binary character of a non-transforming transformer who principally deals with and directs action like the creation of a pure and sinless world. Thus, the unity of the Father's distinct if necessarily inarticulate character is further defined by poles of the act/state and transforming/not transforming (for man) dichotomies.

And there is more! More specifically, since 'God is the be-all and end-all,' God's resolution of distinction into unity must include other Pentecostal oppositions such as male/female.

Its resolution in God is complicated and relates to eschatology. As stated earlier, the figures of the godhead are all male, so fully resolving gender in the godhead involves introducing something female into the divine. Perhaps male Jesus who is God's servant could be viewed as female because he is in the flesh and in this way the female of male/female is incorporated. But in Pentecostal eschatology, that is, in its account of the end of days, we have an explicit incorporation of the female into the male God. This implies that it is believers who are incorporated, it is believers who are the followers (female) of God's manly authority, it is believers who have received the Holy Ghost in their hearts and who are saved; it is these people who become at one with God in this end time. They become as God themselves. Those now divinized human beings were impregnated earlier with the spirit and had joined the Church which is married to Jesus. This female element, these saved believers now are as God themselves. In the end of days, when Pentecostals say history has reached its conclusion, Pentecostalism incorporates and resolves the female spouse of the church by way of its formerly in the flesh (female) individual believers entering into the now even more whole godhead. Thus, the male/female opposition contributes not only to the ultimate character of God which includes them; it also helps direct the structured diachrony of Pentecostal history.

Another fundamental, Pentecostal opposition is the in/out contrast which also contributes to the character of the godhead by giving the godhead an interior character. How so? Realize that the Deity is in a spiritual domain and not in nature or the world at large. Since the world at large is defined in Pentecostal as the outside or external world, it follows that the spiritual realm has an internal aspect. This internal aspect relates to the godhead's singularity in which distinct figures that are in some sense historically external to one another are unified timelessly in one another. We see internal-external in the Trinity. Each member of the deity is predominately in the other even though each member is also external to the other. This "in" quality defines a unity; there is a unity of in-ness in the context in which the distinctiveness of the divines should be viewed.

God, moreover, reflects the resolution of spirit/flesh by His unifying and internal nature. He reconciles the two distinct and articulate persons of the Trinity by being at one with both. That is, He is internal to and identical with but different from Jesus and the Holy Ghost. He also is unknown; He cannot be described since the articulate poles of the system's principal opposition, spirit/flesh only clearly apply to His Son and His Spirit. Moreover, the other categories of the system are inarticulate to believers: state/act, male/female, internal/external. These are unconscious structures for believers in a typically structuralist sense. They are as invisible as sentence structure, whereas the spirit/flesh contrast is used with awareness by Christians on issues of a religious nature. Thus, the Son and the Holy Ghost may have relatively detailed characters, known to informants through the principal contrast. But God, mediating between the fully articulate categories or oppositions of the system cannot be adequately described in these terms. Perhaps the Jewish Scripture (not believers) described God's distinctiveness best when it said, "I am that I am" (though it is perhaps better translated as "I am what I will be")

God the father, however, is known to people in the time of the Jews. He is known only in a very indistinct way - He has no form in the Jewish Scriptures -and for most Jews of that time he is known only from a great distance. Thus, God is to the Jews as Jesus and the Holy Spirit are to Christians. That is, close and far are incorporated here in the Trinity and this incorporates a division of Jew/Christian. It expresses the Jewish distance from an indistinct God compared to the personalized presence of Jesus and the Holy Ghost in the Christian period. The godhead encompasses the Jewish and Christian Lord, with three divines being as one — God the father being associated, however vaguely with the time of the Jews.

168

Moreover, just as the spiritual realm is inner and above, the Trinity also involves the individual/collective opposition. Clearly, the persons of the Trinity can be thought of as partly individual. This is especially true of the Holy Ghost and Jesus when they are agents of God on earth. When the godhead is viewed purely as above, this individuality may become a collective unity. God is one with three persons and the persons, while collectively whole, are also discrete. The plurality in the unitary godhead articulates the individual/collective structure reinforced by the above/below structure.

However, one key to how the Trinity's structure works principally lies in the spirit/flesh and up/down oppositions. These two oppositions with four poles produce the threeness of the Trinity – and illustrate how structure produces a triune God. These two oppositions provide the framework, illustrated in the diagram, in which the oppositions in the Trinity form a triadic unit of diverse characteristics.

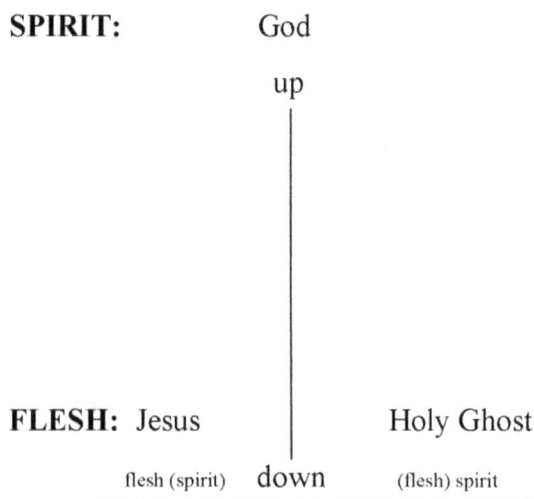

SPIRIT: God

up

FLESH: Jesus   Holy Ghost

flesh (spirit) down (flesh) spirit

ILLUSTRATION 7

The four poles of the spirit/flesh and up/down oppositions form a triad and each point of their combined structure is articulated by a divine. The triad also articulates a total or singular divine personage, with each godhead person expressing the constituting structural elements spirit and flesh of the whole.

A structural accounting for the Trinity must also include more elaborated or structurally diffuse believer ideas – and this structural framework here helps explain many of the adjectives informants used to describe the various divine persons. These were acquired in the ordinary course of attending church each Sunday. I approached church as a new believer might. I learned what believers thought was important for me to see and hear. I heard endless adoration with adjectives like great, mighty, all-powerful, and exalted. In the interpretation given here, these reflect encompassing aspects of the Trinity. The diagram on the preceding page suggests that the Trinity reflects and organizes the oppositions that structure all the items touched by Pentecostal thought, including work and family relations. (The existence of the family's structure in the Godhead's structure is discussed below.) Hence God's encompassment of such fundamental, underlying principles gives a 'most' quality to Him, hence the descriptive adjectives which appropriately describe the greatest and the best. The point, for now, is that God encompasses or expresses the structures found not only in religion but also in kinship, giving him a majestic presence, one that is great and complete and full, the adjectives about God's greatness and majesty stemming from His structural wholeness.

Furthermore, the diagram shows that the Trinity is composed of structure organizing structure, for example, up-down organizing spirit and flesh. This doubly structured or processed condition gives rise to adjectives that stress the terms fully transformed quality. God is sometimes referred to by informants as "honey in the rock" as is Jesus who is also called sweet Jesus. It, therefore, seems appropriate to link His sweetness with honey. Significantly, honey is a fully transformed (red) substance – it is processed and highly refined. And Jesus is a man of the flesh in the (white) spirit, His flesh being eventually fully transformed or processed into spirit. Further, the phrase "honey in the rock" is also descriptive of God, who as we have seen resolves and is the sum of all differences. As stated, a transformed/untransformed difference lodges in the term God and in the phrase "honey in the rock "as well. Like a rock, God is the untransformed, (transformer). His spiritual transformation is made real in Jesus. It can be represented by honey, which is transformed, and therefore Jesus may be called sweet Jesus. He is a fully transformed, natural person just as honey is a fully transformed, natural substance. In this context, He is in God just as honey is in the rock. Both Jesus and God, especially through God's singular encompassment and his untransformed transformer character, are appropriately called "honey in the rock". Rocks, unlike honey, are untransformed.

Other descriptive terms for God, such as Father" or "love" can also be understood in structural terms. For example, if Jesus is love and if Jesus is the spirit in the flesh, then love as a relational term should tie together qualities of the flesh and the spirit, which it does in "pure" and "carnal" love. We see this in marriage where a spirit-flesh unity is constructed into the bride and groom where there are both acts and states of love, a unity of coupling that mirrors the Godhead's spirit and flesh. Love then is a unity of spirit-flesh; certainly, we see this structure in the Trinity. The God term by itself contains the structure spirit-flesh. Therefore, God can be love. Jesus is love. As for the description of God as Father, the structural basis for the Father term, as the previous chart indicates, shows that God is associated with up where Jesus is associated with down. Fathers are obviously a generation above their sons, who are their descendants down in time. If God is up in this relational system, He may be called Father relative to Jesus. The father term is from the kinship relational system, but it has the same structure for father in the flesh as we see for father in the spirit. The one domain repeats the other in its relational terms because they are composed of common differences of spirit and flesh, up and down. Jesus in turn being below God may be called a son as a fleshly representative in the godhead, who thereby links to God by way of kinship and religion, which commands common terms.

One question this analysis raises is: Does a term from the kinship domain exclusively express up-ness or can terms in the religious or even political domain do this as well? The answer is partly that God is also called King, so upness in God is commonly expressed in a political domain. Yet, the kinship connection is especially crucial because it gives rise to other questions. First, why do Pentecostalism and the Trinity, in particular, have the structures discerned in this analysis? These structures include act/state, male/female, in/out, and up/down. Second, given these structures, why does the Trinitarian godhead encompass them – is this necessary and/or arbitrary way of organizing their oppositional character?

Turning to the initial question – how can one explain the presence of these oppositions, I believe the answer relates to this: As the use of the word Father for God suggests, the kinship terminology and especially family relations bear upon the meaning of Pentecostal ideas. An examination of the cultural construction of American family relationships will shed light on the structures used in Pentecostalism.

I use David Schneider's cultural account of <u>American Kinship</u> as the principal basis for this examination. Schneider notes that intercourse between spouses sets the parameters for what constitutes a nuclear family. That is, the traditional family unit is defined by a state of marriage between people of different genders who may properly have acts of intercourse to produce states of relatedness between themselves and their offspring. So, intercourse is central to the scope of the family. In its founding act and subsequent state, the family finds itself meaningfully organized by an act of love/state (of relatedness) opposition. The people who are married and who have intercourse, moreover, are male and female, a relationship meaningfully organized by the opposition male/female, which exists in nature as well as in culture. The intergenerational relations produced from lovemaking involve an ascending and descending generation: up/down in structural parlance. Relations between parents and children involve one group, the parents, helping the other to "grow *up.*"

Thus, for American kinship, or rather traditional family relations, the act/state opposition relates to the male/female opposition and to the generational up/down opposition at play when there are children. Marriage, moreover, is in the spirit, it is a spiritual union as is made clear in most, even secular marriage ceremonies. Informants also perceive marriage as meaningful or in the spirit. This meaningful spirit sanctifies private acts of intercourse. Further, the married couple, who once were two fleshly or corporeal people, now in marriage and, having been transformed in the spirit, are joined as one. Their spirit/flesh personages, either as male or female, become united as male-female, through their common spirit and separate flesh. Hence, we see the spirit/flesh opposition at work, spirit-flesh unifying the differently gendered people who otherwise are principally and distinctly in the flesh. A married couple, moreover, stands together against the external world, -- internal domestic life as a collective unit is made meaningful by its contrasts to practical or economic domains, where people act individually and instrumentally in rational pursuit of self-interest. This contrasts with the collective sharing in family life. The spiritual nature of private couples and their collective posture vis-à-vis the external world embodies an internal/external and collective/individual opposition. Spirit's presence is suggested or at least articulates well here because spirit is internal. Believers also pointedly said that theirs were Christian families, suggesting that a Jewish/Christian opposition also differentiates family relations. More generally, informants use the term 'spirit' as the arena of religion while kinship is the arena of the flesh. This strongly connects religious and kinship spheres. The spirit/flesh opposition posited here between religion as Pentecostalism and kinship as in American family relations uses the key opposition of Pentecostalism. This suggests a systematically binary relation (spirit/flesh) between the two domains in which the structures common to religion appear in the family's meaningful or cultural oppositions.

As previously shown, the Trinity is constructed from spirit and flesh, up and down, internal external, Jew and Christian, and male and female. The existence of so many important Pentecostal structures within the American kinship family suggests a deeply structural relation of religious thought to family life. This relationship is not the social structural one Lloyd Warner envisions in "The Family of God " although we are witnessing a fundamental connection between the social, i.e. kinship, and the religious domain. There is of course a connection but it is not the one Warner proposed. Instead, the suggested relationship between kinship and religion is a binary structural one, governed by principals of cultural logic. The structures appearing jointly in Pentecostal and family life that we have shown are act/state, internal/external, collective/ individual, male/female, and up/down in addition to spirit and flesh. Religious thought, as demonstrated in the Trinity, is constructed of and organizes oppositions that are principal factors in American kinship concepts, as a structural interpretation of Schneider's work shows.

Religious structures build concepts like the Trinity through intensive use of structure. We see multiple oppositions working in tandem, demonstrating a more fully transformed or operated-on thought than one finds in kinship. Traditional kinship terms such as 'brother', do not combine structurally distinct features like in and out, Jewish and Christian, individual and collective in very complex ways. The term brother (or son) is simply a term signifying male difference from female in a flesh relationship that divides in two and that is descendent in the flesh from a singular, spiritually unified mother and father. Pentecostal terms come from more elaborated structural combinations of up/down, internal/external, act/state, male/female, etc. Take as examples Pentecostal ideas of God and history. Since religious terms combine more elementary structures than kinship terms, the source of Pentecostal structures could lie in binary family structure. For a set of structures to be taken two at a time to order or construct a religious idea, those structures must be present singularly. Collective /individual must be available to be combined with up/down in a religious idea, so the suggestion is that oppositions used in religion had first to be present through kinship terms so that they could be "abstracted" into religious representations.

Hence, we have an answer to the question about the source of the major structure found in the Trinity. They derive from kinship. Since kinship and religion are thusly linked, it is unsurprising that terms in one, like father, appear in the other. They have similar structures. While kinship prefigures religion, it is possible to think that this is no accident. Genesis tells us that the family stood at the beginning, not just of knowing, but also of religious thought. Perhaps for the story to be complete, religion derives from kinship as necessarily as flesh relates to spirit.

Having attempted to give an answer to the question, "Why these particular structures?" the second structural question is, "Why in the Trinity is there an encompassment or identity in a system based

174

principally of difference, on binary opposition or (in older terms) on dualism?" An answer can be found either through the reason the system itself provides, or it can be found philosophically. The Pentecostal reason is that God is viewed not only as a unity but also as the source of life and the end of history, where evil is eliminated, and saved people join in God as divine themselves. God as unity encompasses eschatological history at its end, especially for that surviving number whose character is consistent with salvation. This represents an act of exchange: God gave us the world and our humanity, but these gifts will ultimately return to and become at one with Him. The external world, independent of God and yet like His sanctified being, in the end of days reveals how all things internal and now external eventually find their resolution in God. Therefore, God as one encompasses history as well as all of life itself. He is the unity in diversity, the end and the beginning of the great chain of being, the singularity that creates all difference and resolves them as well.

While eschatological resolution stresses that humanity, a female entity, resolves its distinctiveness in the godhead, Jesus presages this final human resolution by His presence in the Lord. He, too, is part of an exchange: giving his body in death for eternal life in God. Like Jesus, people are fulfilled when they are returned to God. That Jesus was external to God, that is, in the world, also suggests that external/internal together are intrinsic to the Pentecostal godhead. The Pentecostal system rules that distinction from God exists, but that distinction, eventually resolves itself into divine identity. The earthly life of Jesus, for example, is at once distinct from God and resolved in Him not simply by way of crucifixion, but also through his ascent to and into the Godhead. The unity of the Lord exists in this system and all distinctions flow from and to it. God is the source, then, of all distinctions and he is a singular source in which they resolve. Pentecostalism tells us that unity is the beginning and endpoint, and all things flow from it and eventually to it. God makes possible distinctions and He resolves them; His unity is the condition in which created diversity exists.

There is, however, a logic behind the opposition difference/unity, which makes this system of distinction less arbitrary and more systematic. That is, distinctions exist only in relation to likeness and likeness exists only in relation to distinction. This logic applies to one distinction such as up/down which requires a quality like height, and it applies to combinations of distinction. They cannot relate well if they have nothing in common. Multiple relations of related differences meaningfully gain from the existence of a single likeness. This likeness allows for common differences to be in common, in order to form a system. Multiple differences must have a quality or identity in common in order to meaningfully differ from one another. The diversity of differences in the religio-kinship system, then, may relate to one another in an identity to enhance systemic coherence. Identity implies difference and identity or unity in this system may be established through a complicated relationship of multiple differences into one identity or God. The identity or character and even the literal oneness of the Trinity is established through this logic. Its differences which summarize the system of common differences give us the character of its monotheistic representations of God.

Further, for a system of common differences or distinctions to exist, the distinctions should be in relation to each other, or there could be no general commonality. There would be no system if all differences (along with their qualities) were unrelated. Distinctions can relate to each other in many ways, but if God is defined as the source of all distinction (since he is the Creator of unique things) then he may be the identity in which distinctions are related. Thus, a Pentecostal system of distinctions implies an identity, and this identity in God may provide the basis for all differences. It, therefore, follows that distinction may be found indistinctly constructed in God since His identity must be composed of indistinct distinctions, as the very existence of identity asserts. Or He could be all things, the most eternal, and the most glorious because all things or distinctions are in Him.

Within this context, distinctiveness has as its opposite, indistinctiveness, and since the external world is distinct from God, it follows that the internal domain of God or the godhead ought to be indistinct. What is indistinct are the distinctions composing God. That is, instead of spirit/flesh or up/down we get spirit-flesh, and up-down. God, then, expresses the structural principle, identity through indistinction in a cultural system involved with knowing. This identity is ultimately formed by the system's major relations such as spirit and flesh which are expressed as indistinctions in the Godhead and these differences expressed as identities relate to one another in the Godhead as well. God, therefore, is the encompassing backdrop of distinction in this system of common differences and the distinctions expressed as qualities or indistinctions give Him character as well. He is explicitly present, moreover, at the fringes of the system – either at the beginning, at the end, or the above. He is there because, at the fringes, identity or indistinction abides. At its borders, differences cease. God is described, therefore, as the beginning and end of history: He is encompassing and above, and His fullest negation is in the below, in the Devil who eventually disappears from Pentecostal history. Interpretively speaking, he becomes indistinct.

• • •

These observations about the Trinity, its structural character, and the explanation of how and why these oppositions work together as they do, lead to a broader statement about the nature of religious ideation. Thus, the final and perhaps most important question is, "What does a binary analysis of the Trinity as a religious or cultural concept or linguistic referent demonstrate, indicate or signify about religion in general and Pentecostalism in particular?" To formulate an answer, it is appropriate to consider Clifford Geertz's views on religion. Geertz's anthropological definition represents one of the most stimulating and certainly one of the most thoughtful conceptualizations since Durkheim. He writes:

Religion is (1) a system of symbols which acts to (2) establish powerful, pervasive and long-lasting moods and motivations in men by (3) formulating conceptions of a general order of existence and (4) clothing these conceptions with such an aura of factuality that (5) the moods and motivations seem uniquely realistic.

Geertz's definition of religion is concerned less with the specific content of religion than with its symbolic nature. In Geertz's work, this symbolic character is distinguished from social relations, from the social

177

constructions of social actors, and from their psyches. For Geertz, religion is loaded with symbols. Items representing broader meanings have an emotional and not cognitive imprint on believers. These may move social actors at a psychological level, which leads to a mystified acceptance of a reality more true and real than the symbolism itself, namely the actor's social world.

One difficulty here is the narrow definition of symbolism. This definition differs sharply from one where the symbolic is culturally organized and thus is the whole *form* of myth, social action and social life. Geertz offers us a native theory of symbolism that concentrates on a certain use of representational vehicles, like winks or flag. He does not appreciate the equally symbolic or structurally organized aspects of social relations and religious systems. He would see the Trinity not from the viewpoint of its construction and its binary social logic which also creates social relations such as mother, father, sister, and brother. He only sees religion as something besides itself, as something that lends moods and motivation to men and women. Geertz's point of view is Weberian, especially in his concentration on the power of symbols to motivate and impose order in individual minds. He does not approach religion as an autonomous symbolic form with a character independent of its social use.

A problem here is that symbolic systems do less to motivate individuals and build moods to convince people of a system's cogency than they do to cognitively orient those who use and live the sense of a particular system. Religious systems are not imposed reality in an external sense in which a symbol evokes a response. Rather, they are an unconscious reality, a reality which often constructs the very ends, like salvation, which people as specifically constructed elements in these systems, like believers or Christians, may seek. Geertz defines religion as a system of symbols, not a symbolic system, and becomes vulnerable to Sperber's observation:

> The very notion of the symbol is a secondary and cultural development of universal phenomena that is symbolism. (t)here is no need for an analysis of the symbolic phenomena into symbols. The notion of a symbol is not universal but cultural, present or absent, differing from culture to culture, or even within a given culture

Pentecostalism is a witness to Sperber's point, having its own notion of the symbolic and not making the distinction between symbolic and social action, a distinction that Geertz subtly endorses in his definition. Within Pentecostalism, a contrast exists between the symbolic and the real, a distinction that counterposes symbolic water baptism and real Holy Ghost baptism. This use of symbolic/real within a realm of so-called symbolism demonstrates the cultural boundedness of the term symbol. It shows how its social scientific use can violate native reality. Treating the Holy Ghost baptism as a symbol misses the native significance and ignores its Pentecostal construction. Such treatment violates the believer's point of view, imposes a foreign order of conception on the cultural system, and distorts the nature of the data.

The internal construction and significance of the Holy Ghost baptism may tell us how such a baptism works and may more closely conform to the nature of such cultural symbolism. This Geertzian use of the symbolic, which he opposes to social action to which it lends moods and motivations, is an arbitrary analytic device that does not adequately consider the social action formed by symbolic systems or the character of symbolic systems in social life.

Instead, Geertz assumes that symbolic, religious orders impose themselves in individual minds, suspending them in Weberian webs of significance. These become reality for social actors through symbolism's power to evoke and mystify. But symbols and symbolic systems do not necessarily relate to individuals through their ability to create nonpragmatic ideals and moods that individuals might not otherwise rationally pursue. Nor do religious systems necessarily link to objective social circumstances and to an objective need for an explanation either of suffering or good fortune. Instead, theodicies of suffering, for example, define the experience and the possible implications of how people see themselves and their terrible circumstances. The eye is the organ of tradition, and in Pentecostalism when the problem of evil is addressed, suffering (my term) results from sin and being in the flesh. Weber's and Geertz's pragmatic notion of individual experience, as in suffering, hardly applies. It is a different order of conception. Since misery of the flesh is opposed by joy in the Lord, it has a peculiarly Pentecostal character.

A religious system such as Pentecostalism is not an externally imposed general order of existence or cosmology that analytically and empirically integrates with a specific pattern of social and individual being in the world. Nor is Pentecostalism an analytically and empirically "detachable" cosmology that makes meaningful sense of a social life that is fundamentally at another level of existence. Instead, bundles of elements in religion and social system are constructed from the same unconscious cultural patterns and structures. The symbolic forms of social action, as well as its collective representations, are the cultural idioms of social life. They are not the products of individual experience which informs and is informed by the pattern of social existence and ideology found in the individual's society. The cultural system does not become native reality through the evocative powers of a symbol that fits into the individual's social reality; rather, it is reality because it constitutes the very form of social life.

In other words, no qualitative difference exists between the construction of what has been distinguished as symbolic and social levels in Parsonian and other social theory. The category symbol, as used by Geertz, does not exhaust or comprehend the arbitrary and yet systematic organization of social-cultural forms like religion. The key to defining religion as distinct from social life lies not in the assertion of distinctive levels composed either of ideas or acts; instead, it is manifested in the assertion that the symbolic forms of social and religious life are crafted differently by an underlying and common social logic.

A brief, interpretive look at Schneider's American Kinship reveals that religious conceptions like the Trinity are more the products of structures organizing other structures than are terms like father or sister. These kinship terms fix oppositions such as act/state, and up/down in a straightforward manner. The Trinity reveals the up-down, spirit-flesh oppositions working together, while in kinship these structures organize in a simpler manner, love and generational relations. Having established the link and noticed the different use of common differences in kinship and religion we can pursue a structural definition of religion.

Let us build up a line of thought to make this definition. First and clearly, a religion like Pentecostalism involves the organization of the social (kinship) system in the construction of religious ideas. These ideas exist primarily in a representational and non-empirical sphere. By contrast to kinship, there are fewer concrete and practical constraints on representations. Possible combinations of structure may work together in religious representations that would not be referential or normatively desirable in ordinary social activities that kinship may address and define.

That is, religious thought organizes itself by its own principles. It amounts to oppositions on oppositions fixed in terms while kinship organizes along a more empirical line. Religion, moreover, organizes the organizing forms of social life by their organizing principles. If Pentecostalism as practiced in the church in which this study is based is a fair example, then religion involves the major principles of social organization. These elaborate themselves, so to speak, where even their metacharacteristics are stated in the representational constructions of religion. An example of metacharacteristics expressed in the religious domain would be the common Pentecostal statement, "you must be transformed". Transformation is a structural process here and is presented as a metastatement within the religion's language. Further, religion uses organizing social principles like transformation or act/state to build and represent religious tropes. Religion is the more representational medium of structure and religious tropes resulting from structures operate on themselves as in baptism, unrestrained (relatively speaking) by the practical and necessary limits of life in the empirical world.

Pentecostalism, then, clearly involves structures used in kinship but it resolves their oppositions according to goals and transformational possibilities within these structures. Its eschatology and Trinity witness the almost pure working through of structures operating on structures. Spirit/flesh is worked through by up/down for example to produce unity in God, heaven on earth, and flesh unified with and of the spirit. In this interpretation, the Trinity and other religious representations like eschatology are a 'lifting off (*Aufhebung*) of social meanings; here the religious categories think themselves, so to speak. Religion is social thought thinking itself, or social organization organizing itself. Religion is the nonsense of the world formulated by the non-sense as sense, and so, as Durkheim expressed it from a social viewpoint, all religion is true.

This neo-Durkheimian language leads of course back to Durkheim. If religion's structures both organize social relations and are elaborated through the underlying principles of the collectivity, then religion as a system of 'collective 'action and belief may organize actual social relations. That is, the summarizing of structures that occurs in religion may unconsciously represent, re-impress, reinforce, and/or coordinate a system of ordered social relations that may reproduce itself over time. Witness for example the inundation of male and female distinctions within spirit/flesh in the religious representations discussed so far. These, in this argument, act to encourage an abiding gender distinction and cognitive orientation in our Western cultural lives.

How structure summarizes itself in religion creates mind-inundating values and templates- creating structural models of, models for and models that are and become the system existing at the concrete level. These models consciously or unconsciously encapsulate the social representations forms of society. The Trinity is such a template in Pentecostalism.

Essay 14- Godheads

The God concepts, or godheads, found within mystical Judaism and Christianity are significantly related in many ways. There is of course a historical connection (Sholem, 1974 pgs. 96-97) but there is also a logical one, and it rests on a paradox. Both this Judaism and Christianity are dualistic religions. But despite this emphasis on difference or dualism, each religion tells us that their God is an identity, a unity, something beyond difference. How is it possible that unifying Gods exist in systems that can be principally characterized by difference? Why do both this Judaism and Christianity produce singular Gods when distinction is the most obvious characteristic of their thought? The paradox goes beyond this question, however, because each religion has a different idea of God (the ten *sefirot* versus the three-person Trinity). Yet both religions have godheads with essentially the same binary structures at their root. How is this possible?

To answer, we first must find these common structures and then show the differences they construct in their respective godheads. As noted in earlier essays in this book, I make plain what these common differences are. Spirit/flesh, male/female, in/out, up/down, and act/state structure much of the content existent in both religions. Here it will be argued that each godhead -- the Trinity and the God of Kabbalah -- gets its unique character or identity through different uses of the same structures such as male/female or spirit/flesh. As argued further on, these two Gods also differ from one another through these common oppositions: the male Jesus, as we shall see is countered by the female *Shekinah* of the Jewish mystical tradition.

The reader may not readily see how ideas or practices within the Western religious tradition like Pentecostal baptism or Jewish candle lighting, are structured or formed by common differences or binary oppositions like up/down or act/state. What follows is a demonstration of how these differences and their structures work to define different God representations. My focus here is the God of Kabbalah [bracketing out an actual God and only studying a Jewish representation of it instead]; my point will be to show how the structures of this representation relate to those of the Trinity. Let me give you the key structure for the Trinity at the outset. The Trinity is formed by a permutation of:

spirit
flesh

The spirit at the top does not divide but flesh, by contrast, does. Imagine that this flesh is itself divided by spirit/flesh. This may form a triad:

spirit
flesh/spirit

This is a Trinity[4] or a Trinitarian triad. The flesh forms the bottom of the triad, which is divided -- and mystical Judaism takes the flesh of the denominator and divides it also but not by flesh/spirit but by male and female to construct its Godhead and many of its representations. In an especially emphatic way, mystical Judaism genders the flesh of spirit/flesh. It gives us a God with Spirit as a male quality above in a triad that also has a mother and a father quality, or a male and female. It then follows this upper portion with a second portion in its Godhead. This second portion has a male quality or qualities in its above and a female quality in its below, the female being the most important in many respects. In this Kabbalist triad, we have a vertical triad, of a male portion (or spirit portion, also, as shown later, in a triad) with male and female in a second portion below. This is the structure of the Kabbalah godhead, in two parts, the top male, the bottom split between male and female. It is tripartite, like the Trinity and it uses gender where the Trinity uses flesh. The reader, being familiar with the Christian relational triad in the Trinity, will see a Jewish mystical God filled with qualities of male and female based on a similar but gendered spirit/flesh structure.

All this will be demonstrated by showing common differences within and between Godheads. But I jump ahead. I should begin with my choice to study the Jewish mystical Godhead and not the God of the *mignogim*, the central branch of European Jewish culture.

The main reason for this choice to study the mystical godhead was that it is possible to see the structure of this God because it has qualities that are clearly discernable where the main tradition, to which I belong, has a God that almost completely lacks content. This absence of content seems to be a deliberate choice of the mainstream tradition: the *mignogim* abbreviated its ideas of God sometime in the 19ᵗʰ century. It eliminated what it considered irrational elements to appeal to people under the sway of more scientific thinking. The scholar Gershom Scholem writes that a view of God called *Shekinah*, a feminine expression of the deity, was substantially removed from the traditional prayer book for this reason. By returning to an older and fuller notion of the Jewish godhead, we may see more Jewish structures at work.

Secondly, I wanted to study the idea of the feminine in the godhead. My initial theory was that since Judaism is a more flesh religion than Christianity, it should have a God that is more feminine than the masculine Jesus. While Judaism may not be a feminine religion by contrast with a masculine Christianity, a basically female entity, the *Shekinah*, which translates as God's presence, plays a prominent role in the mystical God. It is in contrast to the male Jesus, as highlighted later in this essay.

Kabbalah, of course, is a tradition that developed over an extended period of time. Its beginnings were in Provence, France in the thirteenth century, and it developed over hundreds of years. Since the mystical idea of the Godhead grew over time, a question exists as to what to study. Do we study the "images" of the mystical God found in the Jewish Gnostic fragments, or the *Mirkavah* visions, or the *Sefer HaTemunah, the Bahir*, the views of differing *Kabbalah* writers, or *the Zohar*? The diversity of these sources, moreover, raises a question. Is there one idea of the Godhead in the Kabbalah tradition or several competing ones? Do these texts offer unrelated insights into an idea of the mystical Godhead that simply differ or does the diversity of ideas demonstrate varying insights into a single "real" *Kabbalah* Godhead? What does one do with this diversity of views; what should we study?

Scholars such as Gershom Scholem and Elliot Wolfson assume that there is one Kabbalah tradition that was developed by a variety of thinkers, perhaps differently, but at least consistently. I accept this position; it agrees with expectations coming from my theory of common differences. That is, a common logic behind the Kabbalah tradition should result in a consistent stream of ideas, even if they differ over time. So, I will proceed here by appropriating evidence anywhere within the *Kabbalah* tradition that supports or disproves ideas coming from a theory of common differences. I understand that it would be more anthropological to find a time and place, say Prosteyav Moravia, (Husserl was born there) in the eighteenth century where many of my ancestors lived, and uncover the living Kabbalah culture there to see how it works semiologically. This would give us an actual snapshot of a real Jewish cultural life, while the method I am employing only looks to advance or disprove a theory. But, if and once the theory is supported, more pointed studies can occur.

And here in part is what a theory of common differences expects from the representation of God in the Kabbalah. Remember that the basic contrast between Judaism and Christianity is that of spirit and flesh. In other essays here, the point is made that religion (as a western concept) is in the spirit, and kinship (a native term) is in the flesh. The spiritual domain of religion can be further divided by the distinction of spirit and flesh and so there may be a spirit religion and flesh religions: flesh religions may themselves divide by spirit and flesh. Christianity as a flesh religion then was said to contrast to Judaism in a general way as spirit does to flesh.5 Both flesh religions are equally in the super domain of spirit but various aspects of these faiths exhibit qualities that are either more spiritual (like a preoccupation with salvation) or fleshier (like a preoccupation with the life of a people, its descendants and its kosher nourishment). In terms of Godheads, the argument here is that the Trinity emphasizes the spirit and the Kabbalah Godhead emphasizes the flesh. As already noted in previous essays, since spirit is associated with maleness, the flesh may be associated with the feminine. This suggests that gender is key to the fleshly and feminine themes one might expect to find in Jewish mysticism if its God contrasts meaningfully with a Christian one in a system of common differences.

If, for example, the Trinitarian godhead is dominated by spirited male and impregnating figures, perhaps the mystical Jewish godhead is dominated by its female qualities that get impregnated. Let's explore the spiritual nature of the male, Jewish, and mystical godhead to see if flesh and the feminine are its dominating themes. Let's begin with a logical contention: where the Christian Trinity is composed principally of spirit/flesh and is marked by spirit; the mystical godhead of Kabbalah is constructed more from the flesh element of this opposition. Remember that the Trinity is composed of:

<u>spirit</u>
flesh

in the following manner:

<u>spirit</u>
flesh/spirit

which is the personable triad of the Trinity:

<u>Father</u>
Son/Holy Ghost

The reader should be aware that the numerator here corresponds to Spirit where the denominator corresponds to flesh. Basic to the Trinity and the Christian tradition is the contention that Spirit is whole but flesh divides. The denominator divides flesh into two elements: Son or flesh, Holy Spirit or spirit[6]. If one were to imagine a tradition contrasting against this one, one could imagine a Godhead whose flesh was not being divided by spirit/flesh but instead by another opposition. Since flesh may be gendered, one could imagine it being divided instead by male and female.

I contend that in the *Kabbalah* God, male/female replaces the flesh element in the Christian Trinitarian structure and that a shift occurs regarding where this male/female structure is placed. This substitution and shift give the *Kabbalah* godhead its essential structure. Since this shift from the Trinity's structure is critical to this discussion, the Trinity is the point of departure: it consists of spirit and flesh, spirit above and flesh

187

below. Since flesh divides, it divides by the structure that defines the system: spirit and flesh, to yield the following structure:

spirit
flesh

which yields:

spirit
flesh/spirit

And then something more happens to this structure that goes beyond gendering flesh when the Jewish tradition handles it, and this relates to position or shape. As you can see, in the Trinitarian chart above, the FLESH flesh/spirit line is horizontal. Imagine instead, when it is expressed as male and female, that it is vertical (horizontal and vertical being binary oppositions of course). This gives the following structure:

spirit
flesh

which yields:

spirit
male
female

Here is this structure followed by an uninterpreted diagram of the Jewish mystical God:

spirit

male

female

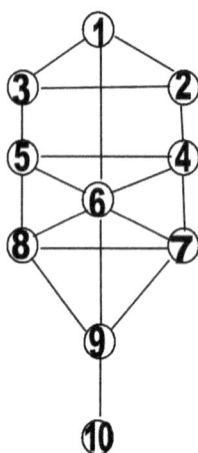

1. **Keter**- crown, will
2. **Chochmah**- wisdom
3. **Binah**- intelligence, understanding
4. **Chesed**- love, goodness
5. **Gevurah**- power
6. **Tiferet**- compassion
7. **Netzach**- eternity
8. **Hod**- splendor
9. **Yesod**- foundation
10. **Shechinah**- queen, presence

Sefirot

ILLUSTRATION 8

Sefirot are the qualities of the mystical godhead, and there are 10. Another word for *Sefirot* is *midot,* a Hebrew word for qualities. These qualities, unsurprisingly, have qualities that will allow us to analyze the godhead's structure. Overlaying the purely structural diagram above with the Ten Sefirot diagram displays the essential structure of the Kabbalah godhead. The top quality *Keter,* it is sometimes called *Ayin* or crown quality or *midot* of the godhead. It is commonly thought of as the spirit which is male and it has two immediately related *Sefirot, Chochmah* and *Binah,* understanding and the upper 3 portion consists of a spirit dominated triad:

<u>male</u>
male-female

189

This is further discussed below.

Then there is a second part of the godhead. It divides into male *Sefirot* and a female *Shekinah*. Wolfson makes the point that each of the *Sefirot* are both male and female, and one or the other gender is emphasized in their *midot*. The thesis here is that the bottom portion is divided by male and female marked *midot*, while the top portion is male, and it contains a triad. So, there is a singular triadic top and a triadic whole structure, with a male and female bottom portion. Again, this makes the godhead three-parted; it is identical to the three-parted Trinity except that it is different, gendered instead of fleshed, and vertical instead of horizontal. And it is filled with qualities, not relations, another contrast.   The chart above was created by my wife from various descriptions of the godhead on the internet and the chart I've studied for this essay comes from the Pritzker edition of the Zohar. I want to credit the introduction to that book for much of my understanding of the *sefirot* or qualities of the mystical Godhead, in case I have understated my debt in the discussion that follows. In any case, let's go further: since this structure is marked by gender, the feminine aspect of this structure, the *Shekinah* should somehow predominate in the bottom half. And of course, if it does, the most general structure of the Kabbalah Godhead would be:

male

female

which is a vertical declension of spirit and flesh in this system by gender.

So, here in these charts is a showing of my thesis: as in the Trinity, the basic spirit/male/female structure for the *Kabbalah* godhead is the critical basis for the Deity's unity. Male and female are commonly present in the top portion and in the bottom portion and in the overall structure giving identity by way of common differences everywhere. Thus, a triadic structure and a common binary distinction defines the unity of the Kabbalah Godhead much as a triadic structure orders the unity of the Christian Deity. Above all, this Jewish structure is a whole, even though its mystical division into upper and lower suggests two-ness. 7

Even the numbers of the qualities or sefirot of the Godhead work into the theme of unity. That is, to repeat, the *Kabbalah* mystical

Godhead is divided into an upper portion which contains three qualities or Sefirot and a bottom portion that contains seven qualities. So, how is this whole? In part this unity comes from the number of sefirot: 3 and 7 are each whole numbers in the Jewish tradition. But more is needed: each of the separate parts of this Godhead must "be the same". So, let's examine the top and the bottom to find unity or better, to find a replication of structure in its different aspects. This repeats what we have just done, but this is a deeper dive into the godhead.

Turning again to the top, we find the three qualities there forming a triad with Keter, as the quality at the very top. *Keter* suggests wholeness itself. It is singular or one just as 3 and 7 are. It is hardly distinct from the *Eyn Sof* from which it emerges. The *Eyn Sof* is the unknowable God that has no beginning and no end; it is complete. While it cannot be known qualitatively by itself, it is best characterized by Keter, the first *sefirot* emerging from it. *Keter*, which archaically means circle, likewise has no beginning and end and this further suggests wholeness. Moreover, the three upper *sefirot* form a whole just in terms of their number, which is 3. Three not only wholly forms an interrelated triad; it is a number of wholeness in the Jewish tradition: it is the number of Abraham, Isaac and Jacob. Here the three are called *Keter, Hochmah and Binah*. Then, there are the bottom 7 *sefirot*, which consists of two triads or two groupings of 3 *sefirot* and a lower or singular *sefirot* called *Malkuth* or *Shekinah*. This *midot* is divided into two (it exists in the godhead and in His Creation). This last is discussed in detail later. The point here is that 7 also expresses wholeness in the Jewish tradition. Seven is the number of days of the week as well as the number of days in which God created the world. He did this in six days, crowning His completed creation with the fullness of rest, of *Shabbat*, the seventh day, the day God rested. Thus, the godhead, at its most basic, consists of two groups; each one representing wholeness, and each also unites in wholeness.

Elaborating on this last point, the top three *sefirot* have a binary and Trinitarian structure which relates to an unknowable expression of the Godhead that prefigures all: it is called *Eyn Sof* which is expressed as *Keter*. *Eyn Sof* as *Keter* sits like a crown at the top of the Godhead, a static and ungendered king from which additional masculine and kingly qualities of God emerge. These qualities are knowable, unlike the King of Kings, and from Keter emerges the qualities Hochmah and *Binah*, a father and a mother. The former signifies wisdom and the later its reflection, which is understanding. Both are a refraction of the light of *Keter* from which they simultaneously emerge as a related pair. They existed as an intention of *Keter*, which has no content or form, and which can only be described negatively, that is, by what it is not. This definition by not (by difference) is, of course, the basic difference-making that particularly exists in the Jewish portion of the system of common differences. More pointedly, the creation of *Hochmah* is a movement from nothing to being. Significantly, *Keter*, the nothing, is not knowable, where *Hochmah* and *Binah* are forms of intelligence, mated and gendered spiritual qualities that contrast with those below. Like husband and wife, they are one, though distinct. And as husband and wife, they suggest the female flesh. They are the female pair in the triadic top portion of the Deity, which is male and is crowned by *Keter*.

This threesome forms a whole, on the top, a pure unknowable spirit or light, and below, a divided but mated pair, again suggesting flesh in the sense that they are an *abba* (father) and an *immah* (mother). *Binah* is the mother, the womb of all that comes below. So, analytically, in the top triad or trinity of the Kabbalah Godhead, we have this structure:

<u>spirit</u>
spirit/flesh

The *abba/immah* characterization of the *Hochmah* and *Binah* that compose the bottom row suggests that the spirit/flesh distinction in this godhead is gendered as male/female. The male *Hochmah* is logically prior to its companion *Binah*, and since *Binah* is the mother of all that exists below, there is a connection of *Binah* with descent: *Binah*, the mother, being down. Hence, the upper 3 qualities of the Kabbalah mystical God express the key structure of the whole godhead which were given at the outset of this discussion:

Structure:

<u>spirit</u>
<u>male</u>
female

Quality:

<u>Keter</u>
<u>Hochmah</u>
Binah

And, just as the Trinity expresses the structure of the kinship family which we have explored earlier, so does the God of Kabballah express the bride and groom in marriage, which is a remarkable structural similarity. But what is emphasized is not its structure or its relations but its shape. Most representations of the shape of the mystical Kabbalah Godhead represent the first three qualities as a triangle.

Returning to the triadic appearance of the upper godhead (which is complemented by a male female division between *Sefirot* in the lower Godhead), it is significant to note that one quality, *Hochmah* is on the viewer's right and the other - *Binah* - is to the left. These qualities are positioned or signified by a left/right structure in the godhead as well. Clearly, the qualities of these *sefirot* can be expressed horizontally as well as vertically.

This is all entirely in the spirit. All three qualities relate intimately to seminal intelligence which is inherently spiritual and the three *midot* (qualities) form a (triangular) whole just as spirit does at various places in this system. As already stated, the fleshliest aspect here is *Binah* and it is mother to all the godhead's lower qualities, yet her profound spirituality is made clear by her main quality, understanding. The unity of the spouses gives us a male-female connection, a binary difference understood as an identity, which is at one with the *Keter* from which they emerge. So, the three elements are one, though created from distinctions, which are distinctions unified in the spirit, much in the way that marriage is described in other essays in this book.

Let's turn now to the bottom portion of the godhead. Keep in mind that the top Spiritual portion has one King keenly united with its two other qualities where the bi-gendered bottom has six male qualities

193

(the actual structure of these male qualities is male over female, marked as male. This will be important to the unity of the godhead, in which all its elements, as in the Trinity, are composed of the same difference). These are separated from its lowest and seventh, which is the female *Shekinah* (which is also composed of male and female, being marked as female). There are six primarily male qualities below and these divide into two triads, which, is, of course, a double that again suggests completion. (See my essay on First/Seconds). As will become clear below, while there are 6 male sefirot, the female *Shekinah* is the source of the unity of these qualities and so casts a female and fleshly form to the bottom portion of the Godhead. But first to the male triads.

The first of these male triads is more important than the second. It consists of *Hesed,* the grace or love of God and it is counterposed by *Din* or *Gevurah,* the judgment of law or the force of power. These two counter one another: they are a pair. *Hesed* is the love that Abraham had for God; *Gevurah,* the fear that Isaac knew. They require a proper balance, and this is expressed in the middle by *Tifferet* which is sometimes called *Rahamin* (compassion) or *Mispat* (balanced judgment). *Tiferet* itself means or expresses the qualities of beauty or splendor. Importantly, *Din* is on the left, *Hesed* on the right and *Tiferet* is in the middle. All these qualities are predominantly male and the three form a triad. This middle is described as the central beam in God's construction of the universe. Jacob is another name for this quality in the middle and so we have the structure of left and right mediated by a central beam or stairway in the middle of the Godhead. Tiferet resolves the tension between *Hesed* and *Gevurah,* between left and right, and between love and judgment.

Also, there is a second triad: *Netsah, Hod* and *Yesod.* Essentially, these *sefirot* are channels through which the light or seminal force, what has been called divine energy, passes on its way into the tenth *siferah.* This last is called *Malkhut* or *Shekinah* and it is the source of all life for the lower worlds, including creation which of course is external to God. *Netsah* and *Hod* are paired as a source of prophecy and little more. By contrast, *Yesod* is foundational; all godly force unites in him, the seminal force of the intellect in the upper mystical Godhead sending its energy through all the male qualities below, including *Netsah* and

Hod, which are likened to male testicles. This seminal force flows to *Yesod's* culminating phallus, which is in the middle of Godhead. The images of *Yesod* are sexual and he unites all the male force of the Godhead in his *midot*. "The seferotic process thus leads to the great union of the nine *sefirot* above, through *Yesod*, with the female *Shekinah*" (the Zohar, Pritzker Edition volume I pg. LI) which becomes filled and impregnated with the fullness of divine energy. She in turn gives birth, like *Binah* above, and her offspring includes the lower worlds, both angelic and human.

As with Holy Ghost impregnation (and this is a remarkable recapitulation), no sin abides in this act or in these *sefirot*; male energy is only fruitful and a blessing. It helps create the unity of the Godhead whose male/female qualities enable this coupling in the spirit. That is, the 9 male *sefirot* find their union and their fullest unity in their intercourse, through *Yesod*, with the female *Shekinah*. Since all the male *sefirot* aim at the *Shekinah*, she is their direction or intention and thus gives a female cast to the below portion of the Godhead. And this act of intercourse is perpetual, giving rise to a union based on an eternal act leading to a constant state. This act is the fulfillment of the entire seferotic system. The great union of the godhead is thus created and creates.

In other words, this union through intercourse is the act that unifies the godhead into one state. A Jewish thought system unifies its God through divine acts of the gendered flesh. Male and female unite as spirit unites them in marriage. It is a perpetual act (of intercourse) that forms a unified state. Upper and lower become one, in an act and in a state. This unity is over-determined moreover, with structural likeness between lower and upper portions of the Godhead further establishing identity in God. That is, if we imagine these male *sefirot* to be constructed of:

<u>male</u>
female

with the emphasis on their male qualities then each is identical. This is so whether the *sefirot* is explicitly gendered male or female or the *sefirot* is in the top or bottom portion of the Deity. The gender identity of all the *sefirot* as male and female is a point I've taken from Wolfson. In this, they are all identical, whatever their marking of gender differences (as either male or female). But these marked gender differences form a binary pair. The top portion of the godhead is male; the bottom portion is (intended as) female, as established in the unity of the intertwining intercourse of the male sefirot with the female *Shekinah*. Since the *Shekinah* is the focus of this unity; she gives the bottom portion its female cast.

Before further examining the 10 *sefirot*, another comparison with the Trinity is in order. The first point relates to how unity is constructed in the Trinity and how this is identical, in at least one respect, to how unity is constructed into the God of *Kabbalah*. That is, in the Trinity, the same binary opposition spirit/ flesh organizes the top and bottom portions of the Godhead. Again, this repeats in the personages of the bottom portion, the Son and Holy Ghost, yielding an identical difference in the two portions of the Godhead and in all three persons of the Godhead. In the mystical God of Kaballah, the top triad and bottom seven *sefirot* portions are organized by male above, female below. In the bottom portion, the six above are male and the seventh is female just as Keter in the upper portion is male in the spirit and the married couple below are in the position of the female flesh. This repetition of male and female portions in both sections of the Godhead also occurs in each of the 10 *sefirot*. Again, while gendered one way or the other, each *sefirot* is both male and female. So the common differences in the *midot*, as in the Trinity, establish an identity.

Secondly, as in the Trinity, we see a summarizing of critical meanings of the system in the mystical godhead itself. All these differences (and many of the qualities as we shall see later), which exist in the worldly expression of Jewish religious culture, appear together in the Godhead just as up/down, in/out, Jew/Christian and act/state exist in the construction of the Trinity. In the Trinity these appear as unities (act-state) and in God of mystical Judaism, these differences likewise emphasize identities.

As observed in the essay "Common Differences", these summarizing structures come from the kinship system, which are defined through the scope of intercourse between male and female spouses. That is, intercourse leads to children: the bonded father and mother, and their distinct children are the nuclear family. The family is composed of identity and difference. Intercourse defines the scope of the family and we see that it defines the unity of the Jewish mystical God as well. In the God of *Kabbalah*, we see the same structures existent in kinship, just as we do in the Trinity. And this includes the structures, act and state, male and female, and these constitute intercourse (as a representation or cultural trope).

To reiterate a key point: if the mystical Jewish Godhead summarizes kinship distinctions; intercourse should exist within the Godhead of the Jewish *Kabbalah* and it does. Where does it exist in the Christian narrative? Clearly, it is present at the Cross, where Jesus suffers his Passion in a spiritual act in which his flesh is put low to raise the spirit of those who come to God through Him. This narrative shows the less than obvious theme of intercourse in the passion of the Christ at the Cross. His passionate act reflects the subdued presence of the male/female theme in the Christian story. This subdued presence of gender is also reflected in the character of Mary. While Mary is impregnated by the Holy Ghost, her gendered character is so underplayed (as is His) as to make Jesus' birth virginal. Nonetheless, there is impregnation, and passion, though the gendered character of these is somewhat muted in Christian thought as is the male/female distinction.

Intercourse forms a part in both godhead narratives, giving weight to the idea that there is a similar process of aggregation in the godheads. The contrast between the traditions determines where these elements are found. Again, the Jewish tradition ought to be more in the flesh than the Christian one and this is more boldly expressed here. The Christian story has His passion not in heaven but on Earth. Likewise, the Holy Ghosts impregnates believers who live on earth, in "the below". Intercourse is separated from the heavenly character of God in the Christian tradition. But intercourse appears in the Divinity in this Jewish tradition. The intercourse of all the male *sefirot* above with the female *Shekinah* below is the dynamic act, the overwhelmingly obvious act which sustains the state of pure unity within the fleshlier Jewish mystical Godhead.

Let me elaborate, in a comparative way, upon the *Shekinah* which is at the root of this God's unity. She has no qualities of her own; she is merely receptive of the seminal energy and light of the *midot* above. (This is the very opposite of *Keter* above who is the source of light) From the standpoint of the Godhead, she is below, and her arousal stimulates and unites the above in an active embrace while she simultaneously is a refracted, enlightened and ruling presence in the below that she herself spawns. She is called, therefore, *Malkhut*, kingdom (of God). She is at one with the *Knesset Yisroel*, the community of Israel. She is the indwelling presence of God in the world, separated from her divine spouse, but a source of Life. She is a font for all blessings. Within the godhead, she is the source of its dynamic union. Within Creation, she is the separated divine that refracts God's light in the world. In other words, she divides in a binary way, being first in the Spirit in God and secondly in the world, being real in the worldly flesh, a feminine refraction of God in His creation.

This implies that the *Shekinah* is a mediator, a part of the Godhead, and apart from it in the created world. She is at one with this refracted creation which she birthed. She acts, therefore, as an entry point to the divine for people, perhaps all people, who live below on earth. That is, as a *Siferah*, (the singular for *Sefirot*) the *Shekinah* is real, the very fabric of creation, and so she advances the process by which God reveals Himself and makes His great name known. She has, therefore, a position between the transcendence of God and the immanence of creation. Her movement is both upward to God and downward toward the earth. As such, she is a mystical expression of the divine immanence in the world. The nine upper Siferah only operate in creation through the intermediacy of the last *Sefirah*, which has received their potency and light and created their offspring on earth. Therefore, the *Shekinah* is the light that has emanated from the Primal light and the whole earth is full of her refracted glory. The transcendence of the above immanently fills the lower world below. Yet, where *Shekinah* is active in the upper world of God, it is inactive on its own in the lower. And where the *Shekinah* actively forms a whole with the God above, it is passively refracted and scattered throughout the distinctions that characterize creation in the world below. This is entirely binary. And while this scattering and separation was the result of Adam's sin, it also can be viewed as characteristic of a creation that was, after Eden, separated from God.

Like Jesus, since the *Shekinah* is in the world, she presents a pathway to God. As God's presence, she is the mediator to the above. The purpose of Hasidic prayer is to excite the *Shekinah* and through this excitement, bring unity between worshippers, who collectively form Israel, and the divine. She is like Jesus, moreover, in that she can be viewed as embodied. This embodiment is expressed in the association of *Shekinah* with the word *komah*, which means form or body in Hebrew. Creation is, of course, formed, and the human form is a body. The body of the *Shekinah* is that of a bride, the marriage partner of God, in which the dynamic and flowing potency of her femininity animates the unity of the Godhead. At the same time, in her refracted birthing of creation, all the powers of the *sefirot* make their way, albeit scattered, into the world.

The *Shekinah's* birthing of a pathway to God means that she provides a way of relating or a relationship to the mystical Godhead. This relating, to reiterate, is analogous to the relating provided at the cross, the place of Christ's passionate act which also resonates with the central role of intercourse in establishing kinship or familial relationships per David Schneider's discussion of American kinship. The place then of intercourse as a central symbol in the two traditions confirms its link to a culturally constructed kinship domain and demonstrates that each is part of a common system of differences.

Significantly, the intercourse represented by and through the *Shekinah* likewise defines a marriage of God with Israel (Sholem, 1974 pg. 111), and connects its Jewish followers to God through Israel. Here Israel is the bride of God. *B'nai Yisroel* (the sons or children of Israel) re-enact this marriage of God and Israel on the Sabbath and thereby participate as Israel in worship or spousal-like devotion. So, since a Jewish believer belongs to the people of Israel, which is the worshipping congregation, he or she may embody or excite the *Shekinah* and therefore relate to God. The congregation congregates and God in turn relates. Israel acknowledges that God is, therefore God copulates. The Jewish Sabbath is the spiritual intercourse of God with his bride Israel which results in a state of spiritual rest or satisfaction for congregants who are the sons and daughters of this union. Israel then is akin to the body of Jesus in Christian systems whose offspring (Christian believers) were born of his Passion for his bride, His church. The symbolic intercourse in the Jewish godhead leads to the existence of the body of Israel in the world. Israel is composed of its sons and daughters - meaningful relatedness once again stems from an act of intercourse. This Jewish system, then, constructs relatedness in much the same way as in Christian and in kinship modes: we find chosen brides everywhere. The church - as the bride of Christ - and Israel - as the marriage partner of God - are both similarly structured. In this respect, there is nothing unique about the chosen Jewish people. The people of Israel are one chosen bride among many, though how this is so is analyzed elsewhere in this book. The centrality of passionate acts, moreover, and their consequences in each system not only constructs meaningful relatedness in the same way, they are clearly related permutations of one another. That is, each not only makes intercourse central to establishing a meaningful connection to God and to other believers, each does so with the same structures. These common structures include both act and state and male and female, each used to a different effect.

And, as previously observed, since the *Shekinah* is the divine presence in the world and a bridge between the upper and lower in the Godhead, she is also a mediator like Jesus. Like Jesus, she is, while distinct, the embodiment of the godhead as a whole. The structural process that produces this identity is also similar to Jesus, though the difference here again between them relates to the significance of the male/female distinction in the Jewish mystical tradition. That is, where Jesus is principally structured by the relations flesh/spirit below in the spirit above, the *Shekinah* is structured female/male below in the spirit above. The male characteristics of *Shekinah* have been studied by Wolfson among others. He writes, "While the *Shekinah* is female, its female emphasis does not preclude its definition from being the same as the other *Sefirot.*" As with the relationship between Jesus and the Holy Ghost, the flesh dimension, which in this Jewish tradition is defined as male/female, is spun or reversed to give a different emphasis of character. Where all the above *sefirot* are likewise defined as male/female distinctions in the spirit, their male character is emphasized, while for *Shekinah*, the female is most stressed. This occurs also with *Binah* above, but as the idea of impregnating *Shekinah* suggests, this feminine *Siferah* can spin its structure to emphasize its maleness even if the lower *sefirot* are characterized as her offspring.

Since the *Shekinah* has the same structure as all the other *sefirot* (the *ot* ending here is a female plural in Hebrew which then identifies all *sefirot* as female from the standpoint of human language and this would be in relation to *Ein Sof*, the unknowable male God from which the *sefirot* emerge), their identity is asserted. That is, they are all male/female in the spirit, whatever the order of male/female might take in *Binah* and *Shekinah*. The male/female character of each *sefirot* can be deduced logically. That is, they must be fundamentally identical to each other to form a whole with differences. And since there is a definite female aspect to two of the *sefirot* while the others are clearly male, the male/female opposition must be present in all, with the female aspect of two of them simply being emphasized. Beyond this quasi- logical conclusion, it is clear all are described as Kings, so they all have a masculine character. For *Shekinah*, the idea of *Malkhut*, of kingdom, again conveys a masculine aspect of a feminine entity. Elliot Wolfson confirms this male and female duality - he repeatedly asserts that *Shekinah* is a duality composed of male and female. In addition to the other ways unity in the Kabbalah godhead is established, we see unity even in the basic gender composition of a *sephirah*. This unity builder exists in the combination of male and female in all the *sefirot*. If the *midot* did not partake of the characteristics of one another, there could not be unity. The 10 *midot* are one—each has all the potencies of the other even as they are distinct. This unity of each *midot* is characteristically represented as a circle, a *Keter*, in most charts of the mystical Godhead even as each *midot* is assigned its individual qualities.

The Jewish mystical Godhead undifferentiates its separate qualities through a common form which is a circle. Therefore, the 10 circled *midot* are structurally identical and qualitatively different, solving in part the problem of their identity/difference. Their distinct qualities express an identical, subconscious structure. These qualities, moreover, are un-differences, so to speak, in part through another relation which has not yet been discussed, and that is left/right which logically has a resolution in the middle.

Common Differences Revisited/Godheads

In the mystical Godhead of the *Kabbalah*, the qualities or *sefirot* are aligned by left, right, and center. The center provides a balance between the opposites of left and right. Perhaps the best example occurs between *Hesed* and *Din*, which is sometimes called *Gevurah*. *Hesed* means mercy and *Din* means judgment and *Din's* synonym *Gevurah* means power. Where *Hesed* on the right embodies the qualities of the love and grace of God, *Din's* judgment is counterposed to it along with the power or *Gevurah* of judgment on the left. So, love and law are contrasted, one on the right, the other, the left, giving the God we love and the God we fear. Where *Hesed* marks the faith of Abraham, *Gevurah* names the fear of Isaac. In between, on the line from *Keter* to *Shekinah* is the quality of *Tiferet*, which means beauty, and which mediates between the virtues of *Hesed* and *Din*. *Tiferet* represents a proper balance between love and judgment and embodies the notion of *mispat*, which ordinarily means religious laws understandable by reason and which here means balanced judgment. It lies neither to the left nor to the right and is part of the central beam in God's constructed universe. It resolves the tensions between left and right, and the result is a quality central to Jewish faith: the idea of completion of personhood, the perfection of character and so is called Jacob, the person who finished or completed the triad of Jewish founding fathers.

Thus, a pure quality, founded neither on left or right nor on a difference of any kind, sits in the middle of the godhead, on a beam that extends from the top to the bottom, from *Keter* to *Shekinah*. Here is an un-difference in a system of difference, a point or line of unity and balance between left and right. And it is here, within this Godhead and here particularly, that qualities of the Jewish religion come for a summary. In other words, within the godhead, the symbolic personages and events of the Jewish religion, like the structures which clothe them with meaning, come together in the unity of God. Qualities crown relations: Moses for example uniquely enters the Godhead through *Tiferet*. More to the major point of the religion, the difference yawning between left and right, between *Chesed* and *Din*, is a place where Moses and his exodus may lodge. They lodge in the middle just as they did in the Red Sea. There, from a unified river a right and a left emerged and the Jewish people, in their full birthing glory, likewise issued forth from the middle. They did not go to the left or the right. This Biblical moment is paradigmatically foundational for Israel and it is summarized, here in *Tiferet*, in the godhead between left and right.

While the Jewish mystical godhead, then, demonstrates the same summarizing found in the Trinity, the content that is summarized, arguably, goes beyond kinship and into peoplehood, though peoplehood may also be a form of kinship, a form of meaningful social relating. The founding and seminal Jewish personages make their way into the Godhead, further showing that it summarizes social or Biblical relations.

This suggests that key Jewish qualities exist among the relations structuring the godhead. We find Abraham, Isaac, and Jacob just as we find Moses yet again between a cleft. Qualities (symbols) abound in Judaism and in this godhead; they contrast with the relations that are so predominant in the Christian tradition and deity. Where the Trinity is a summary of its relations, the Jewish mystical God is a summary of its qualities. While relations summarize in both godheads (and each produces a mediator, in the one case *Shekinah*, in the other, Jesus, and these last differ structurally as female to male) nonetheless a key difference between the Trinity and the God of Kabbalah is between relation and quality. Perhaps a contrast between the Christian Cross and the Jewish Star of David makes the point.

Where the Christian Cross is primarily a relation between two intersecting lines, the Jewish Star of David is a linking of two geometrical qualities, namely triangles. In the Cross, the relations between the lines dominate whereas, in the Davidic Star, the shape dominates. Both are constructed of relations, one between lines and the other between triangles, but, and the point is subtle but real, the lines of the cross relate, whereas, in the star, the qualities of the triangle connect. The first is marked for its relations, the second for its qualities. This last can be seen in its symbolic qualities that express wholeness: the Jewish star is made of a doubled shape. This suggests completeness and this further illustrates a triad divorced from relations and expressed instead as a quality or triangle, which naturally forms the star. In this case, it is a quality or a triangle rather than a relation that fundamentally forms the Star of David. The Cross, on the other hand, is literally a point of intersection between both man and God and heaven and earth. And an intersection is first a relation.

So, the Jewish mystical Godhead, while having a similar structural composition to the Trinity, also distinguishes itself by emphasizing qualities to Trinitarian relations. Again, the shape of a triangle is essentially the shape or quality of a relation. To elaborate again, in the Christian scheme - formed from spirit and flesh- we can imagine a declination of the opposition into a triad:

<u>spirit</u>
flesh

becomes:

<u>spirit</u>
flesh/spirit

If this triadic set of relations is expressed as a quality, it becomes a triangle in the mystical Jewish Godhead. That is,

<u>spirit</u>
flesh/spirit

becomes a triangle.

Thus, the same triadic relational structure is present, but as a quality. There are three such triangles in this Jewish Godhead, one between *keter-hochmah/binah* in the above and two in the lower *Shekinah*: *tifferet - gevurah/chesed* and *yesod-hod/netsah*. The above portion of the Godhead, like the structure of the declined spirit/flesh opposition, is singular, where two-ness, which is both split (one and then another) and whole, appears in the lower portion. The structures that characterize the below repeat those in the above; this further constructs the unity through an identity of the godhead's parts. These three triangles, unlike those in the Star of David, are kept separate; though by identity of structural quality, they form a whole. This hints at the presence of yet another important structure for both the Christian and Jewish deity: that of identity and difference.

In the Christian Godhead, identity/difference appears with Jesus (who embodies flesh in the spirit) and the Holy Ghost (who is the spirit in the flesh). Each is a different expression of identical relations; each of course embodies in the spirit a different emphasis on the spirit/flesh relationship. In the mystical Jewish godhead, this identity/difference opposition also appears, though it is expressed as a quality or a symbol. That is, this godhead is often represented as a tree, with its 10 *sefirot* ablaze in branches that are not consumed by the fire. Doubtless, this not only is an incorporation of the burning bush into the Godhead by way of expressing God as an untransformed transformer (on fire but not consumed), it also expresses the unity of the tree and the separation of its branches. Echoing back to Genesis and the Tree of Life, the mystical Jewish Godhead is symbolized by a tree whose qualities express identity (a full tree) and difference (its branches).

Thus, these qualities are summarized within the godhead and, arguably, they are present within this Unity because it is a concrete or flesh-like godhead, which has little in the way of barriers to most flesh elements within the system. This godhead even is embodied as a mythological person, the Adam Kadmon, whose body, like the tree, gives shape and flesh (expressed as a gendered male), to the *sefirot; yesod,* for example, being his loins.

While the summarizing nature of the mystical Godhead and its use of qualities to distinguish itself seem apparent, it is not obvious why some common elements in both faiths, like intercourse, appear either directly in the Godhead as in this Jewish tradition or somewhere else in the divine narrative such as at the cross and its passionate act in the Christian tradition. Again, the concrete nature of this Jewish God, filled with qualities, embodied by Adam Kadmon, symbolized by a tree, is more in-the-world than the spirit which animates the Christian emphasis. Jesus, for example, following His resurrection, required "glorification" of His flesh to return to Heaven. Perhaps the Christian emphasis on flesh that needs to be in the spirit creates a barrier that keeps more fleshly elements directly out of its Godhead.

Moreover, the near absence of gendered flesh[8] in the Christian godhead suggests that intercourse would be placed "lower" in the narrative. It would be situated here on earth and would be conducted by agents of God who are separated, while behaving thusly, from the unity of God's Spirit in heaven. Likewise, other important elements in this system of common differences are excluded from the godhead itself. For example, in the kosher laws, there is an opposition between milk and meat that I have contended is an expression of a life/death opposition. While a critical Jewish value, neither opposition completely appears in the Jewish mystical Godhead, although creation (and Life) makes its way in through the *Shekinah*. Parenthetically, this milk/meat opposition also appears in a Moslem idea regarding kinship in which the incest prohibition extends to any child that nurses at a woman's breast. The incest prohibition is conferred through this milk tie to all the mother's physical children's prohibited kin. Why this milk/meat opposition appears in Islamic kinship and Jewish *kashrut* in the way it does is unclear and merits future consideration. Milk/meat, as far as I know, do not make their way into the summarizing wholeness of a Jewish or Islamic deity.

The structures of kinship do, however. To repeat by way of concluding, both Christian and Jewish mystical Godheads are structured by in/out, act/state, and spirit and flesh, though, flesh also commonly takes a male/female form in this Jewish tradition. According to the theory behind the system of common differences, this Jewish tradition should contrast in a major way with its Christian sibling by emphasizing the flesh and the feminine. I hope the discussion of male and female within the various *sefirot* demonstrates this point. The *Shekinah*, moreover, has the same mediating role as the male Jesus, and her gender is female.

Fortunately, these predictions are not the only ones that may confirm my basic contention for the system of common differences. This contention, of course, is that the traditions of Islam, Christianity and Judaism are all formed from the same or common differences. The character of each religion depends on not only what differences it emphasizes but also on the particular contrasts that are used to distinguish one religion from another. For example, Islam is the spirit religion in this system, both Christianity and Judaism are the flesh religions; this being divided triadically much as the spirit/flesh opposition is in the mystical Jewish Godhead:

<u>**Islam**</u>
Christianity/Judaism

Judaism differs in some basic way from Christianity as flesh does to spirit. It should be more concrete and divided: in its mystical divinity, we discover that flesh is often replaced by a male/female opposition and that the female element here is emphasized in the fractured flesh or scattered divine light of Creation. Flesh by way of gender is emphasized in the Jewish portion of the system of common differences. The two traditions likewise have divinities that differ over qualities and relations, with the Jewish mystical Godhead presenting its triangular qualities in contrast to the triadic relationships behind the Trinity. Further, the female and fleshly *Shekinah*, like the male but spiritual Christ is a bridge to its religion's God and stands at the fountain of Creation. All these differences between mystical Judaism and Christianity are expressed in their respective godheads, which have homologous functions in their respective traditions. In other words, they summarize and are united in a system of difference. This also, as demonstrated in this essay, is true especially for *Kabbalah*. Likewise, since the system is about relations and relating, these systems should produce ways in which human beings may meaningfully relate to the godhead. I hope I have shown that Jesus and *Shekinah* allow for this.

Another prediction could confirm or disprove my structural understandings of these godheads. Just as triadic structures formed to give the *Kabbalah* Godhead and the Trinity their character, so too should other triadic structures give significance to other ideas in the Jewish tradition. The Jewish tradition should abundantly produce triadic structures because flesh divides. I can think of at least two practices that essentially have triadic structures. The marriage act is in the spirit, encompassing a connection between male and female, of husband and wife. Likewise, there is the lighting of Shabbat candles, a spiritual act by the woman of the house, who raises her arms in circles (3 no less, indicating completeness and a connection to other threeness, so to speak), sometimes splitting her fingers into a pair on each hand over the light (spirit) that encompasses the Sabbath bread called Challah (a word similar to the Hebrew word for bride) which is blessed by a female member of the family while the traditional accompaniment of wine is blessed by a male member. Here is the triad:

<u>candlelight</u>
bread/wine

which is structured by the triad we have seen so many times before: it is the reader's choice to put in male/female or spirit/flesh for the bottom row.

In any case, since the *Shekinah* and the Christ are homologous religious elements, we are presented with an interesting opportunity. We can understand that Judaism and Christianity are declensions of one another, much as active and passive voices in sentences are declensions of one another, and so perhaps they can be reconciled. Each may say the same Salvationist message in its own way. There also is the possibility of translation. Jesus' statement that He is the way, the light, and the truth and that there is no way to the Father except through Him can be taken to mean that He is in the path of the *Shekinah* and that He embodies her Presence. As such, He is an early expression of a Jewish mystical tradition in which relating to God means capturing Her presence in Creation. Theologically, this may allow the Christian tradition to be folded into the Jewish one, with Jesus as its rabbi, with *Shekinah* as its medium, and with Jewish traditions open particularly to all. I naively and perhaps inappropriately say this with the personal hope that the Jewish/Christian distinction, so invidiously used for so long by so many, may be dissolved into a universal particularism that tolerantly accepts the fact that similar differences form our common godheads. But on the other hand, both traditions richly go their own way, and it is not for me to give the reader a preference or suggest changes to the traditions. My real plea is for tolerance and acceptance of common differences that abound in the godheads of both traditions.

Comments

I. If engagement with original sources is essential to the scholarly soundness of an article like this, then this is a very unsound piece of work. I cannot read let alone understand the original material of the Kabbalah tradition and have depended enormously on the works of Sholem cited below, as well as on the introduction to the Pritzker edition of the Kabbalah written by Arthur Green. I have also learned much from the works of Wolfson listed in the bibliography.

2. I am impressed with the possibility that the character of cultural items can be predicted within the system of common differences and that these predictions may confirm the nature of the interpretation I am making. Here is a small prediction. If domestic animals like cats and dogs are given kinship status, that is, they become members of the family, then one of the oppositions structuring the family should signify something basic about the pets. It turns out that dogs are male (whatever their actual sex) and that cats likewise are female. But this is only for the Jewish/Christian families in the system of common differences. Their pets are likely to be more in the flesh (so they can be gendered) where in Islamic families, something more spiritual and connected to the above should occur. In fact, something more spiritual and above should even occur in terms of kinship terms. So, instead of decent being so dominant, ascent should make its way into kinship terms. Fathers, for example, should be named for the sons they bear rather than sons being named for the fathers who sire them. This seems to be true: the term Abu, father of, in the names of male parents suggests this. Ascent, the moving upward in naming, seems to obtain in this naming for the father. Likewise, ascent and spirit might make its way into how family status is accorded to pets. According to this model, birds and not dogs and cats should be the pet of choice for many Moslems, since birds fly in the spirited above. And it should be a male (spirit) bird at that. Perhaps the role of hawks or falcons in Arabic culture may confirm this prediction.

3. Of course, I am personally happy to maintain and have my children maintain their distinctiveness as Jews, and can readily imagine the virtue in Christians doing the same with their children. There is a distinction between making a suggestion and having a conviction that something should be so.

Essay 15- Storied Triads of the Bible

What follows is a "syntactical" study of Hebrew Scriptures: it finds an underlying, grammar like structure -- spirit/flesh -- and shows how it organizes the relationships between persons within many Biblical stories. Declensions of the same spirit/ flesh structure form triads that are used similarly to construct various Bible stories. Where purely grammatical structures in sentences allow speakers to form many different sentences with differing subjects, verbs and objects in different orders, the basic scriptural structure of spirit/flesh likewise allows the Bible to display many different and storied interpersonal relationships. To elaborate, a structure:

<u>spirit</u>
flesh

helps to construct plots or characters in the Bible. When it does this, spirit/flesh may take different forms. These differing forms can be examined independently of any story; spirit/flesh can be examined analytically simply as a structure. The first logical point is this: spirit is complete and singular so it can't be divided where flesh inherently divides or parts in two so it may change to give:

<u>spirit</u>
flesh

a different appearance. It can be divided by spirit/flesh itself to reveal this three-part form:

<u>spirit</u>
spirit/flesh

The bottom portion is a flesh dimension divided by spirit and flesh. To illustrate using the Trinity as an example, the basic relationships of God, Jesus and Holy Ghost are organized or signified by this structure:

<u>God</u>
Jesus/Holy Ghost

or:

<u>spirit</u>
flesh/spirit

which is an expression or declination of:

<u>spirit</u>
flesh

The flesh portion on the bottom is divided into two flesh entities: The Holy Spirit which impregnates flesh nonetheless resonates with spirit, and Jesus, the word made flesh resonates with flesh. Both Jesus and the Holy Spirit are then flesh personages, who are distinguished by spirit and flesh. Again, the flesh portion of the triad divides into two, one personage, Jesus, being first in the flesh and the Holy Spirit being first in the spirit. [9]

Now, the triads formed by spirit/flesh may be more varied than the one described so far. We can also get a structure which reverses the order of the spirit/flesh opposition on the bottom:

<u>spirit/flesh</u>
flesh/spirit

Put diagrammatically and to repeat, we get these equivalents:

<u>spirit</u>
flesh

equals:

<u>spirit</u>
flesh/spirit

which could also be expressed as:

<u>spirit</u>
spirit/flesh

or emphasizing indistinction, we can decline:

spirit
flesh

to:

spirit
|
spirit-flesh

Ironically, dualism naturally produces this tripartite or three-part structure and it gives us others. For example, flesh may divide according to some other opposition --flesh readily relates to gender. People in the flesh have a gender. So, we could imagine another triad or three-part form that expresses the spirit/flesh opposition that looks like this:

spirit
flesh

equals:

spirit
male/female

which could also be expressed as:

spirit
female/male

Of course, these oppositions move left to right. If the triadic forms of spirit/flesh were placed up to down, we would see these triads:

spirit
spirit
flesh

or:

spirit
male
female

We can expect to see all these three-part structures organizing characters and plots in Biblical stories beginning with Adam and Eve.

And in the beginning, we see God talking to Adam and Eve:

God
Adam/Eve

God is without question spirit and the Bible's initial theme concerning Adam and Eve is how they realize their sexuality, hence the importance of male and female difference. Once the sexuality of Adam and Eve is defined as a noted, gender-difference in the flesh, Eve becomes subordinated to Adam, and this has the structure:

<u>God</u>
<u>Adam</u>
Eve

as structure:

<u>spirit</u>
<u>male</u>
female

which is a variation of:

<u>spirit</u>
flesh

as shown above.

Now, at its most straight-forward, male and female refer to sex. But the Bible's use of male and female turns on gender as well. This is central to the stories involving Abraham, Sarah and Lot. While Lot is not a major figure in the text, he is deeply involved in the stories circulating around Abraham and Sarah and he is gendered female at one point even while he remains sexed as a male. So, let us begin our studies of gender and sex in the Lot story by clearly describing the triadic relationships involving God, Abraham and Sara: first, there was God, and then there was Abraham and Sarah:

<u>God</u>
Abraham-Sarah

equals:

<u>spirit</u>
male/female

Now, Lot is Sarah's brother and Abraham is the spiritual leader of this little brood. So, in a different triad, Abraham sits above the two

213

siblings, and this implies that Lot is in a female position relative to Abraham, who is above. Here are triadic equivalents:

<u>Abraham</u>
Lot/Sarah

which is:

<u>male</u>
female

which may also be:

<u>male</u>
male/female

which may be:

<u>spirit</u>
male/female

The logic here is that female divides while male remains whole and female can be divided by male/female, as the diagram shows. Importantly, the male sexed Lot appears on the bottom portion or female portion of the triad. So, the Biblical text could take a male character and gender him female first, male second, but this requires proof, proof which is somewhat provided in the Sodom story.

In Sodom, a homosexual and murderous mob attacks Lot's home just before the city is destroyed by God for its sinfulness. Clearly, these males are only sexed male and are not male by gender. The story makes this explicit: Lot offers them his two virginal daughters. From the Bible's point of view, what could be more enticing, but not to these men who are sexed as male but gendered as something else, which in the binary, Biblical mode of thought could only be female. The gender, sex distinction of the text is made even clearer by what happens further on. After Sodom is destroyed, Lot's daughters conclude that there are no men for them to mate with other than their father. So, Lot's daughters successively mount him, making him the female in this sexual act. Lot is gendered female by his daughters who in each instance of intercourse are male above the female Lot below.

This suggests that structure moves around, making male into female and this theme is further expressed by Lot. As a father and a man, he is associated with spirit and he is a generation above his two-female offspring, who are down. There is a familiar "threeness" to this, but the structure used is not declined triadically unless one takes special note, as the story does, that the daughters, like the flesh, are two. Diagramming, this takes the form:

<u>male</u>
female

and this structure is turned upside down as Lot is feminized:

<u>daughters</u>
Lot

where the daughters play the role of the male in intercourse and Lot the female. Since the daughters mount Lot, the daughters are male/female (sexed female, gendered male), with Lot below as a male gendered episodically as female. While they are two, as the male on top, the daughters are viewed as one; each singularly but together has sex with their father in two acts of intercourse.

This reversing is the point: the text wants structure to move about and be the vehicle of thought, coherence, and significance. It also wants to establish in the mind of the reader that the masculine can also be the feminine depending on gender and not on sex. And it wants to show that structure creates meaningful differences between same sexed persons, much as structure can slot female as male.

This is so in the Cain and Abel story, also. Central to this story is a sacrifice or offering that each male brother makes to God. Cain offers first fruit while Abel makes an animal sacrifice. Fruit suggests completion -- as in something brought to fruition or as something coming to full flower. It is wholesome, fruit hangs above the ground. It is a spiritual offering, a lofty gift, one connoting completeness, and spiritual fruitfulness. Abel, on the other hand, sacrifices an animal. What could be more in the flesh? The story, then, suggests that Cain is to spirit as Abel is to flesh while each as a male brother in kinship is in flesh. Both are making fleshly offerings but one is in the spirit and the other, flesh. Therefore, we now see that male brotherly flesh can be divided by spirit/flesh. We can also see that the two relate to God while in the flesh. The brothers are in the flesh, both are male, and they differ in offerings as spirit does to flesh. Like Lot's daughters, male brothers in the flesh

can be divided by a division within this system, this time by spirit/flesh.
Expressed triadically:

<u>God</u>
Cain/Abel

or:

<u>spirit</u>
flesh

or:

<u>spirit</u>
spirit/flesh

<u>spirit</u>
male/female

The next important figure in the line of descendants described
by the Torah is Noah. Noah, of course, fills the Ark with two of each
kind of living being, to reestablish life on earth after the great flood. So,
Noah is a kind of ruler over creation. All flesh is under his wing: it is
unforced to describe this relation thusly:

<u>Noah</u>
flesh

Given the mating of the saved animals paired on the Ark, this
structure even more obviously can be described as:

<u>Noah</u>
male/female

since all the animals are sexed and coupled as male and female. And, of
course, Noah is the ruler of the ark; hence we can see this structure:

<u>Spirit</u>
male/female.

All these structures are just different expressions of spirit/flesh,
expressed triadically and more details of the Noah tale fit the model. To
wit, God's instruction to put multiple pairs of male and female on the
ark is triadic: every person on the Ark is described as part of a
male/female pair. The ruling structure is:

<u>God(singular)</u>
male/female (pairs).

One could claim that the entire story is formed from a structure that runs from God to Noah -- a spirit to flesh relationship -- and then within this flesh we have Noah ruling a paired or gendered universe:

<u>God</u>
Noah

and:

<u>spirit</u>
flesh

which has the flesh divided thusly:

<u>God (spirit)</u>
<u>Noah (spirit)</u>
pairs (flesh)

Since Noah is in the flesh, which divides; he can be in the spirit and a husband with a female wife. Flesh permits the separated pairing of male and female creatures. Therefore, the unity of the spirit and the pattern of division in the flesh within the system are consistently expressed in the Noah story.

Finally, the centrality of gender in the Noah story comes clear when Noah's 3 sons (all his children were male) see their father passed out drunk upon the ark's having arrived on dry land. One son uncovers his nakedness. This not only highlights the significance of gender to the story (Noah's nakedness obviously exposes his sex) but it also gives rise to other structurally significant points. In this traditional scheme, it is males who uncover females: exposing Noah feminizes him and it strongly defines Ham as male. Noah here is a feminized male and might be characterized as female-male or male-female. The other two sons are passive witnesses to Ham's masculine act, and passiveness is female in this traditional view. So, the one son is male and the passive two are female and we get this structure:

<u>Noah (male-female)</u>
<u>male son</u>
female sons

Now, separation is a structural element and it helps to support triads. The opposite of separation, of course, is unity and this structure, unity/separation, supports triads in many ways. In the Abraham story,

Abraham is described both as Sarah's husband and as her sibling: there is the theme of unity – husband and wife—and separation, brother and sister, which is underscored by a triadic structure based on male and female.

Here is the structure of Abraham's and Sarah's marriage:

<u>God</u>
Abraham-Sarah

where God is encompassing as Spirit, so we have a unified, vertical spirit flesh structure:

<u>Spirit</u>
male-female

In its lower (fleshly and distinctive) part, the male Abraham and the female Sarah, are bound in unity in marriage, which is gendered flesh united. But as siblings, they are separated and viewed as generationally below, with the united-in-the-spirit marriage partners above as this chart demonstrates:

<u>male-female together or one</u>
male/female apart or two

Since the top part is a unity of the spirit, not only is this structure a declension of

<u>spirit</u>
flesh

It is also triad:

<u>spirit</u>
male/female.

Separation and unity are tools working on behalf of this triadic structure, which itself forms a singularity, top with bottom, just as spirit/flesh does.

Furthermore, these structures relate to a highly interesting passage in Genesis which occurs very early on: "In the image of God He created them, male and female he created them" (Gen 1:26-28). This passage forthrightly says that Spirit or God is composed of (a unified) male-female. Adam and Eve are separated and distinctly gendered beings and the structure of the relationship between God and his offspring can also be expressed as:

male-female (God)
male/female (Adam/Eve)

And of course, as a married couple, Adam and Eve are male-female and this structure is highly similar to the one relating to Noah and the creatures on his ark, once we see that male Noah can be feminized. For each of these structural stories, identity prevails in the numerator; difference in the denominator. For example, Adam and Eve become husband and wife so they are much like Abraham and Sarah: brother (/) and sister (of the same flesh); then husband (-) and wife. Common structures reproduce the different characters; repeatedly structure makes possible the story and the characters themselves. And perhaps wherever there is unity, such as male-female, there is or should be spirit even if the unity of differences is in the flesh.

Structure does not move the story forward alone; elimination of a character or a line of descent from the text is a way Jewish scripture protects and highlights structure through a story that it wants to progress. For example, Hagar is sent away by Abraham -- she is eliminated from the story. Ishmael, however, is not entirely out of the structural picture. At the time of Abraham's death, Ishmael, the hunter, meets again with his domesticated shepherd of a brother Isaac. Ishmael as a hunter and a forest dweller is in the flesh and is male, where Isaac, the domesticated camp-dweller, is female. Homebound Isaac was gendered female earlier in the story where he was intended as a human sacrifice to God. As a sacrifice, he is passive and submissive, a female body to be offered up. But Abraham, his father, substitutes a ram in his place. Isaac is like a sacrificial animal. He is not a hunter but more like the animal hunted or the female animal that submits. So, we see this triad:

Abraham
Ishmael/Isaac

where the spiritual father is followed by a male/female pair of sons. Isaac though sexed male and in the flesh, is female here. Again, we see a declination of the:

spirit
flesh

opposition. Ishmael and Isaac later meet again together only to separate, and this separation will later be complemented by the meeting of Joseph and his formerly estranged or separated brothers in Egypt, who unite. A dividing and uniting structure moves the story forward.

In any case, Sarah dies, ending this portion of the text with her lineage extending clearly to the remaining Isaac, who unlike Ishmael is a Hebrew. She is eliminated from the significance of the text before the next set of characters triadically arrives. Remember that Abraham establishes a line of descent with Sarah which leads to Isaac. Sarah dies before Isaac is wed: with this wedding the triad of

Abraham
Isaac-Rebecca

results, but here Isaac is gendered and sexed as male.[10] In the context of being the wedded husband to Rebecca, and though the passive recipient of a wife, Isaac plays his conjugal or male part. He is in the flesh, and therefore female but since flesh may split male/female, his gendered female flesh remains true to his male sex. When he first sees Rebecca enter his father's camp, he immediately beds her in his mother's tent. Both passive and overly domestic, he nonetheless exercises his male sexuality, displaying his male gender in the Abraham, Isaac, Rebecca triad.

But at this point, the text is more interested in the Abrahamic line: his son Isaac and Rebecca give birth to a pair of males, Jacob and Esau. According to the theory presented in this essay, they ought to differ as flesh does to spirit or as female might to male.

Two points to note. First, we have brothers, a horizontal contrast, and second, we have descendants, a vertical contrast. We should see male and female, or spirit and flesh, both ways. From the descent standpoint, the male and female divides, or the spirit and flesh divides ought to go between generations. The above (spirit) ought to be male and the generation below ought to be female, and that means more in the flesh. [11] Abraham, the first Hebrew, is clearly male and so is slotted male or spiritual in the above generation. His two descendant offspring are far more in the flesh, the hunter son leaving to establish another line, and the domesticated son, a propagating but passive (slotted female) male, gives us the gendered triad. But then two questions arise. Where is the spirit in the stories featuring Isaac? Where is the flesh in Isaac's tropes? Clearly, the two sons below Isaac are a twin pair and it is hardly difficult to discern the twin Jacob as smooth female by gender, especially by contrast with the hairy Esau.

More will be said later about Esau and Jacob. The concern now is where spirit lies in the ascending generation. Perhaps it lodges with Rebecca and not the more female Isaac. While Rebecca is sexed as female, her link with water at her father's well raises a spiritual possibility. It is not just that well water is lifted from low to high; it is also that water is like spirit: pure, immaterial and flowing. Rebecca is associated with water, with spirit, and she may, therefore, play the role of father in the text. She may select as a father might, one of her sons as the true heir for example, as she does when she designates the great blessing of Isaac for her son Jacob through her female scheming. Her domesticity may prevail, as when Jacob induces his starving brother to give up his birthright through an offering of her cooked food. While the male Isaac is feminized, the female Rebecca is masculinized. Together they are man and wife, one male and female, each being both male and female, and together they are a spiritually bonded husband and wife, male-female, giving us the spirit portion of the triad in their generation:

<u>spirit</u>
flesh

or:

<u>Rebecca</u>
Jacob/Esau

or:

<u>Rebecca-Isaac</u>
Jacob/Esau

or:

<u>female-male</u>
Jacob/Esau

or:

<u>male-female</u>
female/male

or:

221

<u>male</u>
female

or:

<u>first</u>
second

This deserves more discussion. First, the Jewish scripture is trying to establish a Jewish line of descent from Abraham, and for the Hebrew Bible descent is inherently in the flesh and therefore female. Jacob and Esau, as descendants, are female. They are descendants in the flesh. Their parents are married in the spirit, and spirit is male. While Rebecca could choose which son got the blessing, the male Isaac had to give it. The (spiritual) will of the married couple is ultimately the husband's. Isaac as a male gave the blessing to Jacob, a blessing he received first from his mother and then properly from his father. So, the male blessing went to the more female-gendered son.

Again, Jacob and Esau readily contrast as female to male. Esau like Ishmael is a hunter where Jacob like Isaac is a shepherd. Jacob is smooth where Esau is hairy. Jacob stays at home where Esau wanders. Isaac, moreover, distinguished the brothers thusly, "Your hands are the hairy hands of Esau, but your voice is the voice of Jacob." By his voice, Jacob is male but especially female! Jacob, the female male, is distinguished by voice, which is often associated with the female. That is, voice is the female in the male-female constructing God. It was God who created the world with his voicing of "Let there be". The voice is the creative voice of Spirit; like a fertile female, voice creates and so it is feminine. It is a still but acting, small female voice. This suggests a united male-female structure to the act of creation in the top of the triad:

The Living male God His (female) Voice (creating) flesh or the world
below

with living beings in the world below distinguished by male and female. It also suggests that a voice, Jacob's voice, is like God's voice, a creative feminine. And through the guile of his female voice his inheritance is created. Jacob is female not only as a descendant but also as a brother. This is not to underplay his maleness, his hands are (but only apparently) hairy, but it suggests that the line coming from Abraham, although originating in a male line, has like flesh and Jacob, developed a female gender.

The vertical line of descent going through Jacob, the son who is chosen[12], expresses triad once again. The male founder Abraham sits on top. Vertically below are Isaac then Jacob, two descendants in the flesh, each significantly feminized. Isaac is a male father of a smooth-skinned, over-domesticated, mother- dominated, fair- voiced son. This Jacob is the son who runs like a girl away from a fight with Esau, whose anger with being supplanted understandably displays a combative masculinity. Of these two brothers, Jacob is the more female. Like a woman, he is chosen in the line of descent. We get this line of male descent of a now obvious female line:

Abraham
Isaac
Jacob

which is:

male
male
female

which is an expression of:

spirit
flesh

and:

male
female

Once this story's structure is established with Jacob as the male head of a female, male line stemming from him, Jacob propagates greatly. Arguably, he is also a second, that is he is complete and blessed, and a complete person propagates in the Biblical intellect, as its dualistic alternative, a curse of bareness, shows   He has a huge brood of children, all but one male:

Jacob
male children/female child

a structure that remains in place after Jacob's son Joseph departs from Israel to go to Egypt. That is, Joseph is the female child in this triad while in Israel, and after he leaves for Egypt, an actual female child, Dinah, comes to the fore.

Now, Joseph displays a female character, though sexed as a male. Unlike his brothers, Joseph receives a unique gift from his father, a coat of many colors. In other words, like a woman, he is chosen for something special, a colorful gift. He interprets dreams, and like a woman, his name means food giver. His coat is feminine – it colorfully suggests something refined and not coarse. Dream interpretation appears to be a female gift in the ancient world, just think of the Oracle of Delphi for example. From the perspective of Biblical culture, food-giving is what women do, from breastfeeding to family cooking. The text early on feminizes Joseph. Perhaps this is most obvious in Egypt. There, Joseph is stripped of his loin cloth by the wife of the man who was his slave master. In traditional terms, a real man is not stripped by a woman. In this traditional culture, only women may be stripped. In any case, Joseph had domestic control over this household (Potiphar's) and he does not work in the fields. As a slave, he lives as a female-gendered male who does his master's domestic will.

Therefore, Joseph stands in female contrast to Egyptian men as well as to his male brothers though this changes when he rules in Egypt and when his younger brother appears well after Dinah does in the story. Now at this point, when his brothers appear in Egypt, he forms a triad with Benjamin and his father:

Jacob

Joseph/Benjamin

Benjamin exists in part because the main figure in the denominator level of the triad given by the text requires a pair which can be gendered. And the former slave Joseph is male here. Regaining maleness is Joseph's theme: For one, Joseph is raised up in Egypt, from being a slave to becoming an overseer. He controls the entire Egyptian food supply through seven years of prosperity and then during seven years of drought. Under or perhaps over Pharaoh's visage, he rules. A ruler rules in the spirit (though, since Joseph rules over food, he rules in the flesh as a Hebrew) and the text goes so far as to describe Joseph as the father of Pharaoh, using the Hebrew *AV* for father. Egypt as embodied by Pharaoh is a fertile, food source, so this interesting father of Pharaoh expression, which puts Joseph above Pharaoh, makes Joseph a male father to a Pharaoh who embodies Egypt. Now in embodying Egypt Pharaoh's situation can be constructed as:

Pharaoh
fertile Egypt.

This means that Pharaoh is above the Egypt he rules, and it is a fertile female land that is Pharaoh's. Joseph is the *AV* or father or ruler above this structure. He is male over the masculine Pharaoh and his female and fertile land. This expresses the following triad:

Joseph
Pharaoh
Egypt

or:

male
male
female

which as the reader knows is a declination of:

spirit
flesh

To further clarify how triads structure the text, perhaps the broader Joseph story can be divided into two parts, a time in Canaan and a time in Egypt. In Canaan, the story first presents us with Joseph and his brothers (his sister and younger Benjamin are not discussed at this point.) They are sons, as previously discussed, Joseph with his coat of many colors is female and we have:

Jacob
the brothers/Joseph.

Joseph dreams that one day these brothers would bow to him, that he, therefore, would be ascendant. This expresses the structure:

Jacob
Joseph
brothers

The dream at this point makes little sense (and is rejected by his brothers) perhaps because the boy Joseph is not yet a real ruler. In this dream structure, Joseph the female child is the (spiritual) authority, the gendered male who is above, with the male brothers subordinated, put in a female place. The brothers of course reject the dream, likely on this basis. This dream comes true in Egypt, of course when Joseph is a man. Once Joseph leaves Canaan for the land of Egypt, the remaining male brothers in Canaan relate to their sister Dinah. Dinah becomes the focus of the story when she is raped, and the brothers take revenge on the rapist and his people. Again, Dinah contrasts with the brothers, giving us a triad involving Jacob. Only Jacob reacts to the brutal retaliation of the brothers and only Jacob is consulted regarding the rapist and his people. It is just Jacob and his children sans the mothers. There is only the male figure above, and the actions of the male brothers on behalf of Dinah. We have this structure here:

Jacob
male brothers/female Dinah

Thus, the relationship between siblings is triadic in Canaan, just as it is in Egypt where the story proceeds triadically as previously described. The family fully gathers there; even baby and passive brother Benjamin and father Jacob eventually go down to Egypt where these 70 migrants become a multitude over time.

And there arose later in Egypt a Pharaoh who did not know Joseph, who oppressed the Hebrews and enslaved them. In response, there arose a Jewish leader, Moses, who wished to liberate these slaves. The Moses story exhibits triadic relationships and it begins with Pharaoh's attempt to kill all newborn male Jewish babies. Moses' mother hides her male child, and after three months, puts him in a straw basket; she floats the basket along the Nile River where Pharaoh's daughter finds him and adopts the baby as her own. Moses' mother has her daughter Miriam spy on the water-born child, and it is Miriam who tells the mother that Moses has been drawn from the water by Pharaoh's daughter, and she later volunteers the baby's real mother as a surrogate for the child's breastfeeding.

So, in this story, we have a mother, a daughter, and a baby brother. Moses' father is not present, and a triad exists here between the mother, Miriam and her brother Moses:

mother

Miriam/Moses

This triad has a female on top in the traditional male position; the mother in fact is the authority figure, the decision-maker, and this genders her male.

Pharaoh's daughter is part of a similar triad; here, she substitutes for Moses' mother. There is only a single female on top, and when the triad involves Pharaoh's daughter, she is surrounded by her female servants who are below her, as is her adopted son, Moses, who is lower in the water and lower by generation. To illustrate:

Pharaoh's daughter

Moses

female servants

Of course, the female servants, like Miriam in the preceding triad, are servile and therefore are below at the bottom in the triad. They contrast against the male Moses, whom they also serve.

This story produces other relationships involving Moses. The first is the relationship between God, Moses and Aaron. The background is that Moses has fled Egypt after killing one of Pharaoh's taskmasters; he then lives with Midianites, one of whom he marries. When he arrives in Midian, he chases male Midianites from a well, Midianites who had threatened the daughters of Jethro. The structure for Moses, Jethro's daughters and Jethro is:

Jethro

Moses/daughters of Jethro

Of course, the daughters in this triad are later replaced by one of these daughters. This daughter becomes Moses' wife, thereby forming a male female bottom to the triad, against the male ascendant Jethro whose wife is totally missing from the text.

Later in Midian, God tells Moses to return to Egypt to free the Hebrew slaves; Moses refuses at first, making several objections that God overcomes. Finally, Moses says that he is slow of speech and could not possibly orate well on His behalf. God becomes annoyed, and then provides him with his brother Aaron as his spokesperson, telling Moses that "he shall serve as your spokesman, with you playing the role of God to him" (Exodus 4:14-16)

Until now, little is known about Aaron, so it is hard to argue that he is gendered female. This is required if Aaron is to be part of a triad of God and Moses where Moses plays the role of God. And the text insists on:

<u>Moses</u>
Aaron

which is:

<u>God</u>
man

which is:

<u>male</u>
female

which is:

<u>spirit</u>
flesh

Of course, the two of them are under God, which then gives us the triad:

<u>God</u>
Moses
Aaron

which corresponds to:

<u>spirit</u>
flesh

(But again, this only works if Moses and Aaron are male and female in the flesh). This works because Aaron is female since, as a spokesperson, it is his voice that characterizes him. His voice is female, as discussed above. It is the voice of authority, the creative feminine of the male authority, Moses being God to him.

Now Moses goes way down to Egypt, leaving his father-in-law behind and returning to Pharaoh's sway. Alongside Aaron, he appears before Pharaoh, and the relationships here are again triadic. First, they are appearing before the ruler of all Egypt, two Hebrew supplicants with one demand: the liberation of their people. Before Pharaoh, the male ruler, we see:

Pharaoh
Moses/Aaron

but that is not how the text leaves it. God says that Moses is to be a God to Pharaoh, (The Lord replied to Moses, "See, I place you in the role of God to Pharaoh, with your brother as prophet" Exodus 7:I) Moses and Aaron are to prevail. Thus, Moses is to be like God above and this position is always singular, and Aaron as God's female voice prophetically commands Pharaoh. This gives us a vertical triad:

Moses-Aaron
Pharaoh

Moses is male, Aaron (especially his voice) is gendered female, and Pharaoh is the male ruler of Egypt in the feminine flesh. Moses and Aaron should be represented as Moses-Aaron since Aaron's voice is Moses'. Like God, there is unity in the brothers. Pharaoh listens to the two of them and lets the Israelites go. His acquiescence may be viewed as female. Then, the Hebrew slaves are led to freedom by a new triad:

Moses
Aaron/Miriam

Miriam leads the people with a timbral and harp as well as poetry, all-female things from the standpoint of the text. She sings. Aaron, though gendered earlier as the female voice of Moses, is nonetheless sexed here as the male prophet, and so we have two siblings in the flesh, one male brother and one female sister, where Moses, playing the role of God, is above as a man in the spirit.

In keeping with this line of thought, Moses brings the Hebrews to freedom by following the Lord's instructions and we may have another triadic relationship in:

God
Moses
Israel

Moses leads Israel, revealing God's commands to His people, a tri-partite relationship sculpted deeply in the text. Israel here, of course, is female, as her key descending lineages are female. Here she is female as she is a bride of God, and a people in the flesh. Moses is a man in the spirit, so this triad is based on the:

<u>unified spirit</u>
<u>divided flesh</u>

or gendered flesh pattern used by the Torah to structure good relationships: here Moses and Israel divide and gender the same flesh, Moses as male, Israel below as female.

Joshua follows Moses. He is a military leader who replaces a prophet and Joshua has the same position in the triad as Moses but to a lesser consequence. In the end, he conquers his way to the Land of Israel, eventually dividing it among 11 of the 12 tribes. The priestly tribe of Levi does not get any land, and this suggests a triad:

<u>Joshua</u>
priests/rest of Israel.

The priests, like Joshua and unlike Israel, are (all) male.

Once Israel receives her land and her laws, new characters come to the fore, the period of judges follows, and among them are some noteworthy people and relationships. There is Deborah, the female judge who rules over Israel as a prophetess, who says that Sisera, a Canaanite General, will die by a woman's hand. Sisera engages in battle with a Hebrew army roused by Deborah, and he is defeated. He flees and is lured to his death through the crushing female guile of Jael, who is kin to Moses, and who stones him to death while he sleeps. Perhaps Sisera takes the role of Pharaoh here, a dominated and defeated power, the subordinated feminine, with the structure looking like this:

<u>Deborah</u>
<u>Jael</u>
Sisera

Deborah is the singular ruler where the killer and the killed form a pair. The killer is sexed as female and gendered male (what gender kills? Clearly one nurtures); the killed is sexed as male and gendered as female. He is a (female) victim.

In this context, Deborah plays the role of general, a male role, and so arguable is a prophetess gendered male in the spirit, which makes her a candidate for rulership, and the singular, top and male position of the triad.

The story of Ruth and Naomi illustrates the text playing with the triad to define what is proper both on top and below. It answers a question, "Where does two belong?", and it shows that two belongs below and one above. In this story, Ruth, a Moabite, follows Naomi and returns to Naomi's Israelite people and land. The land in question is a field managed by Boaz, yet it is owned by Naomi who could be taken as the natural spouse-to-be for Boaz. But to continue with the story, the text clearly shows that Ruth is a follower, someone who is subject to Naomi. Naomi is even a surrogate husband to Ruth in the sense that Ruth has lost her husband, who was Naomi's son, and now she follows Naomi as she would have followed him. Naomi, moreover, is a landowner. She likely has gained this land through inheritance. In Biblical law, women may inherit land when male heirs are not available. Thus, arguably, by inheriting the land, Naomi is cast in a male ownership role. She is the land-owning boss of Boaz. So how can she marry him? She is on top. The text then has Boaz, a man meant for a Hebrew woman, marrying Ruth the Moabite instead. Structurally, the relation between Naomi and Ruth is male to female and up to down:

Naomi
Ruth

And Ruth as the female here can be married. So, we get a marriage below:

Naomi
Ruth=Boaz

The bottom gives us the difference of two even if they are united as one in marriage. Two belongs below and Naomi is alone, the ruler so to speak, above.

Ruth's marriage begins a female line: Ruth is the denominated woman here and the line leads to David and later to Jesus. The path to David as King of Israel also comes from the prophets, Samuel in particular. Samuel is the prophet who gave Israel a King; he is the man who more formally separated religious and political authority. He does this by navigating a series of triads involving himself and others.

First, here are the triads related to Samuel: Samuel is God's prophet to Israel, and this is a triad:

God
Samuel
Israel

which we have shown to be:

male
female

which expresses:

spirit
male
female

Israel is the female nation of God led by its male prophet. It is Samuel who anoints Saul as first King and this is easily understood as a triad:

God
Saul/Israel[13]

or:

God
Samuel
Saul

In this first triad, Samuel can be slotted into the role of God – he is after all God's voice. Later, the Biblical text rids itself of Saul (he failed to genocidally destroy the Amalekites per God's murderous command, the semiological reason for this is beyond this essay' scope) and he is replaced by David, whom Samuel selects as the king to be.

David is the son of Jesse, who has seven other male children. Perhaps these basic relationships can be described triadically

Samuel
Jesse
David

(David who contrasts with seven other male sons)

David is in the female position here and he is established as female in a variety of ways. First, there is this triad:

Jesse
7 sons/David

232

which puts David in the female position. The number of other male children is emphasized in the text, and 7 is a number of wholeness where David is a singular difference so we clearly have a binary relationship. (Please see the discussion of binary trees in an earlier essay to see that 7 is whole and the essay about Firsts and Seconds to see how the number 1 in Torah text expresses difference). Second, the history of David and Saul helps establish David as female. While David is chosen (again being chosen as opposed to choosing is female according to the Bible's thinking) by the prophet to be a second king, his kingship is established politically only through a complicated relationship with King Saul. Importantly, King Saul at one point was anxious before battle and wanted spiritual comfort. David, like Miriam before him, comes forward to play the female harp. A battle with the Philistines then ensues; David is sent by his father to the battlefield with food for three of his brothers who are present:

<u>Jesse</u>
3 brothers/David

(As a food giver and harp player, David is female).

While on the battlefield, he fights Goliath with stones he has selected from a brook. He uses a slingshot, which was not the expected male weapon of battle. Smooth stones are not ragged and rough, slingshots are not manly weapons, and before the battle, David played the harp and provided food. This suggests a female personage and this female personage is used in the following relationship: On the battlefield, he swears eternal friendship and brotherhood with Jonathan, Saul's son. This gives us the triad:

<u>Saul</u>
Jonathan/David

again putting David in the female role, almost as a wife who is, of course, an eternal friend.

While Saul is the first King of Israel, David begins a new line and is likewise a first. Solomon, his son, is the second. Perhaps this relationship is constructed triadically:

<u>Saul</u>
<u>David</u>
Solomon

233

Expressed in terms of spirit and flesh, Saul is the singular ruler where David and Solomon are a pair. Saul was anointed in the spirit, David likewise was anointed but is female by comparison to Saul and as the true line of kingly descent in Israel, both David and his son are in the flesh. Hence, we have this triad above being a permutation of:

spirit
flesh

with flesh divided by David and Solomon,

female
male

To elaborate, David has supplanted Saul; David prevails over attempts to trap and kill him and comes to Kingship through guile, a female characteristic in traditional Torah thought. Later, his masculine son Solomon comes to Kingship with a personal weakness: his over-charged sexuality. While he uses his wisdom to judge, he also builds a great Temple in 7 years, writes psalms, proverbs and songs, establishes new cities and mighty fleets, and has a throne of ivory overlaid with gold. He also promiscuously gathers for himself a great many women. Unlike his feminized father who exposes himself like a woman in at least in one instance, Solomon is heterosexuality personified. He is a male, perhaps blindly so. He loses sight of the Lord as he makes room for the gods of his harem. Yet this man completes Israel by building a great tabernacle to God in Jerusalem. Where David was a female male in the flesh, Solomon is a masculine second who concretizes his spirit by building the Temple. While he lives, Israel is encompassed by the physical spirit of Solomon, a completion of Israel that the Torah enshrines. Under Solomon, a priestly class arises, and it has a proper place in Israel as this triad shows:

Solomon
Priests (of the temple)/Israel

(or Israel could be placed below the Priests). As the Jewish scripture completes one of its most important stories, it ends on a triadic note.

There are at least two more triadic instances in Hebrew scripture: in the Book of Esther, we have:

<u>King Achashverus</u>
Mordechai/Esther

That is the King triadically rules over Mordechai and Esther and this supplants:

<u>King Achashverus</u>
Hamen/Vashti

his triadic rulership over Hamen and Vashti. Later, Hebrew scripture ends with the triad of:

<u>Torah</u>
Nehemiah/Ezra

That is, the Jewish text was rediscovered after the Babylonian exiles returned to Israel and two figures structure the significance of that return: Nehemiah and Ezra.

Nehemiah is the military leader while Ezra is the priest, and so they follow in a complicated way the distinction between priests and King which Samuel the prophet indirectly bequeathed to us. How these two are gendered is unclear, though prophets live by their voice and so do priests, each then being female in their way. But they certainly form a triad with the masculine military leader in the flesh and the female-voiced priest in the spirit. Significantly, the Book of the Torah takes the role of God in this triad.

Triads extend to the Christian thought as well, and not just in the obvious one of the Holy Trinity. The apostles, for example, are a male group, who are counterposed by the younger Mary, giving us a triad of:

<u>Jesus</u>
male apostles/female Mary

It is especially noteworthy that the Christian as well as Hebrew traditions produce more than one triad.

• • •

And to review, the Hebrew Bible is storied with triads. As demonstrated, these take different shapes. We move from the:

<u>God</u>
Abraham/Sarah

triad to the:

<u>Abraham</u>
Sarah/Lot

triad, all of which express the:

<u>spirit</u>
male/female

triad (though this last reverses the male and the female). This extends to the Noah story where we see a vertical triad:

<u>God (spirit)</u>
<u>Noah (spirit)</u>
gendered pairs of animals (flesh)

This same structure orders Noah's relationship to his sons and displays the distinction between gender and sex which triads use throughout the Hebrew Bible. We then see additional declinations of spirit/flesh into male-female-together male/female-apart with the possibility of female taking the lead place in both the numerator and the denominator.

The point here is that different declensions of the same spirit/flesh structure form triads that are used similarly to construct various Bible stories. This is, therefore, an analysis of relational elements or structures that form meaningful Biblical stories: this is a syntactical study. The structures make the different stories possible and are in part an explanation of how meaningful elements populate the Bible.

This discussion is incomplete in noteworthy ways. First, showing the existence of the triads in stories is different from uncovering the deepest use the text intends for them. My guess is that Bible readers are subject to endless varieties of the same structure so that they take them in cognitively as a kind of mindedness. This encourages the believer to think in these terms, to think in terms of the tropes that structure creates: of sanctification, blessing, Israel, the importance of descent, kosher food, God, etc. In my view, the structure might be more important than the stories: structure is something the text wants to convey to readers.

Structures ultimately signify, constructing life as lived in the flesh and sanctified by the spirit, thereby conveying the Jewish possibilities of blessings, of other sanctifications, and even of kosher eating. A Christian view would emphasize that structures make possible conceptions of salvation and even the Trinity. In addition, the Hebrew text wants to lead its reader to a time in history when God no longer is present, where instead His Presence is replaced by His recorded revelation. In historical time, there is not God but Torah, spirit made flesh (it literally is written on the skins of animals and in its public readings, its chanting often imitates the bleating of sheep). At the end of Hebrew scripture, this spirit is then disseminated by priests (who were the forbearers of Rabbi's in the rabbinic period) and so on in the flesh. The terms, I am arguing, come to the fore even in change: we see the world through spirit/flesh by repeatedly reading stories made up of its triads.

Next, there is a problem with the simplified discussion of the male/female opposition; this is best pointed out in relation to the mystical Jewish godhead of Kabbalah. People familiar with this godhead might readily argue that when I call a *sefirot* male, it really is male/female though its emphasis might be male (in the image of God He created them, male and female he created them). This certainly is true of all the qualities of the godhead: each is male-female and for most, only one gender comes to the fore, though this is not true for all. For *Bina* as well as for *Shekinah*, the availability of each gender is taken advantage of under different circumstances. Therefore, here, spirit is not male: it is male-female, emphasis male. Perhaps this description of its structure is what makes possible the seeming incongruous assumption of females in the upper, male-appearing position of the triad in different stories that have been described.

Finally, there is at least one aspect of spirit/flesh that has been under-discussed: while spirit/flesh is the system's stalking horses, behind it is a more fundamental opposition. Spirit is an expression of identity and flesh an expression of difference. Logically speaking, identity/difference is the basis of all knowledge systems (as argued for in an earlier essay entitled "First Thoughts"), suggesting that this system is a particular and living way of knowing. As for the universal role of identity/difference in knowing, it is true that if all qualities were identical, then nothing would be distinguished, and we would know nothing. If every quality was simply different, then there would be no coherence, no comparison and no perspective. We would not be able to distinguish anything. Both similarity and difference are required to know and the two are co-dependent. What we have here is a particular system of identity and difference distinctly expressed in spirit/flesh. It is unsurprising then that this issue of identity and difference is in play particularly and endlessly, even in its godhead and even in the storied triads of the Bible which immerse the cognizing reader in spirit/flesh.

Essay 16- Unity through Common Differences

Triads abound in the Hebrew Scriptures and their flesh portions often are gendered as both male and female. Likewise, triads dominate the godheads of the religious traditions based on Scripture. Both the Trinity and the Kabbalah godheads are explored in more detail elsewhere in this book of essays, but I thought a separate piece on the common differences expressed by each godhead might be useful. The purpose here is not a complete analysis of the Trinity or the God of Kabbalah; it is instead to show that certain common differences form the unity of each godhead. This is meant to supplement the observation that spirit and flesh fundamentally form the basic elements of our culture: other differences such as male and female are common throughout as well.

Additionally, the godheads in the system are in the spiritual domain of religion so the identity of their inner structure reflects the theme of spiritual identity (or indistinction of differences) despite their differences. Their distinctiveness in the spiritual domain otherwise presents a problem since the spiritual should emphasize unity yet there are three traditions with different godheads. But it is common structure (though decline differently) that overcomes this issue. There are common differences in the godheads and at this essay's end, a brief discussion of the religious term Allah makes this clear.

In any case, the Trinity, as the first example, takes the spirit/flesh opposition, places the spirit on top as the Father or God and has the Holy Ghost, an impregnating spirit, on the bottom as spirit along with Jesus, a spiritual but dying mortal man in the flesh. Hence, we get:

<u>Father or God</u>
Holy Ghost/Jesus

as an instance of:

<u>spirit</u>
flesh

expressed triadically as:

spirit
spirit/flesh

Jesus is a spirit in the flesh, the Holy Ghost is a spiritual impregnator in the flesh and God is spirit-flesh, an identity through a difference as other essays establish. Not only are all three personages composed of spirit and flesh, but the top portion and the bottom portion are declinations of spirit and flesh. The entire structure is composed of this repeated, common difference, so it is entirely the same, a unity of differences identically or differentially expressed.

With the mystical Jewish deity of Kabbalah, we also witness a three-part God with the same repeating structure, this time of male and female, giving it unity in a similar way through common differences. But instead of being one triad like the Trinity, it contains several triads, though these also work through a repeating structure to give unity. In this Godhead, the top portion consists of spiritual qualities or *sefirot*, and they form a triad of Godly qualities or *midot*:

Keter
Hochmah
Bina

which expresses:

spirit
male
female

or:

spirit
male-female

or:

male
male/female

To explain, the quality *Keter*, having the position of spirit or God in the Kabbalah Deity may also be characterized as male-female here emphasizing the male (male and female He created them, in the image of God He created them,). This three-part spiritual top of the Godhead also genders *Hochmah* and *Bina*, since it refers to them as father and mother respectively. Their spirituality is clear: both indicate intelligence, wisdom and knowledge but importantly here, by being a mother and a father, they are gendered male and female within this triad. That is, *Keter* is on top, the *Hochmah* and *Bina* qualities of the top portion of the Godhead are on the row below. This implies that the row they appear on is female in opposition to the male *Keter* on top. Now, *Keter's* spirituality is so pronounced that its qualities cannot be described. He, therefore, is an identity, an indistinction, and a unity of opposites like flesh-spirit or male-female. His character is expressed and only somewhat knowable in the two *sefirot* He is directly linked to, and they are again also male-female. While the top triad of the Kabbalah God has this male-female pair, the 3 triadic qualities nonetheless are strongly in the spirit and so are a masculine triad, even if some mystical accounts of the top three sefirot refer to them as mothers, which of course confirms the use of female gender as well.

While the top portion of the Godhead has 3 *sefirot*, the bottom has seven, and these can be divided as six and one. The six are marked as male (even if they are also male-female as discussed elsewhere) while the bottom-most *midot* or *sefirot* of the mystical Godhead is the most pronounced, flesh portion, or female portion. She is called *Shekinah*. She is encompassed or dominated by the above 6 qualities which then form a spiritual, male above and a single flesh below. That is, after the top 3 unified qualities of the mystical Godhead come six explicitly male qualities, they are opposed by a seventh at the bottom, the *Shekinah* which is also explicitly female. Gender is emphasized here because there is spiritual copulation between these *sefirot* and *Shekinah*.[14] The seven qualities below are also a unity. They are in an act of perpetual intercourse. This act is frozen into a constant state of connection, unifying the distinction of act and state as well as male-female in the spiritual intercourse occurring in the Godhead. Thus, just as there are the three above, (again, 3 and 7 are whole numbers in this tradition) the bottom 7portion replicates the top in that like *Keter, Hochmah* and *Bina*, they are a male 6 and a female seventh. Male and female repeat themselves! Hence the top portion is made of:

<u>male</u>
<u>female</u>

expressed as Male-female as a singular unit where the bottom portion is:

male
female

also is a singular but identical unit. All 6 mid-section *sefirot* are male but also are male-female in that they are identical to the *Shekinah* below to which they are united. This is much like the unity of *Keter* and *Hochmah-Binah*. And, the unity of the bottom seven sefirot in a frozen copulation act/state brings us male-female throughout. So top and bottom are identical -- and they are different, we have common differences top and bottom and a unity just as in the Trinity. The top portion is male, the bottom, emphasizing *Shekinah* is female. Males occupying the bottom portion form triads in the form of 2 triangles. This entire bottom unit replicates the structure of the top, it being male and female. So, we have a common male/female difference everywhere along with common triadics throughout. Reiterating my theme, the mystical God of Kabbalah is a religious construction that demonstrates a varying use of spirit/flesh, in its more gendered and vertical triadic expression. And its fundamental structure repeats the unity of the Trinity, using male female instead of spirit and flesh to establish its unity through common differences.

Finally, Allah is the godhead term in Islam, the religion atop the common differences system (religious domain triad as seen in **Illustration 4**), making it the 'purely' spiritual of the three religions. This spirit religion godhead should show the most apparent unity of the three divinities since it is marked as spiritual. Yet it still must still exhibit triadic structure given our hypothesis: a unity of spirit and flesh difference must compose unity, since unity requires difference of something to be unified. Since it contains differences and is united, it must be triadic no matter how indistinctly. Significantly, Allah is one word, composed of two sounds, al and la. As a singular word it is especially spiritual and unified. As two sounds that are oppositional, al being the reverse of la, we get a distinction indistinctly in the singular name Allah. Different binary sounds compose one word giving us a triad. The God trope Allah is triadic in a singular, spiritual word. Like the godhead of mystical Judaism and the tripartite God of the Trinity, we see a unity through common differences, structurally, triadically and unconsciously expressed.

Essay 17- Pentecostalism and Transformation: A New Approach

Transformation as a conceptual tool of structural analysis is discussed and employed by Levi-Strauss and others, but it remains a relatively underdeveloped idea. Considering it here in the context of Pentecostalism, I will devise an abstract description of its logical processes. In current usage, transformation refers to a switch of some sort, whether in states, activities, or relationships. I suggest that transformation may be analyzed as a complex process involving its apparent opposite - that is, a reverse of transformation, or formation. While transformation involves a switch to something different, formation involves an association of cultural elements with something similar. I will show that likeness is the key to difference, that formation is key to transformation. Transformation then involves both identity and difference.

The processes of transformation and formation can be illustrated by the Pentecostalism of the small Church of God that I studied in Chicago. In Pentecostalism, a flesh → spirit transformation is basic to the religion and the process of formation in this transformation involves the association of like or similar elements: flesh → flesh and spirit → spirit as analysis will show. In the structural process of formation, like or similar entities go to like, and an association between similar cultural elements is the route by which a transformation or switch to a difference such as flesh → spirit takes place.

To elaborate, when it comes to a transformation, the spirit/flesh opposition displays four possible orderings of cultural elements:

TRANSFORMATION

flesh → spirit

spirit → flesh

FORMATION

flesh → flesh

spirit → spirit

The latter two pairs are formations of likeness. Association of like cultural elements may be illustrated by such statements as "an eye for an eye, a tooth for a tooth," "dust to dust and ashes to ashes," and "render to Caesar the things which are Caesar's." In Pentecostalism, things of a like nature associate unproblematically without any requirement for elaborate cultural structuring.

The first two pairs in the diagram, however, represent transformations or switches which problematically associate different things. In other words, flesh is not spirit; they are opposites in Pentecostalism and differ as much as damnation and salvation do. Yet to be saved in Pentecostalism, a person -who is, by cultural definition, in the flesh- must become of the spirit. Such a conversion is problematic in the sense that it is incongruous by the cultural nature of things for a person in the flesh to become a living person in the spirit. The concept of flesh in the raw is the opposite of pure spirit. This problematic association of the two is affected through a systemic device called here a rule of formation. In this case, Jesus, who is a man in the flesh, makes possible a human spiritual transformation through His experience on the cross. As God in the flesh, Jesus provides, through flesh, the association of humans and God or Spirit which permits a person to be converted and enter a spiritual domain. Thus, cultural elements that are alike-here (human) flesh and (Jesus's) flesh-are a bridge, though not the only one, to a transformation from flesh to spirit.

Therefore, transformation involves a movement toward difference; the complementary aspect of transformation involves identity. The claim here is that to create a difference (obviously, a switch or transformation) the movement to a difference necessarily involves cultural elements that display likeness which is a form of identity. To further illustrate these lawful processes of transformation and formation,

244

both the process of conversion and Jesus's experience on the cross will be examined in detail. These two aspects of Pentecostalism are highly interrelated: each shows an orderly arrangement of cultural elements per the rules of transformation and formation.

• • •

To begin, conversion involves an individual's initial acceptance of Jesus Christ into his or her life. It affects a change or a transformation (also a Pentecostal term as in statements like, "Ye must be transformed") of the believer's being, which the system initially categorizes as in the flesh and as natural. To understand the notion of conversion, it is important to first understand the Pentecostal notion of the natural man. for the switch from damned to saved, from sinner to saint, necessarily involves contact between the opposed states. Therefore, through an examination of the natural, sinful state, transformation and formation may be analytically discerned.

According to believers, people in the flesh are born with a "speck of spirit." This spirit is part of the natural condition of man, which nonetheless is of the flesh and sinful. The natural man, say believers, is untransformed and unfulfilled. He does not know the spiritual possibilities in his own nature, which if realized, may make him whole. It is the spiritual life which makes a person complete. Life in the flesh is divorced from the spirit. Thus, the unconverted man is alienated from God and lacks His spiritual grace and salvation. Flesh encompasses the natural man's being, although it nevertheless includes spirit. The state of the natural man's being at birth and throughout his unconverted life can be illustrated as:

flesh / spirit (in the flesh)
flesh

The flesh, whether or not it is in the denominator, is encompassing. From a Pentecostal point of view, this state requires transformation and is unstable.

An individual then is always composed of spirit and flesh, and Pentecostalism maintains that one can be basically of the flesh or in the spirit. The problem that Pentecostalism addresses is the problem of conversion and spiritual transformation. It is directed in part at natural and sinful people who are born to suffer the mortal fate of flesh and aims to make them spiritual Christians, who, in a binary fashion, will have eternal life.

To do this, the system works in part toward a switch in the encompassing dimension of the individual's nature. This switch is only possible because, within the natural individual, as we have seen, there exists a germ of spirit. This spiritual seed in human nature is one of the keys to effecting a change in the individual. In conversion, a Christian term for initial spiritual transformation, the Holy Ghost is a divine agent of transformation. He affects an increase and dominance of the spirit in the individual by entering him or her and filling his or her soul or inner vessel. This entrance is possible by virtue of the individual's innate spiritual yearning; the inner nature is transformed by a divine act, which is spiritual. The result is a transformed, internal state which must at the same time also act externally for the Lord. The new spiritual encompassment of the believer's being can be diagrammed:

Encompassing: flesh   spirit

Encompassed: flesh/spirit→spirit/flesh

ILLUSTRATION 9

This illustration represents a transformation occurring by way of likeness. That is, the spirit in the original state on the left allows spirit by way of the Holy Spirit to encompass the second or transformed state. The formative movement from the Holy Spirit to the human speck of spirit does not, however, exhaust the rule of likeness as expressed in conversion. For example, in conversion acts link up with acts; both the Holy Spirit and the converting individual act to effect a spiritual transformation.

Further, the internal/external opposition also applies here consistent with the law of formation. In other words, the individual's being is defined within Pentecostalism as having an internal as well as external aspect. Pentecostalism defines the person's inner self as the appropriate home for the spirit; the Holy Ghost, who as spirit carries with Him a sense of innerness, properly works conversion in the individual's heart. Thus, the interior aspect of the Holy Ghost and the individual have contact within the person, so this unproblematic association is one of like to like, or in this case, inner to inner.

The alignment of elements in the Christian transformation of conversion, however, is not as simple as these spirit → spirit, act → act, and internal → internal formations indicate. The spoken word in the personal appeals of Christians to nonbelievers is also an element of Holy Ghost transformation. These words, spoken by Christians to unbelievers or potential converts, commonly convey the Word of God and its linguistic message of salvation. Thus, the spirit is conveyed through words: words → words is an instance of like to like. However, since spirit is essentially internal in Pentecostalism and spoken words are in a sense external, religious words may appear incongruous in the external world where speech events occur.

This problem is addressed by eliminating it. In the conversion process, the worldly aspects of speaking are not marked in a meaningful way: the essential aspects of this interaction are considered inward. When the Holy Ghost is internalized by a convert through a linguistic message delivered by someone through a speech act, the conversion is accomplished through a linguistic medium. This Christian message is unmarked as external but spiritually marked as internal. Thus, the comprehension of a divine, if linguistic, message is an internal act appropriate to the soul and inner heart of man. Divine spirit goes to spirit in human flesh conversion, illustrating the law of like to like within a transformation. The human speaker is the flesh aspect of this communication though he or she acts in the spirit, while the Holy Spirit is the spirit, so spirit and flesh are part of the conversion communication as well.

The seeming incongruity of the external aspects of proselytizing or speech in the experience of an internal spiritual conversion raises the issue of the place of elements such as exterior in this transformation process. Since elements like outer and flesh are oppositionally connected to internal and spiritual acts, what role do they play? How do they also express rules of likeness in the transformational process?

To provide answers, it is useful to examine the fleshly dimension in conversion pleas: the persuading and embodied believer must perform acts of faith, ordinarily inviting the Holy Ghost into his or her heart to assist in conversion. Further, the corporeal believer, acting as a physical being, may contribute to the conversion process through fleshly and worldly action.

This in-the-flesh aspect of communicating about the Word is clearly structured in the Pentecostal system. Critically, concrete speech acts transform just because a believer can appropriately associate in the physical world with the unbeliever. Remembering that a spiritual Christian is also in the flesh —as is the fleshly state of the sinner with whom he speaks, and remembering that conversion involves physical acts of a Christian who has a physical state, we can diagram the nature of this worldly and interpersonal speech act with the sinner:

a man in the spirit	a man in the flesh
saint	sinner
inner...outer	outer...inner
word....word	word....word
state.....act	act.....state

ILLUSTRATION 10

Clearly, the culturally encoded outer aspects of human interaction (in contrast with the Holy Spirit's action, which is internal) relate not only to words in speech acts but more broadly to the general external life of the nonbeliever. The nonbeliever may be contacted by a believer who also is a person in the flesh. Sharing outer-worldly activity, they can interact through like natures and this ability leads to the culturally structured possibility of transformation by words. Fittingly, words may be exchanged in interaction because language is an attribute of people in the world. At the same time, words may also internally mediate the Word. Words may be brought inside because an individual has within him a speck of spirit, and words are comprehended internally. This contiguity permits the spirit to enter the nonbeliever's inner vessel by way of a relationship not only with the spirit but also with a human in the flesh.

Transformation occurs as the spoken word conveys to the nonbeliever the complex of meaningful associations assigned to it within Pentecostalism (spirit, light, acts, purity, perfection, sanctification, etc.) with the Holy Spirit acting to aid the comprehension of the potential convert. Thus, conversion involves a transformation and appropriate contacts of spirit with spirit and flesh with flesh, as well as other contacts of likeness.

Converting, however, is not just a matter of speaking and listening to the Word, nor does it simply involve a switch in the encompassing dimension of one's being. It also involves following the way of Jesus and experiencing His crucifixion as one's own. Christ's cross is the altar on which individual conversion is achieved; the additional aspects of converting depend on the nature of Christ's death and on the cultural appropriateness of Christ's sacrifice. When a nonbeliever converts, he or she is joining the body of Christ, which makes that person's salvation possible. This possibility and His sacrifice also demonstrate the structural principles of transformation.

• • •

The believer first sees the light, so Pentecostals sing, at the cross; and the cross is where Jesus shows mankind the way in which sinfulness can be laid low so that people may rise in the spirit. The burden of all human sins, including those which necessarily arise from human, fleshly natures, is upon Him. Jesus is in the flesh and in the agony of His death He personifies the torment and pain that sin causes man. His death is described as a passionate act through which God's love for the world is realized. And in His loving agony, Jesus, like the Godhead (this cannot be fully developed here) summarizes a crucial opposition of the system, namely individual/ collective. That is, not only does His death mark a transition from the collective age of the Jews to an individual dispensation of grace to Christian individuals, but He is also both an individual and collective representation of humans in the spirit. His individual crucifixion may be the crucifixion of all persons: the way Jesus lays low His flesh for the spirit shows how all individuals may switch from mortal, carnal existence to immortal, spiritual life. Crucifixion, therefore, is a spiritual act in which spirit is elevated and flesh is lowered:

spirit: above
flesh: below

It is an act for all mankind done by one man, and for those who likewise follow the cross, there is a reward, namely a state of grace. So, the crucifixion affects a switch that occurs in the form of an exchange: in exchange for individual acts (by Jesus) the church and its believers collectively receive states of grace. But in consequence, the individual believing person is the church's or the collective's unit or agent. He or she acts on his or her own part to be saved. Previously, Jewish priests collectively made sacrifices to God to remove sin. In crucifixion, God gives Himself to man and individuals who through their collective identification with His act receive His uplifting. Crucifixion then involves a second act of exchange: like Jesus, individual people give over life in the flesh for a life in the spirit. Where Jesus gave his life (or flesh) for mankind, people also make this sacrifice. They give over their flesh to death- death is of the flesh and intrinsic to the human condition - to receive eternal, spiritual life.

Humans may follow Jesus because of the nature of His body in crucifixion. As Jesus initiated a new period of grace in history, the church which in Pentecostalism is defined as the body of Christ, became a collective means of grace. God gave His body to death, and so interpretively, to man. Through this gift, man gains a mode of likeness by which he may enter the spiritual realm. Christ's body goes to man- flesh to flesh-and man, who identifies with the body in the collectivity of the church, becomes Jesus's bride, and so may follow and receive Him. Individual believers may identify with the crucified God and uplift their spirit by submitting their flesh just as He did. Thus, as part of the new and systematic mode of salvation affected by Jesus, the church is married to Christ and His body, submitting to His submission and gaining the salvation He affects, with individual believers being the core of the Church's collective submission.

Therefore, the movement from human death to spiritual life, which is, of course, the essential transformation in Pentecostalism and which is initiated at the cross, involves modes of identification by likeness on the part of the believers and God. It is through the flesh that mankind shares in God's salvation. God initially makes this contact by coming to man as spirit in the flesh. This coming in a medial form is necessary, an informant said, to bridge the gap between human and Godly nature. Similarly, His death and rising complete the medial significance of Jesus's nature. He shows how to move from being in the flesh to being in the spirit. His body, perfect and yet representative of all bodies, is the point of identification and association through which people in the flesh may gain access to spiritual blessing in the new period or age of grace.

The collective identification with Jesus's body is in fact individually performed by discrete, moral agents. The collective aspect of identification with the crucifixion initially allows all individuals access to God's ultimate blessings. But concomitant with the rules for like associating with like in the crucifixion, this access is further developed in two ways. First by the particular element through which contact between God and man is established -namely through His blood, and second, by a major contrast, namely the inner/outer dichotomy. People who become saved by acts-their own and God's, and especially by Jesus's sacrifice- are, as believers repeatedly said, in the body of Christ. They are not exterior to it. Here flesh is generally conceived of as exterior while the spirit is interior. People connect with Christ and His salvation from the inside but through the flesh. How is this contact effected?

It is established principally by the blood Jesus shed on the cross. Believers rhapsodize in song about the saving power of Jesus's blood and people say they are washed in the blood or that they are in the blood of Jesus. What are the properties of this blood and how is it consistent with the transformational process as described here? Blood obviously is of the flesh; equally, it is also inside the body, liquid and flowing. The spirit is associated in Pentecostalism both with the internal and with viscous fluids that fill one's inner vessel or the soul. Blood is also associated with Jesus: it flows downward when He is hung on the cross. It, therefore, comes from above, as must the Godhead on Earth, and it is without sin, as is its source. Somewhat speculatively, blood is also associated with healing, certainly according to my informants, but not in any concrete way. As we also know, spirit makes people religiously whole; blood associated with spirit, miraculously though that association be in Jesus. Blood then offers healing and the possibility of wholeness to people and so the blood of Jesus has a transforming power. It is His blood that saves and this internal, saving and transforming power is obvious in the ways blood, which is also internal like spirit, is described. Therefore, like Jesus, His blood is in the spirit even if it also is in the flesh.

Further, Jesus's blood cleanses, and the Christian who is in it is whitened whiter than snow. Ordinary blood stains rather than cleans and so the spiritual nature of purification by blood immersion is patent. It is miraculous, this blood of Jesus, and it flows down on the Christian from above. The Christian-who is below Jesus at the cross-then becomes under the blood, as Pentecostals say. As a marked spiritual but unmarked flesh component of Christ, blood is low, compared to the spiritual aspect, which is high. Blood is also in the flesh of the believer who, as a human, is low compared to Jesus. Blood's fleshly aspect, moreover, is underlined by the natural effect informants say it has on the untransformed, Jews in particular, whom it collectively and naturally stains, even as it cleanses individual Christians. Jesus' flesh then is divided by flesh and blood, which is a spirit and flesh distinction in the flesh, blood having the character of both.

Thus, these two low elements of blood, one in a spiritual realm in Christ and the other in a fleshly domain of people on Earth, meet at the foot of the cross, much as the humble woman of the street kissed Jesus's feet. Blood, which associates with the heart and so with the loving death and agony of Christ, meets believers in a dimension of likeness. Believers then become Christians in the blood of Christ. The internal, in the flesh, aspect of this meeting is spiritualized by another co-occurrence: Jesus or the Holy Spirit then enters the believer's heart. This meeting of spirit in the flesh of Jesus and in the believer is especially appropriate in the light of human nature which, as discussed above, contains a speck of spirit within. We have, therefore, an outside-to-inside connection in the blood which transforms the believer from an outward, fleshly person to a more inward and spiritual Christian. This flesh connection through blood is complemented by the work of the Holy Spirit. (The Holy Spirit is in the spirit in this conversion process and Jesus is in the flesh). For the person under the cross, this splitting of spirit and flesh is a division brought about by Christ's sacrifice. Division, of course, is oppositionally appropriate to a binary scheme; in a sense division or separation is a binary opposition. Here, division works to make people whole and greatly multiplied in the blessings of the spirit through separation from the flesh.

This initiates a long cycle of spiritual growth that ultimately transforms the flesh more fully, eventually making it wholly compatible with spirit, and eternal life as well as compatible with the experience of glossolalia. Conversion, with its division of blood in flesh, and spirit through the Holy Ghost, begins the process of uniting spirit with a spiritualized flesh. I suggest that this two-fold process reflects the spirit and flesh opposition as well. Where conversion through preaching or linguistic acts is associated with words and so is especially associated with the spirit, conversion at the cross is a physical or fleshly aspect of that process. It is a relationship building act in the spiritual flesh and so it is a form of spiritual intercourse in this world, spiritually procreating for all, establishing Christian brotherhood and sisterhood in the spirit, and mirroring intercourse in the family which likewise is relationship-building. Both initial conversion and the experience at the cross are possible through the likeness of the convert to the preaching Christian and to Christ in both spirit and flesh. Likeness is married to difference yet again. Transformation takes the philosophic observation that difference requires identity and uses likeness or identity to establish a difference. The complex of elements that makes possible a conversion transformation in Pentecostalism forms a structural chain, linking differences by similar, bridging elements that permit switches from one structural link to the next.

This point can be demonstrated logically. A transformed element is assigned the value of Y. This Y represents a switch from X. The switch, consistent with the binary nature of such systems, involves a difference. Then it follows that the original element had to have something in common with the resulting element Y in order that the two elements be structured as opposites. Were elements X and Y totally random elements, the system of opposition or transformation between them would be nonexistent. Transformation and opposition would have no coherence in such cases. In fact, a difference between the two elements is only discernible or coherent through their "common" character. Thus, to move toward a difference or to establish a transformation necessarily involves a point of identification between related elements. In this case, the quality that unifies spirit/flesh relation or difference is God who appears as the speck of spirit in the flesh of the believer and Christ's body on the cross.

• • •

Given the argument for rules of transformation and formation presented here, one important question is: How are similar and different elements abstracted from the field material I gathered in studying this Pentecostal church? I believe that relations of likeness are known through their actual, unproblematic association with one another in the statements or actions of believers. Where, for example, elements a, b, or c, like spirit, the Word or transforming blood, are associated with y, and where they are not in any immediate sense contrastive relations, this web of elements has a relation of likeness. This likeness may exist by arbitrary cultural fiat: these elements go together and can be contiguous. Nonetheless, this arbitrariness is systematically developed in a transformation, which uses this likeness to make a meaningful difference.

In any case, given this definition of similarity between cultural elements, which may be uncovered by the nature of their unproblematic association within the given cultural framework, the path of likeness through which difference can be affected becomes discernible. The concept of likeness in transformational processes, therefore, is a concrete corollary to the notion that, within a cultural framework, meaningful relatedness always involves commonality among the associated elements.

Identity and difference, known as spirit and flesh, then, stand at the root not only of Christian knowledge but also of Christian transformation, as viewed by the Pentecostals I studied.

Essay 18- The Eucharist, the Passover, and the Word

If Western religion is to Western kinship as spirit is to flesh and if, within this spirit domain, Judaism is likewise to Christianity as flesh is to spirit, then is it possible to make a prediction? Is it not possible to predict that both the Jewish sub-domain and the Christian sub-domain are also divided in a major way by a flesh/spirit distinction? After all, the kinship system takes the spirit flesh distinction and elaborates basic domestic family terms through it. Husband and wife are wed in the spirit and united in the flesh. Their spiritual act of marriage produces a state of spousal relationship, with their acts of the flesh likewise producing children whose state of relationship in the flesh defines the scope of the family. Flesh and spirit further elaborate relations outside the family. There are relations by blood (and flesh) and relations through marriage or in-laws. These in- laws, who are in the kinship domain, are nonetheless defined through the spirit. But consistent with the concrete nature of kinship flesh, spirit is viewed concretely as law or in-law.

Therefore, in kinship, relationships are elaborated principally, though not solely, through the flesh/spirit dichotomy, in the context of flesh. Could major distinctions of the same sort exist in the spiritual or religious sphere? Using a flesh spirit principle, it is predictable that both Jewish and Christian domains can be divided or elaborated by the flesh/spirit distinction. In Judaism, it predicts that traditional orthodoxy, which is concretely bound by commandment and law, a flesh expression therefore of Jewish spirit, would have a spiritual opponent. This opponent would make *ruach* (spirit) more important than the literal practice of the law. Perhaps Hassidism is that happy opponent. In Christianity, the obvious distinction is between Catholicism and Protestantism. Our theory suggests that a defining difference between these two religions should occur along a flesh/spirit axis. If Catholicism is the fleshly version of a spiritual Christianity, then Protestantism expresses a spirit version of Christianity. Perhaps the difference in focus might be an emphasis on Christ's body in Catholicism and the Word of God in Protestantism. My theory, then, predicts that Catholicism should have a fundamental focus, however, it develops and changes, in the spiritual flesh of Christ, and this is so both in terms of what the Church is, namely the body of Christ, and of what the mass celebrates, namely the Eucharist.

The Eucharist is the central Catholic sacrament; it is the end or ultimate telos of the mass. Mass is the religious service Catholics undertake on Sundays. It celebrates Christ's sacrifice on the cross, which it enacts in the Eucharist. In the Eucharist, the sacrifice of Christ is essentially embodied in the wine and wafer which are consumed by believers and priests. This is the Eucharistic act and it is called taking communion. Christ is literally present in the two signs: the wafer and the wine. It is His crucified flesh and blood which are eaten or incorporated into the faithful. The Eucharist signifies the crucifixion of Christ in a literal act of eating; it is the sacrament of the cross. This eating sacrament has a connection to the Jewish Passover, which not only reveals the structures constructing the Eucharist, but it also shows how both the Passover and the Eucharist are essentially of the flesh, while nonetheless as different as flesh is to spirit.

The Eucharist has its roots in the last supper Jesus shared with his followers before being crucified. During this Passover meal, Jesus said to his apostles, "Do this for a commemoration of me": the eating of bread and the drinking of wine were introduced at the Passover Seder before He died. He took the bread, blessed it, gave it to his disciples, and said, "Take, eat this my body". Then He took a cup of wine saying, "Drink this for this is my blood of the New Testament, shed for the remission of sins." Now, the bread of the Seder is flat-it has not risen. It is bread untransformed much as Jesus had not risen from the dead nor undergone the deadly transformation of the cross. In these respects, the *matzah* or flat wafer of bread has much in common with Passover celebrating Jesus. It is literally like the living Savior-it is untransformed. Jesus says exactly this: eat my body for the bread.

Now, *matzah* is not an ordinary religious symbol in Judaism. It marks an extraordinary event and a holiday that begins the historic existence of a Jewish people with a law and eventually a land. This historical theme contrasts with the theme of God's creation. That is, historical events such as leaving Egypt and coming to Israel, assisted though they may be by God, are nonetheless the actions of people, who increasingly take responsibility for the law and the land. By contrast, God's creation is not human-historical; it is divine only, the natural act of a Lord Creator. Not only is there a nature/culture distinction here, but there is also difference in terms of completeness or fulfillment.

In other words, Creation was completed in seven days and is marked and completed by the Sabbath. The Passover, like Creation, is also a beginning, but it is not complete. Leaving Egypt is not getting to Israel, and that is not even the whole story. So, in a sense, the *matzah* reflects this incompleteness: it is untransformed; it has not risen. The bread that marks the Jewish Sabbath celebration, however, celebrates a day that remembers a complete creation. It, therefore, is a full bread. It is made from dough that has risen. It is called *challah* and its completeness is accentuated by its shape. It is twisted bread that comes full circle, especially on Jewish holidays, when it is made in a circular rather than in an elongated fashion. Circles, which are twisted, suggest completeness. Its blessing remembers creation and even Passover. It is complete.

Therefore, when Jesus says to eat this bread in remembrance of me (and my soon-to-occur crucifixion) he is like *matzah* in the sense that He is at a beginning which is not complete and not transformed or risen. But He is very much like the *matzah* because he is concrete and, in the flesh, food not fully cooked. As Sabbath bread marks creation and incidentally, the Passover also, so too will Jesus complete the themes of creation and history by beginning a new period of salvation. This is not a religious statement, but a structural one. *Matzah* is a bread with a contrast: *Challah*. One is untransformed or flat, the other is fully cooked (transformed) or risen. Jesus can be like the flatbread, which is untransformed because He, from the standpoint of Christian constructs, is a fulfillment which has a beginning, a life in the flesh, and an end or completion -- transformation in the spirit.

He is like flatbread but like risen bread also. He rises; since he is complete, i.e., like both, he can liken Himself to *matzah*, though as a flat symbol it only partially represents His nature. It represents his flesh but as a symbol, it requires something additional, something transformed and more spirit-like. It requires wine which is a hallmark of the Seder. Regarding the Seder's wine, its ceremonial place here and within Judaism generally marks life or spirit. In the Seder, it provides the intoxication that celebrates the freedom to be as a people, which is the tale and message of Passover. This intoxication, based on the four full cups of wine each participant is commanded to drink at this meal, lets the participant's state be at one with the Seder's message: with Passover, Israel is full of life, as is the tipsy Passover participant. And the life of Israel as a nation now begins with an Exodus. This is a separation, a splitting of Israel away from the Egyptians. It affects a transformation, a change from slavery to freedom. The kosher Passover wine celebrates the life in this. Jesus, too, is like this wine. Wine is a fermented substance, a transformed body that gives *ruach* or life. Jesus also gives life, in the Catholic scheme, life eternal by permitting his transforming body to die for the remission of sin. Where Passover wine is transformed, Jesus's body is transforming. Thus, the Seder's bread and wine as a symbolic replication of the bread from Exodus are similar but different from a bread and wine of the Eucharist.

These last two are literal symbols in the sense that they not only represent Jesus, they are Jesus. They re-present Him. The *matzah* of the Seder does the very same: it is the bread of affliction Jewish forefathers brought out of Egypt, yet it is recently made *matzah*. Still, big differences exist here. Perhaps the most telling is the kind of transformation effected. The Jewish transformation in Passover is one of separation. The Exodus from Egypt changed or transformed the enslaved Jews into a separate people, later to be a people with a revealed law and land. It is a historical trans-formation of a particular people by way of separation. The crucifixion, on the other hand, affects a difference, the salvation or new life of believers, by a transformation for all time and for all peoples, through the dying Christ on the cross.

In Judaism, a separation (from the Egyptians) affects a transformation by creating a different Jewish and collective or whole people. But in Christianity a transformation (the dying Christ) affects a different state for individual believers, from sinner to whole individual, who become equals or siblings in the Christ. The emphasis on transformation and difference work in opposite ways. But importantly,

258

in the food of the Seder and the food of Eucharist, we can see the spirit/flesh characteristics of each faith.

In other words, the bread and wine of the Seder are primarily bread and wine even if they are meaningful symbols. They are consumed as food and drink, they remember a 'factual' history of a particular people and they are the basis of a ceremonial meal. The bread and wine of the Eucharist, on the other hand, are not the basis of a ritual meal. They are not food for the body. They do not remember a historical event critical to a particular people but instead herald an event for all times and all places, a story for all peoples. While the bread and wine are eaten, it is really the incorporation of God into the believer, a communion with his sacrifice by way of food that takes place. It is a foretaste of the future; an experience of faith and it is the opposite of remembrance. Faith and crucifixion go forward, and remembrance and Passover go back in time.

Clearly, there is a systematic opposition between central Jewish and Catholic motifs. Judaism is historical, particular, collective and remembering. It is focused on the flesh; it sanctifies its believers in part through eating. Judaism even remembers with food. Just as eating is of the body, Judaism is of the flesh, though this does not negate its spiritual, sanctifying religiosity. It sanctifies things in this world: its God is firstly a living, not a dying God; it emphasizes life, which it blesses and holds forth to its practitioners as a Jewish way of life. Catholicism maintains continuity with this of-the-flesh religion while essentially reversing its character. It transforms in the spirit the fact of death in the flesh. It challenges the separating character of Jewish particularism by its universalizing salvation. Yet it begins, as does Judaism, with the flesh. Most significantly, crucifixion as embodied by the Eucharist involves eating. The Eucharistic meal is the body and blood of God. The spiritual salvation of this act emphasizes, as the outset of this essay predicted, the flesh in the spiritual or Catholic religious dimension. The Eucharist, like the crucifixion itself, is about a sacrifice of a body, and sacrifice by its very nature is of the flesh. This nonetheless is a religious or spiritual concern even as the believer enters a relationship with Christ through his body, the principal commonality between man and God. Flesh goes to like flesh to effect a transformation in the spirit. In Catholicism, by consuming the body of Christ in the Eucharist, each Christian partakes of the crucifixion and its triumph over death.

It is noteworthy that traditional Jewish worship on Sabbath contains a service called *Shacharit*, which means sacrifice. This service is based on the sacrificial service in the Temple of Jerusalem conducted by the high priest, alone in the holiest of holies, where animals were ritually slaughtered. This sacrifice has been 'spiritualized' in traditional Judaism in the sense that Hebraic prayer progressively substitutes for actual sacrifice. By comparison to Temple days, the service has been democratized and universalized as well, its religion allowing for a moral advance from Biblical practices. All Jews may participate in the 'sacrifice' or service through collective prayer. Just as Jewish High priestly sacrifice is remembered in the *Shacharit* to spiritually renew the present Jewish community, Jesus's historic sacrifice represents a founding act of spiritual salvation, through his fleshly offering.

So, yet again, we see a systematic contrast (and similarity) between Jewish practice and Catholic rite. Here, sacrifice looms as a central to both worship services: while each is based in the flesh of a dead offering, both spiritualize this. Judaism moves from a single priest to collective worship and from slaughter to prayer. With this movement from sacrifice, there is also a sub- theme: the incorporation of death-for the sake of completeness in bygone priestly practices- into a religious system that celebrates life. Catholicism moves from the slaughter of a single "High Priest" to individual salvation for all mankind. The oppositions in play include single/collective, flesh/spirit. In terms of structural emphasis, both are rooted first in the sacrificial flesh dimension of spiritual life.

Protestantism, at least the Methodist offshoot Pentecostalism with which I am familiar, on the other hand, does not root itself in the flesh dimension of spiritual life. Instead, its focus is on spiritual gifts and on the Word of God. Apparently like other Protestantism, it bans visual signs, such as statutes of Jesus. It drops the overarching importance of Mary, a mother and a personage of the flesh and childbearing, and it eliminates the Eucharist as the centerpiece of religious worship. Instead, it emphasizes preaching the Gospel and the experience of the Holy Spirit. The Gospel, of course, is made up of words, as is the preacher's discourse.

Even the experience of the Holy Spirit in glossolalia involves speaking in tongues or word-sounds. Words and word-sounds are endlessly spiritual; they are spoken in a spirited manner and they are even noisily appreciated. The aim is salvation, and without any value judgment, it is apparent that even a superficial description of Pentecostal practice shows it to be a religion primarily in the spirit. Its contrast with Catholicism follows a spirit/flesh distinction. And this is high- lighted in the differing use of words in the two subsystems. In Pentecostalism, the preacher's use of words is different only in degree from those of a revivalist or those of an ordinary believer. In other words, like any Christian, the preacher uses the word to convey the message of salvation preached by Jesus. He, as an agent who is spirit in flesh, uses spirit - Word – to connect to sinners who also have a residual speck of spirit or soul that can respond to his message. It is a message in the spirit which can transform the fleshly sinner who, under conviction, undergoes conversion and begins an ascending life in the spirit. Any time any Christian speaks the Word to the unconverted, the same structured act of communication takes place. Any Christian can be a preacher or revivalist; the message of Jesus's salvation is spread spiritually by the Word. Here this aim at conversion, or its doubling in the continuing work of the spirit in the fleshly lives of believers, is the heart of the Pentecostal religious service. Preaching affects a spiritual blessing and experience; it is what Pentecostal worship is all about.

By contrast, the priest in the mass uses words to a different effect. His audience is not composed of individual equals; the priest is above the total congregation. He is an individual to a collective mass; he is high to low, and he speaks words that would have no effect were they uttered by congregants. The priest is like Christ to the Church; he is His embodiment and he speaks the words Christ spoke. In the Eucharist, in the traditional Latin mass, for example, the priest holds up a wafer of bread and says, "Behold the Lamb of God", and then gives the communion or the meal of the Eucharist to each worshiper. The physically present priest prays, "May the Body of our Lord Jesus Christ preserve your soul for everlasting life." The priest consecrates the Eucharistic meal and he does this by using words which Jesus Christ Himself uttered. As the Council of Trent's doctrine of the Eucharist clarifies, it is through the words of consecration and not through the believing communicant's faith that transubstantiation occurs. That is, the priest's words affect the actual transformation of the bread and wine into the body and blood of Christ. But it is their reality, the actual presence of Jesus in the bread and wine that are most important. The words of the priest bring the reality of the sacrifice to bear to the believer. The Eucharist begins with the idea that Jesus is God made man, the incarnate of the Word. His incarnate Word remains active and present until the end of the world through the literal signs of Eucharist. So, to repeat, there is the sacramental presence of Christ, a presence that is both real and simultaneously contained in a sign under the appearances of bread and wine. The words of the priest are secondary to the symbolism of the mass. They identify what is primary: the body of Christ and its literal symbolism in food.

Therefore, there is the sacramental eating of the Eucharist and through it the action of Christ on Christian souls through His body. Believers consume Christ and perfect their incorporation into him. This sacrament consists of a double sign: the bread and the wine. There is also Christ's broken body, delivered for salvation, with His shed blood. Not only is the Eucharist a sacrament of the body of Christ present and acting as food at a collective feast, it is also a sacrament on His sacrifice, the sacrifice on the cross.

What is this sacrifice? It involves the immolation of a victim, who suffers and dies. It has an external and an internal aspect. In the mass and in the sacrifice of the cross, the external events were private for Jesus, and the internal experience of these events are public for Christians. The priest may publicly perform this sacrifice externally so that the community of believers may realize the internal spirit of the outward sign or performance. Structure is omnipresent here. The most obvious is spirit and flesh. In the Eucharist, the believer, a person in the flesh, relates to Jesus through the flesh, which he eats. Flesh goes to flesh, effecting a spiritual transformation. All the other structures, such as internal/external, which have a complicated play here, are governed by the master spirit/flesh relationship. The believer comes to Christ through His body, which he eats, and which likewise is the Church. Just as Judaism, a religion in the flesh, thinks with food, so does Catholicism's Eucharist. While its purpose is spiritual, its similarity with Judaism confirms that Catholicism is a fleshly expression of a spiritual domain. This is highlighted by the importance of eating in the Eucharist and even is confirmed in relatively small details. When the Biblical Jews saw God in all His Glory in the mountain cleft as they first approached Israel, they celebrated by feasting. Likewise, Catholics celebrate God through the food of His body and in the body of his Church.

Catholicism represents a fleshly expression of a distinction within a spiritual-religious domain. This is simply a different use of the same structures. Judaism seeks spirit in the flesh; Catholicism, in a complicated way, emphasizing the flesh in the spirit. Through its affinity and difference with Judaism, Catholicism sets a similar table albeit with a different meal. One could argue that the use of systematic differences here is overextended. How, for example, is the difference between Protestantism as a spirit version of Christianity and Catholicism as a flesh version established by differing emphases on the use of words. Doesn't Quakerism use silence rather than sound in its worship? Certainly, Quakers are Protestants. Doesn't this undermine the argument?

In answer, I hold that these systems and subsystems simply turn over structure to establish themselves as distinct. That is, if the word is primary in Protestantism, it invites differentiation in how words are used. They may be spoken or thought, articulated or withheld (Pentecostals use words loudly, Quakers use silence). This is Levi-Strauss's bricoleur at work, endlessly combining and separating, turning over and fixing, accepting and rejecting ever new combinations of structure. Take a structure like spirit/flesh. It may be separated or combined, and the main differences between Judaism and Christianity fix different uses of identical structure. Consider, for example, something as central as the concept of God. In a system based on spirit/ flesh, at some level, either the Deity combines these two or separates from humankind along this dimension. Clearly, the godhead in Christianity combines the spirit and flesh, especially in the personages of Jesus and the Holy Ghost, as my essays argue. In mainstream Judaism, by contrast, God is an unknowable, spiritual entity who cannot be known through an image. Here, God is viewed as a radical other, an "I am that I am" or "I am what I will be" who nonetheless formed humankind after His image. The exact meaning of this is unclear to believers, proving not only the spirit and especially flesh connection here but also confirming a radical separation between the two for Judaism, though as other essays establish, this becomes complicated in Jewish representations.

Thus, structures play on structures, fixing and fixed, ultimately along a difference/identity plane. Judaism and Christianity are both identical and different from one another, both being in the spiritual domain, one emphasizing the flesh, the other spirit. Within the Christian domain, Catholicism likewise contrasts with Protestantism, as Jesus' body might to Jesus' words. Both Jewish and Catholic religions display opposing tendencies, as Catholicism also does within Christianity. Finally, in light of these comparisons, we see yet again that differences are arising through similarity, and similarities depending upon differences. This the reader may discern for himself in the following example: upon death, traditional Jews may present food to the bereaving family where Christians may present flowers.

Essay 19- The Torah as a Cultural Object and Text

The Torah, or the physical object which records Jewish Scripture, is not simply a practical object in which an ancient text resides. It is a significant religious object that has a place within a deeper system of cultural meaning in the system of common differences. The triadic nature of many of this system's tropes has been emphasized throughout this book. This triadic structure and the fleshly expression of religion that Judaism represents in this system are the keys to understanding Torah as a trope in Judaism.

To begin, the Torah resides in the Jewish portion of the system of common differences. This system is a network of religious and kinship terms and relationships based upon a distinction between spirit and flesh. The religious sphere for each of the religions in this system (Christianity, Islam and Judaism) is the spiritual one while kinship is in the flesh. Both kinship and religion are further structured by flesh and spirit. This might be most apparent in kinship marriage, which spiritually unites two people in the flesh. In the religious or spiritual domain, spirit/flesh appears in many different representations, including the separate religions themselves. The separate religions in this system are distinguished from one another and are themselves developed on a structural basis, using spirit and flesh. This understanding is key to analyzing the Torah as a cultural trope. The Torah may be constructed as a meaningful object through some declination of spirit and flesh, of some declination of a deep structure.

To elaborate on the broader use of spirit and flesh, to eventually analyze the Torah as a cultural object, let's examine how spirit/flesh

defines the religious (spiritual) character of each religion. To begin, if
the spiritual or religious domain is structured by:

<u>spirit</u>
flesh

there ought to be one spirit religion and two flesh religions. This is an
expectation-prediction: the system of common differences should
produce 3 different religions. In other words, the top portion of the
spirit/flesh opposition should produce, structure, or undergird an
(overwhelmingly) spirit(ual) religion. The bottom should produce two
religions, one likely a spiritual religion (perhaps of salvation) dependent
on a body and the other being a sanctifier of the flesh. This is so because
spirit is whole or singular and flesh divides or splits. Here is the triadic
declination of the opposition illustrated above, using spirit and flesh to
structure the bottom portion of the binary opposition:

<u>spirit</u>
spirit/flesh

     I contend that this structure constructs a general relationship of
Islam, Christianity and Judaism, giving each religion its most dominant
theme. To explain and to put it simply, Islam is a religion of spiritual
encompassment. Everywhere it celebrates the oneness of God. Both
Judaism and Christianity are flesh religions. Christianity is a religion
about God's body, the word made flesh or Jesus, where Judaism celebrates
a people, a land, food, descendants, sexual sanctity, ethical behavior
(*mitzvot*) and Torah, which is the object we are trying to elaborate or
culturally construct. Judaism's flesh concerns are the context in which we
must understand the Torah. These are concrete and this-worldly.
Christianity by contrast focuses on the individual's spiritual salvation.
Since salvation is possible through the body of Christ, it is a religion of
the flesh with a spiritual concern. By contrast, Judaism wants to sanctify
this life; it is a religion of sanctification, of *kiddushin* (holy acts) and
kashrut (food sanctification) and so it is spiritual -- as religion is -- but
focused on the flesh.

     Now, flesh religion may appear as a contradiction to many
people, who think that religion is only spiritual in its concerns. But within
a spiritual domain, not only is there spiritual religion, but there also is
flesh religion. Christianity's spirit exists with its bodily concern for Jesus;

Jewish fleshly religion nonetheless is sanctifying even if its objects are physical things in daily life. This spirit/flesh divvying up of religion can be illustrated with a spirit religion above and two flesh religions below. They form a triad:

<u>Islam</u>
<u>Christianity/Judaism.</u>

Of course, if common differences are pervasive, then each religion and many of its concepts, objects, and stories might be fundamentally composed of spirit and flesh. It turns out that each religion has branches that differ or divide by spirit and flesh. I suspect that Sunni and Shiite differ in this fashion, one being the flesh versions of Islam and the other the spirit: one representing authority charismatically (i.e. spiritually) while the other representing authority institutionally (concretely in the flesh, Max Weber take note!). If there is an undivided, spiritual version of Islam, the spiritual religion, it is likely to be a mysticism such as Sufism. Within the Christian tradition, one might expect a spirit version stripped of traditional custom and filled with words and lofty aspirations for salvation of the elect or the believer. Protestantism takes this form. Catholicism, with its Church as the body and bride of Christ, its bread and wine, and its traditional ways is the flesh version of Christianity. It might be interesting to see if Orthodox Christianity is similarly rooted in the flesh, its differences with Catholicism only being institutional and historical and not cultural. Likewise, with Judaism and its branches, whose Torah is the focus here. Indeed, Judaism divides between its traditional forms (Sephardic and Ashkenazi orthodoxy, modern conservative and reformed Judaism) and its mystical tradition. The mystical tradition exalts its book, *Kabala*, which, by way of its spirituality, makes traditional custom a secondary concern and it exalts *ruach* or spirit. Further, in the traditional forms of Judaism, not only do we see a dominating theme of flesh religion, but we also see spirit/flesh structuring its basic concepts. God and Torah, for example, are structured somehow by spirit/flesh.

Perhaps we can see this structuring in the most basic statement of faith in Judaism: the Jewish prayer called the *Shema*. It says, "Hear O Israel, the Lord your God, the Lord is one". Here we have God or

Spirit which is one and Israel, an entity in the flesh which listens, a physical act in the flesh, and Israel in the flesh ought to be two, as the flesh is two and divided.   And Israel is a land and a people; it is two. This gives us a basic triad:

<u>God as spirit</u>
Israel as a land/ Israel as a people

A few things to note.   God and Israel relate, and the relating is constructed by a structure: it is a spirit/flesh relation. God relates to Israel as Spirit does to flesh -- which Israel is, as a concrete and divided people-land entity. That makes both Israel entities in the flesh. Israel as a people, for example, may represent the spirit part of this fleshly portion: The Jews are or are meant to be a nation of priests, a holy people and a people of the book. And as a land, Israel very concretely exists, so it is in the flesh.

Israel the people and Israel the land are not, however, simply spirit and flesh, in the flesh within the Jewish tradition. Jewish flesh often takes on the characteristics of gender. Flesh may be gendered. Divided flesh can be male or female rather than spirit or flesh. This helps us further characterize the spirit/flesh relationship of God and Israel described above. Spirit can be viewed as male (The Lord as King is male); flesh may be viewed as female and since Israel like flesh divides in two (land and people), and while Israel overall is female, the people may be male and the land female, both generally being in the flesh and female. Thus, we get the triad:

<u>God-male</u>
people male – land female

which expresses:

<u>male</u>
female

Relations occur between God and Israel along a male/female dimension which is a declension of spirit/flesh.   And the triad immediately above could be viewed as in the spirit and/or as one since both top and bottom are structured identically as God (male-female) and Israel (male-female) That is, Israel - at one with people and land - is like God who is composed of Israel's two underlying distinctions, male and female, as previous essays show. This male female triadic structure is also available to construct other relationships, one of them being the relationship between God, Israel and Torah, which are also traditionally thought of as one. It this last statement, that Israel, God and Torah are one, that I wish to analyze, since it will tell us about Torah as a cultural object, and the observation that the spirit domain is divided into a triad is helpful here. That is, the Torah may exist in a spiritual triad of God, Torah and Israel and this triad may be one, as the relationship of people in marriage may be one, and especially here, as Israel and God are one. This last relationship is the key to the place of Torah with Israel and God since these three are also one.

Gender again enters this discussion since it also is expressed in the marriage of Israel and God. Since Israel is a people in the female flesh, she may marry God, who as a male chooses her. The significant relationship between them is male/female which expresses spirit/flesh.[15]

So, what form does this union of Israel and God take? Again, Israel is God's chosen bride (parenthetically, so is the Church), so the form is one of husband and wife and it represents marriage and unity. In this marriage, God, in light of Genesis, can be understood as male-female, and here Israel, as land and people can be understood as male/female or male-female, below. This gives us an identity between the two (by way of common differences), and therefore Israel, as a bride, as male and female, as a coupling of land and people are married, coupled with God and are one with Him. They are the same despite their differences. To illustrate, we get:

<u>male: spirit-flesh</u>
female: spirit-flesh

as:

<u>male: male-female</u>
female: male-female

as:

<u>male: God</u>
female: Israel

as:

<u>male: male-female</u>
female: land /or- people

so that spirit above is the same as the flesh below, it is a unity in marriage
and a unity of common differences. It is in one unified structure. This
unity is in the spirit domain of religion so the differences between male
and female, top and bottom, are also identities.

Again, this structure is best expressed as male-female over female-
male. This structure can be expressed using royal terms – King and
Queen -, to give us: **male King – female Queen.** And this relationship
can be expressed vertically as:

God as King

|

Israel as Queen

which can be expressed horizontally as: **God as King – Israel as Queen.**
Please remember that these declensions of structure are really giving us
new and meaningful sentences within the parameters of the system of
common differences.

Of course, God could be viewed as married to Israel here, giving
us:

<u>God as King-Queen</u>
people-land

which can be elaborated as:

<u>King</u>
people

|

land

or:

<u>King</u>
people-land

where God or King is the male-female unity. This gives us a male people
in the female flesh married to a female land and connected as a spousal
unity with the God above, God being a connected unity identical to the
married unity below. Hence unity, God and Israel are one. Israel then is
God's bride.

These relationships or marriages are all variations of spirit/flesh
which is a unified distinction by itself and as such, these various structures
while different are nonetheless similar. Therefore, the marriage of God

and Israel is like the other marriages. This marriage is distinctly structured by male-female which can be declined into male over female, a unified structure containing difference in and of itself. In this marriage, Israel is female, and that relates to the place of Torah in this system. Remember, we began with the statement, which comes from the tradition, that God, Israel and Torah are one. If God and Israel are one in marriage and Israel is married to Torah, the marriage of God and Israel is the key to understanding the Torah's place in the system.

And let's say a few words about Torah before placing it in the various triads we've demonstrated so far. Torah is God's revelation - His words recorded in His Book. It is a concrete book so it readily has the characteristic of flesh. And is full of words! Words which we have seen are the female, creative voice of God, in the initial act of Creation. So, in relation to God, we can imagine that the Torah is female at the level of the male God, whose female voice Torah is. So, Torah can fit into the structure above in which Israel is married to God as His Queen. That is, just as God has the gendered structure of male-female, God as male can be at one with or married to the female Torah: God-Torah which is male-female in structure. Now, while this structure is both male and female indistinctly linked or married to one another, it is a male structure. This is so especially as it faces the world, where spiritual God is an authority over or in relation to worldly flesh, and let's take the unified, male-female people of Israel as the flesh. This gives us a structure of two marriages, in a single structure:

<u>God - Torah</u>
Israel the land - Israel the people

This displays male over female or spirit over flesh, it consists of two marriages identical in the male-female or spirit-flesh identity differences they express and, in this structure, Israel, the Torah and God are one. Each horizontal level is formed of male and female and the vertical is also male and female. This unity is like the unity of the Trinity and the God of Kabbalah. In this unity, the Torah in relation to God is male to female. But the Torah also faces the world.

Torah is the female voice of God, but when facing people external to God it is the Godly male in the triad and so we can readily get another relationship of Israel and the Torah:

271

Torah
People of Israel-Land of Israel

The Torah sits in the position of God in this triad, in part because she is married to and at one with the male God. (In some parts of the world, the Torah is robed or adorned in dresses.) And as one with God when facing the world, the Torah is a He. Parenthetically, there is a similarity between the *Shekinah* and its relationship to the mystical God of Kabballah and her relationship to creation, where she is a female expression of an essentially Male God in the world! Both Torah and *Shekinah* have a male/female character, casting the one gender over the other depending on where they find themselves.

Again, God is spirit, and as spirit He is male-female. So, the spirit can have a flesh or male and female expression in Judaism (as the mystical Godhead makes plain), and this goes to Torah. She likewise is male-female, female in the God male-female structure, as has been shown. But in facing people and not God, that is, as separate from God (and in the flesh world below) the Torah may be viewed as concrete spirit, a male expression of God in the flesh and this male object has a female voice.

Remember, the female people Israel is also married to Torah – a fundamental religious statement -, which suggests that the Torah is male or that Torah is a homolog for God which Israel is likewise married to. As homolog for God, Torah is a flesh expression of His spiritual being. So, it is male, a possible groom while at the same time it is female, flesh or a concretization of God. Torah is the divine law, God's word as revealed to Moses. It is a concrete, in-this-world expression of His historic (and perhaps ancient) will. So, while God is in the Spirit, the concrete Torah is in the flesh as God's word. As written, it is concrete and male but as His voice and since He is in the flesh as Torah, Torah being an embodiment, the voice of the male God, Torah is oddly female too. God then is composed of:

<u>spirit</u>
flesh

or:

<u>God</u>
Torah

or:

<u>male</u>
female

     All this is in indistinction and in the spirit: and so is indistinctly one. And as single oppositions, these are all one, an identity with distinctions. Moreover, the distinction or line between them is indefinite, though the terms above are incorporeal, and the others below are concrete. Flesh Torah and female are simply married to or at one with Spirit or God or male. This is like law is to Spirit or, as I am suggesting, His female voice is to God, as Torah is to God, or as female----male. That is, Torah --as inseparable from God -- is masculine in authority as God is for people, but in its relationship to God, as an aspect of God, it is female, and its voice is female. As such, it is like the *Shekinah* of the mystical Jewish tradition: the female expression of the male Godhead. For its followers, Torah then is authority, God in the flesh so to speak, and so it is a male authority with a female expression. Israel is in the flesh and in a religion of likeness, Israel may relate to God's female authority: Torah as flesh to Jewish flesh. Just as God marries Israel in the spirit, Israel marries the Torah in the flesh. This suggests a simple structure:

<u>Torah</u>
Israel

and this relationship not only is one of:

<u>spirit</u>
flesh

or:

<u>male-female</u>
male-female

it is a relationship of male over an indistinct female in that Torah is an authority and a husband or King like the male God, likeness through spirit. The Torah in every synagogue wears a crown, no less. But the Torah is not just male. It is a Jewish book and since this is flesh religion, the Torah must be female. Hence it is male-female. Beyond what has been said so far, and in the interest of elaborating, how is this true?

     First, the Torah is God's revelation or book. It is God's law in the flesh, given by the hand of Moses, written down on parchment, filled with laws, and constructed of words. In creation or *b'raishit,* God, who is male-female, has a voice. Spirit is formless; voice is a shapeless physicality, and it uses words. In the Torah, words form flesh and establish Creation. To create the world, God says in words, "Let there be Light". So, God -- who is made of spirit-flesh or male-female -- is also (in)divisible into Spirit and His Words, words that are fleshly even if they are in the spirit. Conceive of this spirit/flesh structure as God--Words. This makes of His words spirit in the spiritualized flesh. Further, if God's words exist in the flesh religion of the system of common differences, we would expect them to be concrete expressions of spirit. Law is a concrete expression of spirit.

What is more, these laws came from the hand of Moses. Here is a penned law in the flesh made of words, and not only were these first written in stone, but they are also recorded for the generations on parchment. Parchment consists of animal skin which is dried and written on. What could be more in the flesh than animal skin? Moreover, the Torah is covered and uncovered, suggesting a body which is dressed and undressed. The argument and contrasts continue: the ink must be black and the Torah parchment is white. Each expresses fire: black fire and white fire, so there is difference but identity, unification then in the brilliant spirit of fire. The ink is made in part of gall nuts, which are wasp eggs and other natural things like honey. This natural theme is in the flesh. It expresses life, which eggs embody and which a female body produces. Even the use of honey in the Torah's ink suggests the flesh, which perhaps can be discerned in the interpretation I give to the expression "milk and honey" as code words for spirit and flesh. Honey of course is produced by the female bee.

All this suggests that the Torah is in the flesh and so is female and we can see its structure in this version of flesh/spirit:

<u>male</u>
female

or:

<u>God</u>
Torah

But it is more likely that the Torah is God's (developing) intentions made flesh. So, the Godly or spiritual structure would be

274

male-female or God-Torah, all of this being in the spirit, the Torah being God's law at one with the God of Jewish Scripture. In a religion of the flesh, which is separate from God as it is in this world; his Presence would concretely be known through his Torah somewhat differently. In this world, the Torah concretizes the Being of God for the Jews. In the world, it is male in relation to the people who observe Torah. For them, the words of the Torah are like the words of creation. They are a logos: and where God's words once created the world, even now the Torah gives forth Jewish law. We see here the female logos of creation become the female voice of God's commandments embodied in the Torah. This mirrors the way the *Shekinah* makes its way in the world and this was described in the essay on "Godheads" earlier in this book.[16]

Since the Torah is a physical embodiment of God's words, we expect the shape of the Torah to reflect a unity that somehow is divided into two. It should triadically express spirit (one) and flesh (two). The physical Torah should have the symbolic form of spirit-God and His flesh relations. It should have a triadic form. Again, its physical unity should be a triadic two and one. The Torah is one scroll with two poles, poles which are called *etz chayim*, which means tree of life. Life, of course, is the created world of the flesh which again suggests the female but more importantly here, the Torah is a single entity with two poles forming a single scroll. It is a physical triad, just what we should expect from something composed in a complicated way of spirit and flesh in the system of common differences.

Thus, with Torah, we get a female authority in the male Spirit and it relates to people. Torah is above while relating Israel -- people and land -- is below. Here is another important triadic relationship:

<u>Torah</u>
Israel the land/Israel the people

Therefore, we can easily describe Israel as married to Torah, much as Israel is married to God. The reader can plug in the relationships in the structures for this marriage as previously discussed. From a structural perspective, a great many relationships that exist between Torah and Israel may be understood through the structures we have developed. Torah, in the flesh but existing at God's level of spirit, should have 2 entities below it, one in the spirit and one in the flesh, or one gendered male and the other female. Let me express a number of them, at the structural level.

First, the Torah is supposed to be an authority for Israel's kings. This takes the form:

<u>Torah</u>
<u>king</u>
people/land

Second, the Torah is an authority for Israel's prophets:
<u>Torah</u>
<u>prophet (or prophetess)</u>
people/land
Third, the Torah is an authority for Israel's rabbis:
<u>Torah</u>
<u>rabbi</u>
The Congregation of Israel
All three of these structures are permutations of:
<u>spirit</u>
flesh.

This last triad is very interesting in that the Rabbi, though a man in the flesh, is constructed in the spirit. His prayers and more importantly here, the prayer books that the rabbinic tradition produced are in the spirit. In the Jewish service, the spirit of the rabbinic tradition meets God's Torah in the flesh. It is an interesting and odd combination of spirit/flesh and the rabbinic tradition spiritualizes the fleshly Torah it reads.

This leads to a final thought about the Torah. If it is constructed in the semiological manner I have described, the text itself should also be loaded with these triadic structures. This has been clearly illustrated in my essay here on "Storied Triads in the Bible". Perhaps this insight will allow secular people to read the text not as literal truths but as meaningful stories. These stories can be interpreted, as the rabbinic tradition has done, through the spirit of the Torah itself. Instead of seeing Torah literally and only as revelation, it can be viewed as a cultural text. It can be viewed as a religious literature that gives secular people access to culture, access to the spirit/flesh relations which construct our marriages, form our communities, gives authority to our Rabbis, and allows people within the limits of language to meaningfully relate to God and also to one another in love. Our lives have increasingly been emptied of cultural life and for non-Jews as well as Jews, this seems to have led many to a paucity of the spirit and a rise of strident and righteous politics. But in truth, humans are cultural beings and a commitment to cultural life refocuses people on personal relationships and the private domain. This is a tonic to a life dominated by public life, economics, and politics. We need to realize that the support of private, meaningful relationships should be one purpose of public life. Culture and private life should often come first and I hope these essays bolster an interest in regaining this focus. While this essay has focused on the Torah, its perceptions might well apply to a reading of the New Testament. In my view, spirit-flesh is our culture's relationship of love which we cannot do without, and when Scripture's flesh perspective becomes ugly, should aspects of the Bible's text become morally repugnant, we might view it as literature (our western literature) whose Bronze Age edges we can smooth. Take the famous Biblical portion or *parsha* called *Shofetim* which begins in Deuteronomy XVI 18. It contains the profound injunction, "Justice, justice, thou shall pursue", a verse that could not be more concretely in the spirit. But in the same *parsha* or portion, we are told that when a city resists Jewish settlement of Israel, "And if it will make no peace with thee, but will make war against thee, then thou shalt besiege it. And when the Lord thy God delivereth it into thy hands, thou shalt smite every male thereof with the edge of the sword.... And thou shalt eat the spoil of thine enemies which the Lord has given you" (Deuteronomy XX 12-14) If we view this as literature, set in the bronze age with a different standard for the survival of peoples, and if we view this as premodern, we can put these injunctions aside. We can view them as in the Torah's harsh flesh, not as something in the light of its Spirit. As semiological literature, the Bible can be ours but thankfully, not completely so. Its meaning is more important than its literal truths in my view. This is so because it is a constructed text, not a historical document, with a place within a system of common differences, that presents itself as God's message in the world, one open to a spiritualization that comes of the very spirit/flesh distinction it gives to the world.

Conclusion

The essays in this book attempt to explain Western religious and kinship tropes according to their deep cultural structures which are governed principally by spirit and flesh. They show the compositions of the religious and kinship domains and many of its tropes. This includes an explanation of the character of its godheads, which are constructed and hence explained by the same structures that construct family life. The Trinity, the God of Kabbalah, the western family, and the unity of God, Israel and Torah are based on similar triadic structures. These structures create identities in very similar ways; though each trope is different: each has a unique and unified character that arises from structural processes and distinctions in common.

These essays also show how male and female articulate with the distinction of spirit and flesh to better understand how tropes like Christian eschatology and Jewish peoplehood are constructed. Other common differences like in and out, act and state, and up and down have their place in the constructions of many religious tropes as well. The system then creates a whole serious of religious meanings from common differences, common binary distinctions, the most important of which is spirit and flesh which is expressed in a variety of structural declinations including many different triads.

Along the way, something even deeper than spirit and flesh is uncovered as basic to this cultural system: identity and difference. It is the epistemological basis for spirit and flesh and it helps these essays describe the system of common differences as involved with knowing and identity. Identity and difference even add to the notion of structure used here: identity is the tool by which difference in structural transformation as in Christian conversion is established. Moreover, binary difference, in light of the logical and epistemological necessity of having identity connected with difference, led to a notion of binary identity. These are examples of binary identity: spirit-flesh and male-female; and these complement the binary character of the deep structures like spirit/flesh and male/female that explain the cultural tropes examined in these essays.

The essays were written episodically over a very long period of time and most predated the development of the triadic concept used here to explain so much of the material in the system of common differences. It was not very difficult to revise the older material to reflect the new idea. And its basic idea is simple: a deep structure, based principally on spirit and flesh, generates a variety of structures, many triadic, which act as a grammar that enables religious ideas to find their expression and express their character. Common differences are at the root of the plethora of religious tropes found in western religious life. This discovery, hopefully, is what this book of essays accomplishes.

INDEX

BIBLIOGRAPHY

Benedict, Ruth. 1934. Patterns of Culture. Boston: Houghton Mifflin Company

Berlin, A. (2013). The Levite Rebellion Against the Priesthood: Why Were We Demoted? TheTorah.com. https://thetorah.com/article/the-levite-rebellion-against-the-priesthood-why-were-we-demoted

Bourdieu, P 1973 The Berber House. In Rules and Meanings. Ed Mary Douglas PP 98-110 Baltimore: Penguin.

Bradley, F.H. 1969 Appearance and Reality London: Oxford University Press

Carrol, James 2001 Constantine's Sword New York: Houghton Mifflin Co.
Cartwright, Peter 1956 Autobiography of Peter Cartwright. New York: Abingdon Press

Douglas, Mary Purity and Danger 1966 (Routledge Press, United Kingdom)

Durkheim, Emile 1915 The Elementary Forms of the Religious Life. New York,; McMillan,

Feeley-Harnik, Gillian 1981 The Lord's Table Washington Smithsonian Institute Press

Feinberg, Richard and Ottenheimer, Martin eds. 2001The Cultural Analysis of Kinship Urbana and Chicago University of Illinois Press

Feuerbach, L. 1957 The Essence of Christianity New York: Harper Torchbooks.

Foster and Ranum Food and Drink in History, vol.5., John
Hopkin Press, Baltimore,

Gaines, M.C. ed. 1979 Picture Stories from the Bible. New
York: Scarf Press

Geertz, Clifford 1966 Religion as a Cultural System. In
Anthropological Approaches to the Study of Religion. Ed. Michael
Banton. pp. 1–46. ASA Monographs, 3. London: Tavistock
Publications.

Heidegger, Martin 2002 Identity and Difference (University of
Chicago Press, Chicago)

Leach, Edmund 1969 Genesis as myth and other essays
(London: Cape)
1960 "Levi-Strauss in the Garden of Eden
(transaction of the New York

Lieber D. 999 Etz Hayim: Torah and Commentary. The Jewish
Publication Society:
New York
Levi-Strauss, C. 1967 Structural Anthropology. Anchor:
New York

Marx, K. and Engels F. 1974 On Religion. New York:
Schocken Books

Matt, Daniel (translator) 2004 The Zohar Stanford, California:
Stanford University Press
MacClancy, Jeremy 'The Milk Tie' 2003 Anthropology of Food
issue 2
Morris, Charles 1975 Foundations of the Theory of Signs
University of Chicago Press: Chicago

Pettit, Philip
    1975   The Concept of Structuralism.   University of California Press: Berkeley

Pritzger edition, The Zohar

Schneider, David American Kinship 1968 Englewood Cliffs, Prentice-Hall: New Jersey
Scholem, Gershom Kabbalah 1978 Penguin Group: New York
Scholem, Gershom Major Trends in Jewish Mysticism 1974 Schocken Press: New York
Scholem, Gershom On the Kabbalah and its Symbolism 1965: Schocken Press: New York
Scholem, Gershom On the Mystical Shape of the Godhead 1991 Schocken: New York
Sweet, William Warren 1944 Revivalism in America: Abingdon Press: New York
Turner, Terrence   N.D. Draft Essay on Kyapo Myth. Unpublished
Weber, Max 1958 The Protestant Ethic and the Spirit of Capitalism.   Charles   Scribner   and Sons: New York

Wolfson, Elliot R.   Along the Path 1995 Albany: State University of New York Press
Wolfson, Elliot R.   Circle in the Square 1995 Albany: State University of New York
Wolfson, Elliot R. Language, Eros, Being 2005:   Fordham University Press: New York

---

FOOTNOTES

[1] And it is unsurprising that the issue of knowledge, the introduction of difference, is also at the Bible's outset since structural meaning and knowledge are among the Bible's fundamental if underlying themes.

² And triads apparently exist in Islam, also. Take the name of God: Allah. It is one word. It consists of AL and LA, an obvious binary opposition. Since this distinction is combined in one word, it is a triad, expressed in a word, which clearly is unified linguistically in the spirit. Moreover, the word Allah is in the feminine, though Allah is referred to as a He. This seemingly replicates the male-female structuring of spirit found in Genesis. And significantly, as in Kabbalah, Allah is known through 99 qualities or names, suggesting that Allah Himself is the relation unifying the qualities.

³ Found in Food and Drink in History, vol.5. Edited by Foster and Ranum, John Hopkin Press, Baltimore, pg.• 121-138.

⁴ Please note that this Trinity in its raw structural form emphasizes relations, spirit/flesh being a relation. The opposite of a relation is a quality and we will see that the Kabbalah Godhead emphasizes qualities or *siferot*. This contrast of qualities and relations helps define the character of both Godheads and is another example of how contrasts or relations construct the character or qualities of religious ideas, in this case, of the Trinity and the Kabbalah God.

⁵ Christianity is marked as a flesh religion since it is founded on the body of Christ

⁶ It is appropriate to ask, at this point, "How is the Holy Spirit of the flesh"? The Holy Spirit impregnates souls. That is the impregnated answer. It is spiritually of the flesh at this level in the system.

⁷ This two-ness as wholeness could be expressed as a singular difference, which sounds like so much jargon except that it is a way of thinking about the opposition identity/difference. It has two parts, but it is one difference that turns out to be the distinction that makes possible a unity of differences. The identity/distinction difference is behind the two-ness of the Kabbalah godhead, each distinct or different part essentially being identical to one another as the forthcoming argument hopefully demonstrates.

⁸ Gendered flesh is not glorified flesh, I suppose.

8 Importantly, both Jesus and the Holy Spirit are themselves structurally identical in the sense that they are both composed of spirit/flesh, Jesus being spirit in the flesh and the Holy Ghost being a spiritual impregnator of people in the flesh. There is identity here because they are using the same structure to express their personages and it is the same structure that gave rise to the triad of God, Jesus and Holy Ghost, hence another source of identity.

¹⁰ Isaac, then, is sexed and gendered male and also female by gender. One aspect of his gender becomes marked under different circumstances. This seems to be how the *siferot* of the mystical Jewish God wield their male-female attributes as well.

¹¹ Of course, descent is primarily in the flesh, it is a biological tracing of one generation from another and later the Jewish tradition will counterpoise descent in the flesh with spiritual Torah ascendancy in each generation but that is for later.

¹² As is discussed in other essays, males choose and females are chosen. The female Jacob is chosen as the heir in the line of descent. And of course, this observation about choosing and chosen as male and female applies to the Jewish people, a female

body, which is a chosen spouse to God (with all the moral duties this implies as a chosen people), but that is for another discussion. But one point here in case I forget to make it later: note also that Christians choose individually where Jews collectively are chosen, a purely structural or binary distinction. Christians are choosing life after death and Jews choose the sanctification of this life, which in part takes the form of an emphasis on marriage and childbearing, the hallmarks of traditional Jewish life (which is sanctified and in the flesh)

[13] To repeat a point, Israel is female, and she is sometimes referred to as the chosen people. If men do the choosing, and females are chosen, then the fact that Israel as a people is both chosen and female becomes understandable, at least from a structural perspective.

[14] Giving us a copulating (acting) God that or who IS: an act/state unity.

[15] Where individual Christians choose to join the body of Christ or the faith, people born as Jews don't choose to be Jews. They are passively Jewish, and so by contrast this can be viewed as Chosen. They are collectively chosen as a chosen people: choosing/chosen as well as collective/individual are simply contrasts, distinctions along a common dimension. It is the same thing, just different.

[16] In another essay I make this clearer: God's voice is the source of creation. It an immaterial but an actual expression of God, its creating is essentially female – God's voice births the world. His voice is inseparable from Him. The unknowable male singularity has a creative female voice which makes the world. God says, let there be light, and so light was. God then consists of male---female. The Torah, as God's voice, is likewise female, an indivisible extension of God in the spiritual flesh.

www.ingramcontent.com/pod-product-compliance
Lightning Source LLC
Chambersburg PA
CBHW070759280326
41934CB00012B/2984